To Percy
with best wishes
Alexander
October 2020.

CHEERS!

DRINKS AND DRINKING IN JERSEY THROUGH THE AGES

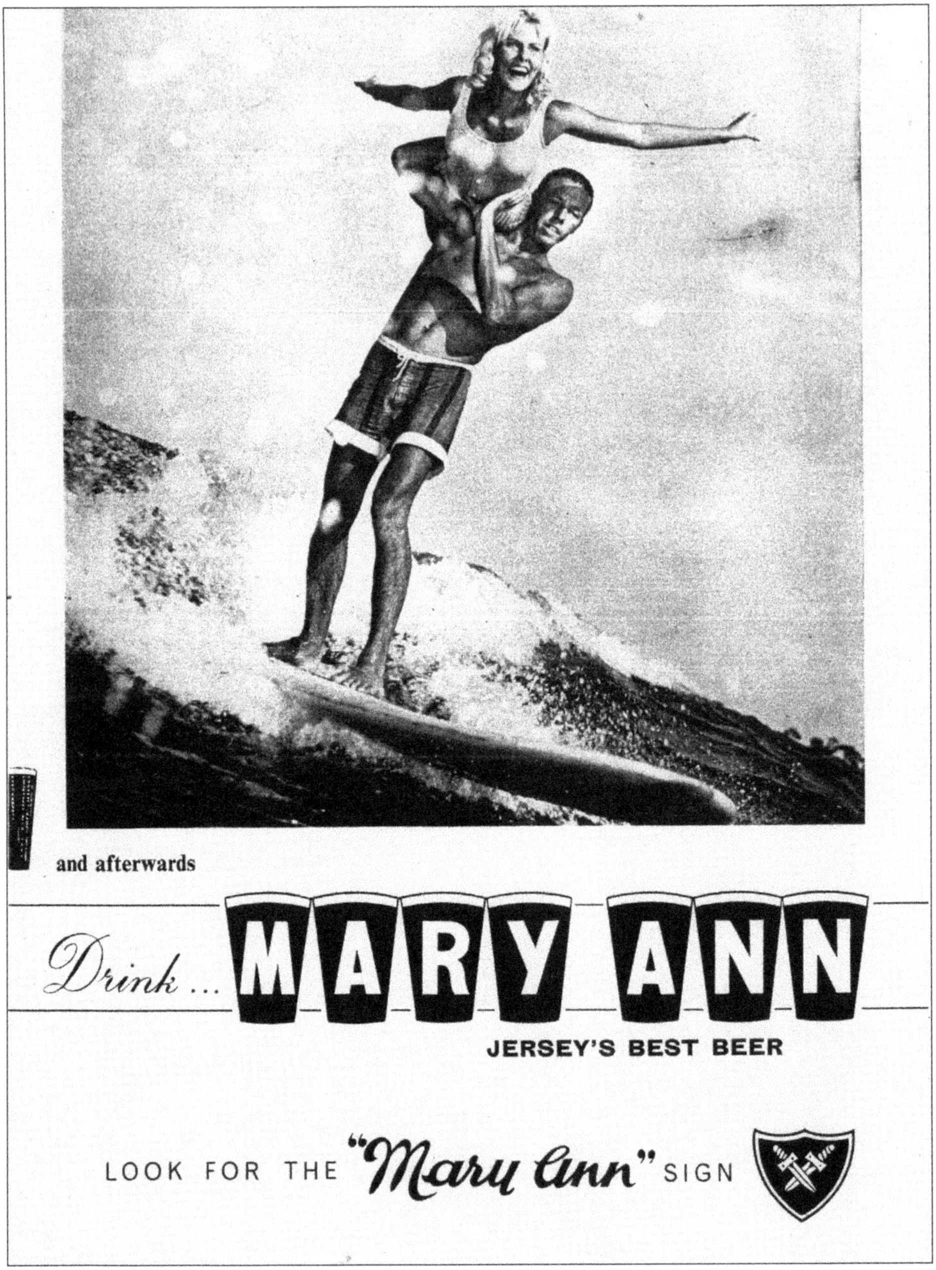

and afterwards

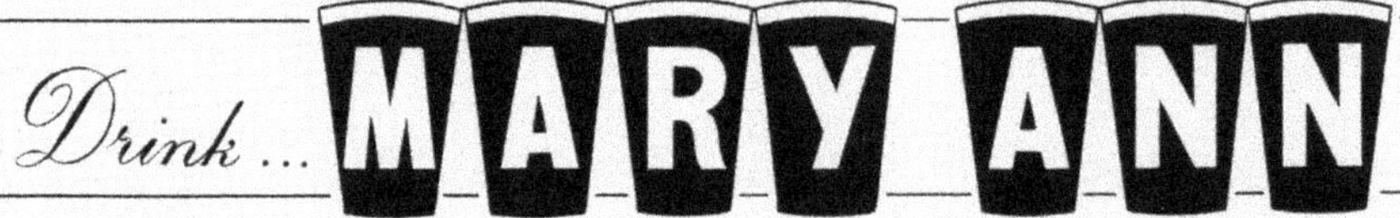

JERSEY'S BEST BEER

LOOK FOR THE "Mary Ann" SIGN

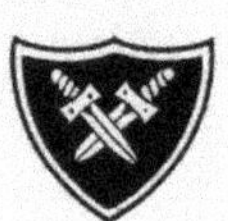

Advertisement from 1965

Cheers!

Drinks and drinking in Jersey through the Ages

ALASDAIR CROSBY

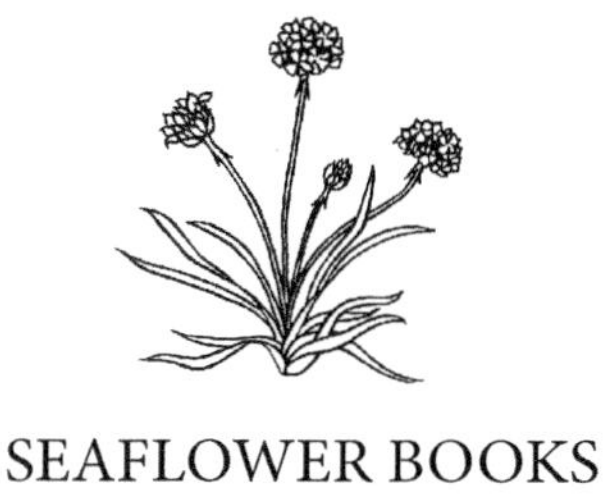

SEAFLOWER BOOKS

Published in 2017 by
Seaflower Books

www.ex-librisbooks.co.uk

Origination by Seaflower Books

Printed by Anthony Rowe CPI UK Ltd
Chippenham, Wiltshire

ISBN 978-1-912020-71-3

Contents

Acknowledgements

For help in research, the author is indebted to a great many people. In particular to:

Howard Baker
Robert Blayney
Mark Crowther
Tim Crowley
Patrick Dean
Martin Flageul
Derrick Frigot
Alex Glendinning
Gary Grimshaw
Paul Hurley
Geraint Jennings
Roger Jones
Chris Lake
David Le Maistre
David Le Quesne
Hamish Marett-Crosby
Heather Morton
Gavin Reid
Al Thomas

Howard Baker deserves a special note of gratitude to himself, as without his help the book would never have been written. So also does Mark Crowther and Roger Jones, for their support and patience during the frequent periods when the author got distracted from the job in hand.

And as always, my thanks to my wife and family whose own lives were disrupted during the times when 'Daddy is doing his drinking research again'.

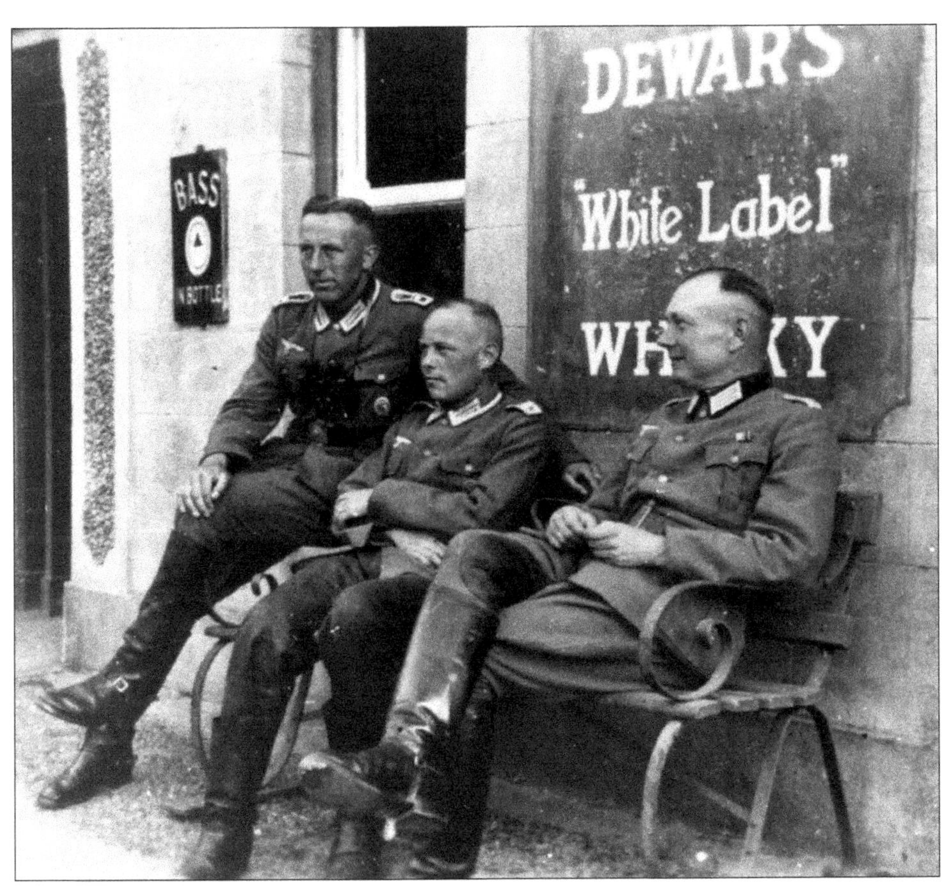

Uninvited guests during the Occupation relaxing outside the Carrefour Selous, St Lawrence (© Bundesarchiv)

Introduction

She was young, possibly in her early 20s, pretty, and was sprawled on the pavement, drunk.

Earlier in the evening she had obviously taken great care with her clothes and appearance; Saturday night was party night. She was now a total wreck.

As the evening had worn on, her very high, high-heeled shoes must have made standing upright more difficult than it should have been. She still had one shoe on – the other had been lost somewhere in the course of the long, boozy evening in the pubs and clubs of the old Weighbridge and Esplanade area.

She was not alone; her male companion was making every effort to carry her to a bench. Unfortunately he was also very much the worse for wear, and every few paces he collapsed under her weight so that they both fell down together on the pavement.

'Such a waste of good alcohol,' I thought in my caring way, as I side-stepped to avoid treading on them.

But why was I, the author – at a time of life that I prefer to call 'middle-aged' but at which unfortunately many of my age contemporaries seem to be already grandfathers – out and about in town in the small hours of the morning, looking at young women becoming incapably drunk?

The reader might be fully justified in demanding an explanation – but do not think too badly of me: I had been invited by 'The Street Pastors' to observe their work.

They are indeed good angels – a Christian and public-spirited body of men and women who make a point of being there, in the thick of the crowds, to help those who have taken too much alcohol for their own good.

As for that young pair, who were so much the worse for drink – the final stages of their current predicament must have developed quite quickly, otherwise they would doubtless have been noticed and assisted by the emergency services. But at that moment and place these services were not on the scene.

As they staggered and fell about, Street Pastors were quickly at their side. They were helped to a bench; they were made comfortable; they were given water to drink; Pastors stayed with them to take care of them and ensure they got home safely. Things were not as bad for them as they could have been –

although I imagine waking up sometime the following day would not have been a pleasant experience for either of them.

Cold water, and flip-flops to wear for those who could no longer cope with their high-heeled shoes; picking up broken glass that would otherwise cut the feet of those who had lost their shoes; in short, comfort and help without judgment – the Street Pastors do a worthwhile and commendable job.

They are the latest body who have taken on the help of those affected by alcohol, which wreaks such havoc on people – especially young ones – who have not learned to drink wisely and moderately, or whose curious idea of pleasure it is to drink, as much as possible in as short a period as possible.

As temperance advocates have never tired of emphasising, excessive drinking can lead to violence. Over the years there have been cases beyond counting at The Royal Court concerning young males whose consumption of beer and spirit chasers have led to 'glassings' and GBH.

'This behaviour was totally out of my client's character and entirely due to his unwise consumption of alcohol,' the defending advocate says. 'He bitterly regrets his behaviour.'

'Drunkenness is no excuse for violence' is, of course, the presiding judge's reply.

In short, it might appear that the hours of darkness are not suitable for law-abiding and prudent members of society to be out and about, a conviction reinforced by those tragic cases of violence and rape that intermittently hit the headlines and lead to people saying that the streets of town are becoming ever more dangerous than in previous eras.

But that opinion is demonstrably wrong; the story of the consumption of alcohol is not a one-sided story of foolishness and violence. It might be argued that things have improved considerably since the early Temperance campaigners of the 19th Century inveighed against 'the demon drink'.

For every horrible incident caused or exacerbated by drunkenness, there are countless other incidents of people using alcohol wisely and responsibly and just having a good time before going back home at the end of the evening. In a night spent with the Street Pastors – very much a typical night for them at a busy time of year – there was certainly evidence of boisterous high spirits. A cap of one of the Pastors was snatched from his head and removed by one joker who found this very funny; comparisons with Bertie Wooster and his friends stealing policemen's helmets on Boat Race night spring to mind. The two young people described above who were practically incapable were the only serious victims of drink that could be observed. Many revellers were merry; few had seriously over-indulged.

What a contrast from previous times!

What a contrast, for example, from 1945. A lady who was a young woman during the days of Occupation once told me that she felt completely safe walking alone in the vicinity of a soldiers' canteen; the German troops were always scrupulously polite and deferential. That was in marked contrast to the days after Liberation, and the behaviour of off-duty Tommies in town.

What a contrast, for example, to the 19th Century, when St Helier was a commercial port as well as a garrison town, and the streets were full of taverns and brothels and there were often night-time riots in the streets.

What a contrast to the 18th Century, when demonstrations on a Monday against an unpopular States measure were preceded by 'the mob frequenting the cider houses from Friday night to Monday morning' and Members of the Royal Court wisely made themselves scarce so as to avoid their drunken fury.

And although a walk through the Weighbridge area on a Saturday night in modern times might have its moments, one is not likely to be accosted by a drunken leper, as was one person's misfortune at a fair near Mont Orgueil during the Middle Ages.

At its best, the enjoyment of moderate drinking is a welcome temporary remission from the cares and stresses of daily life. From the mead enjoyed by the early inhabitants of the Island, to the cider of later years and the beer, wine and spirits of modern times, alcohol has always been part of Jersey people's daily life.

The history of its production and consumption is an integral part of the history of the Island, which it is the aim of this book to chronicle.

Our attitude to alcohol has improved over the centuries; today a greater danger to society is not so much the negative effect of the over-consumption of alcohol, but the New Puritanism of the modern age, which emphasises only its bad effect and forgets the words of the Psalmist: 'Wine maketh glad the heart of man'.

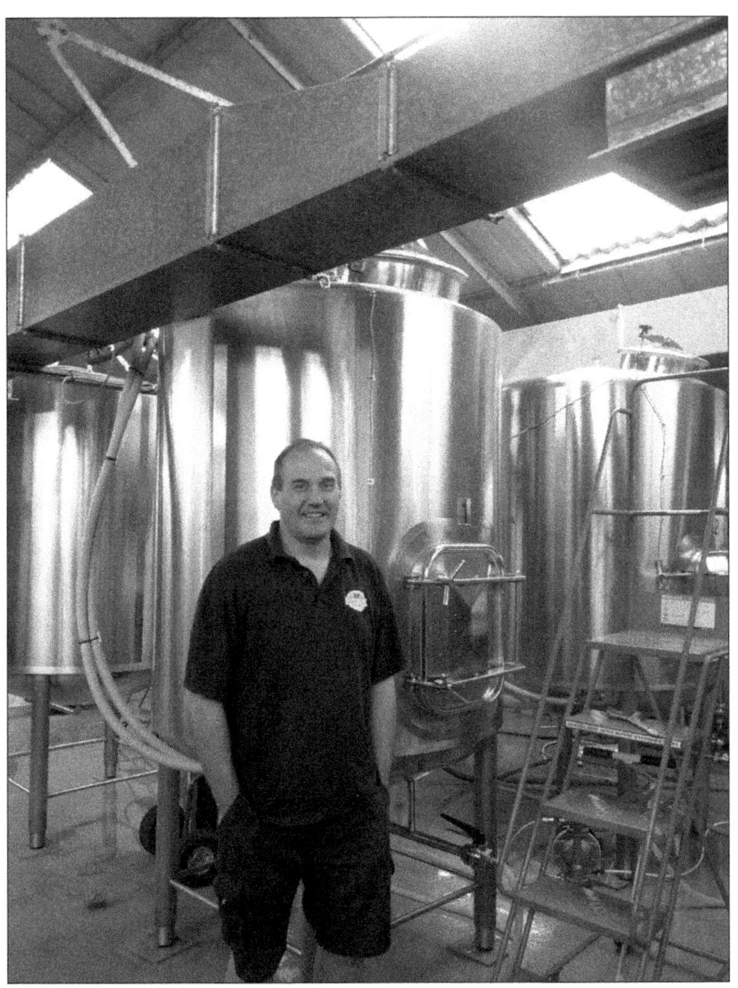

Patrick Dean, Head Brewer at Liberation Brewery

~ 1 ~

In the Beginning

When Noah came out of the Ark after the Flood, he planted a vineyard. He made wine and got drunk. Opportunity, aspiration, failure – the history of mankind throughout the ages.

For many thousands upon thousands of years, humanity lived as hunter gatherers. Although they used and took advantage of caves, the popular idea of them as 'cavemen' is grossly unfair; from the drawings the Magdelanian culture left behind on the walls of caves in southern France and Spain, we can begin to approach some slight understanding of their civilisation: glorious works of art that showed they understood the meaning of perspective; cartoon head and shoulder drawing of themselves showing clean-shaven chins and wearing tailored clothes, carved horses' heads showing what could be harnesses; fine and precise flint tools. By circa 16,000 BC these people were visiting Jersey – using the higher slopes of what is now Les Varines as a hunting camp overlooking the lower ground that in due course would become the sea between Jersey and Normandy.

The hunting of large prey species may have been the preserve of testosterone-filled young men; a more regular and dependable source of food and nourishment – as well as medicine – may have come from the members of the tribal community who were available to forage the countryside near their homes or camps: wild grasses, fruit, wild honey, herbs and culinary and medicinal plants. Perhaps these were the womenfolk and their children, together with the older and slower men.

It suggests that originally there was a wholly different way of perceiving the landscape. A modern person might stand, for example, on the high ground above St Ouen's Bay overlooking the wooded slopes, dune land and foreshore, and exclaim: 'What a lovely view!' A person transported from the Palaeolithic era, or indeed Neolithic, Iron Age or early Mediaeval times, might reply, 'Maybe, but will I be able to get my dinner from here?'

Where we see a landscape to admire, our early ancestors would have seen the equivalent of a shopping mall.

'Foraging' has recently come back into vogue, and in Jersey, 'professional foragers' such as Kazz Padidar give instruction into to the properties of herbs and plants and show how drinks such as 'birch wine' can be made.

The plants collected by early mankind of what is now Europe would have included specimens of the raw material of modern drugs. With no sanction against their use, the effects of eating these plants would have seemed like a religious or transcendental experience. Some of them would have been known to be dangerous, or to be used only with great care by their shamans and medicine men. Others, such as grapes from wild vines, or the heads of certain wild grasses, could be processed or left to ferment into alcoholic drinks – perhaps proto-wine and proto-beer. And as any effect on health of these drinks was only temporary, they could be used with greater freedom than other herbal preparations. Honey, if stolen with care from wild bees, could be mixed with water and if left for sufficient time to ferment; the alcoholic drink of 'mead' is the result.

Humans learnt how to make mead before they learnt how to plant seeds or keep animals. It marked the passage from nature to culture. Fermented honey was the first way humans discovered of intoxicating themselves through alcohol. It predates wine by thousands of years.

Prehistory is an era of which we know little for certain, but can surmise much – and we can surmise a family or tribal group relaxing together after the rigours of the day, sitting around a roaring fire and passing round a jug of something alcoholic and agreeable. The sense of ease and contentment engendered inspires intimacy and conversation, inspires stories to be told and the music of flute and drum to be played, inspires the discussion of plans for the future and for increased co-operation – in short, we see the genesis of civilisation and culture.

ONE day, the hunters left Les Varines for the very last time, tramping off across the flatlands, probably eastwards and southwards, and maybe impelled to move quickly by a biting wind from the north. The climate was worsening: from the safe perspective of today, we know that the geological equivalent of a prolonged cold spell was imminent. We call it the Younger Dryas. It lasted for perhaps a couple of thousand years – the last bite of the Ice Ages. By the time it was over, around 10,000 BC, the glorious Magdalenian culture was no more; perhaps they were driven southwards toward the sunnier and warmer climate of the Mediterranean.

In Jersey, the Younger Dryas came and eventually went with no human inhabitants to witness it. In due course the climate warmed again; the future Island (it was still an integral part in the west European mainland) was covered with forest. It would take perhaps 5,000 years for the Island to be re-inhabited; when it was, it formed part of the impressive – and mysterious – Neolithic culture that would in time build La Hougue Bie and the other megalithic monuments around the Island, as well as the great structures at Stonehenge, Carnac, Newgrange and countless other places along Europe's western seaboard.

Considering the scale of their constructions and the precise astronomical knowledge that the creators of these megaliths apparently had, it must surely be undeniable that this was, of its type, a cultured society. There are too few facts and too many suppositions, but it seems reasonable to surmise that the survival of the essence of the human spirit – and ways to ensure that survival – played a major part in their culture, much as it would in the culture of ancient Egypt and its own tombs and temples that would still be some 2,000 years in the future when La Hougue Bie was constructed around 4,500 BC.

What would have been available to refresh the toilers and hewers of stone as they worked to construct La Hougue Bie?

Certainly tea: leaves infused in hot water would have produced pleasant and refreshing teas, including mint, elderflower, heather flowers, wild strawberry leaves, or any fruit steeped in boiling water. Other drinks or tisanes would have been made from the dried flowers of lime, elder, chamomile or woodruff, and the fresh flowers of gorse and sorrel. Incongruous as it might seem, dandelion and burdock might already have been the basis of a drink. The dandelion roots by themselves, and chicory, would have produced warm drinks analogous to coffee.

Barley would have been cultivated in the small fields and the grains, if allowed to sprout in a warm damp place, could have been boiled in a pot, the water drawn off, sweetened with honey and drunk as barley water, or allowed to ferment into beer. There is every possibility that the Neolithic peoples grew apples and brewed cider.

AS the millennia rolled onwards, Jersey's megalithic civilisation seems to have waned. A different sort of society took its place as the Neolithic merged into the Bronze Age; the times seem to have become more uncertain, with defensive structures being built for protection. We seem to sense something of the heroic, or even Homeric, about this new form of society: chieftains in their fortresses, small kingdoms defended by warriors with bright spears, sheep nibbling the grass, ponies ridden along the trackways, feasting in the chieftain's hall. In time, the culture we call 'Celtic' established itself and iron became the material for weaponry.

What would there have been to drink at a feast at the chieftain's table?

The brewing of beer was well understood, and common ingredients were spruce, nettle, dandelion, and barley.

The Celtic year was marked by festivals, and the most important of these were quarterly, such as the New Year festival of Samhain in late October or the spring festival of Beltain. If a new wine was made after each festival, it would be ready in time for the next one, three months later.

Samhain was also when elderberries ripened, a berry that is one of the richest natural sources of wild yeast in northern Europe. This yeast, from the fermented berries, can be used as a wine, beer, or yeasted bread starter.

The early 3rd Century writer, Athenaeus of Naucratis, stated in his monumental book *Deipnosophistae* (which has been called the world's oldest surviving recipe book) that in the Celtic north:

> 'the poorer people drink a type of beer called *corma*, which is sometimes flavoured with honey. They pass around a common cup taking small but frequent drinks. The cup is passed to the right, not the left, and by turning to the right in this way they honour their gods.'

Corma was probably a beer brewed from barley. The Celts would have made wines and ales from elderberries, birch sap, blackberries and raspberries, rosehips and heather – the latter romanticised in Robert Louis Stevenson's famous poem 'Heather Ale', once known to every schoolboy.

Honey was the only available sweetener. Beekeeping was already understood and beeswax was also important to seal up containers of jelly, verjuice, ale and – importantly – mead, perhaps the most famous drink of early history, popular with northern cultures from prehistoric to mediaeval times. Honey also produced metheglin – honey mixed with a fruit or juice – and they are known to have used the juice of the hazel tree.

We will have more to say about mead in the next chapter.

Although hops were known in Europe from prehistoric times, and occur naturally in Jersey, they were not used in England for the purposes of making beer until the 16th Century.

But whatever the attractions of mead or other drinks, it was wine – from grapes – that became quickly the most popular and the most high status drink of the

Celtic people. Quite simply, it tasted better than anything else.

The 1st Century BC Roman author, Diodorus Siculis, wrote on this fondness for wine, specifically among the Gauls:

> 'They are exceedingly fond of wine and sate themselves with the unmixed wine imported by merchants; their desire makes them drink it greedily and when they become drunk they fall into a stupor or into a maniacal disposition.
>
> 'The Italian merchants, with their usual desire for a quick profit, look on the Gallic love of wine as their private source of wealth. [The merchants] transport the wine by boat on the navigable rivers and by wagon through the plains and receive in return for it an incredibly high price for a single amphora of wine they receive a slave – a servant in exchange for a drink.'

Diodorus was not impressed by Celtic manners:

> 'Some shave off the beard, while others cultivate a short beard; the nobles shave the cheeks but let the moustache grow freely so that it covers the mouth. And so when they are eating the moustache becomes entangled in the food and when they are drinking the drink passes as it were through a sort of strainer.'

The 1st Century BC geographer, Strabo, damns the Celts with faint praise: 'The whole race is war-mad, high-spirited and quick to battle, but otherwise straightforward and not of evil character.'

What was very unimpressive for Romans and southern Europeans was the Celts' 'primitive' habit of drinking wine neat, whereas the civilised peoples of the Roman world always added water to it.

But the contribution of the Celtic tribes to the Roman economy was significant and very beneficent to Italian wine producers. Just as in later times, there was generally more wine produced than could be consumed by the available market. Italian estate owners could dump surplus wine on the Celts and received, in return, profitable slaves.

There are analogies here both with the slave trade of the 17th and 18th Centuries and with the sale in the American Wild West of 'Fire Water' to native Indians. History always repeats itself.

'Many Italian merchants, prompted by their usual cupidity, regard the Gauls' taste for wine as a godsend,' wrote Diodorus.

The distinguished archaeologist and authority on the Iron Age, Barry Cunliffe, in his monograph titled *Wine to the Barbarians*, said that at a time when Gaul and Britannia were still beyond the frontiers of the Roman empire, one of the main routes for wine exports from Italy was from Massilia (Marseilles) and then via Narbonne, Toulouse and Bordeaux up the Atlantic coats to Brittany.

Amphorae have been found around the Baie de Quiberon around Quimper, and at Saint-Servan in the estuary of the River Rance.

> 'The clear implication of this distribution is that loads of Italian wine were being carried across France by cart and river boat to the vicinity of Bordeaux where they were then trans-shipped into sea-going vessels to be sailed northwards around the Bay of Biscay for the main ports and *oppida* (settlements) of Armorica. Since the Armorican massif is rich in metals, particularly silver and tin, it may fairly be assumed that these were some of the commodities that the Roman entrepreneurs were intent on acquiring.
>
> 'From the mouth of the Rance estuary the route would lead up the coast of Normandy and then, the final leg, across the channel to Hengistbury Head, the headland flanking Christchurch harbour on the borders of Hampshire and Dorset. From there, the Rivers Avon and Stour lead deep into southern England.
>
> 'What is clear is that in the first half of the 1st Century BC Hengistbury was the place where Mediterranean luxuries were offloaded to be distributed to the courts of the British Celtic elite: Italian wine, Mediterranean figs, Breton luxury foods, olives, fabric and fine metal work.'

In return the traders would buy grain, leather hides, hunting dogs and slaves. Contrary to the sentiments of 'Rule Britannia', Britons frequently were slaves – and sold at an agreed exchange rate of one amphora for a slave.

> 'The impact of trade on the native economy must have been considerable, for not only was a totally new range of luxury commodities made suddenly available to the elite of central southern Britain, but slaves became a marketable product, almost overnight.'

In 1994 Professor Cunliffe delivered the Joan Stevens Memorial Lecture in Jersey on the theme: 'Jersey in Prehistory – a Centre or a Periphery?'

In his lecture he said: 'It is inconceivable that Jersey did not feature prominently in these 1st Century BC enterprises.'

The thrust of his lecture was that Jersey was indeed very much at the centre of a long-standing and important trade route. The treasures that have been dug up in recent years reinforce the view that Jersey was a stable and safe place to store wealth – so perhaps nothing much has changed there, and as a stopping point on the cross channel route, there would have been, at least by the elite among its inhabitants, an appreciation of the finer things of life – including wine.

Strabo can have the last word on this fascinating subject:

> 'They [the Celts] also drink beer: but they are scarce of wine, and what wine they have made they speedily drink up in merry feasting with their kinsfolk.'

~ 2 ~

Drinking in the Middle Ages

'In Jersey, the year 1066 was only the year between 1065 and 1067.'

For this insight, we are indebted to the former Jersey Heritage head of community learning, Doug Ford. By that year Jersey had been part of the Duchy of Normandy for over a century. There were almost certainly Jersey soldiers at the Battle of Hastings, but most Islanders would not have been at all affected by the invasion of England by their Duke.

At that time Jersey people would have looked back on some six hundred years of history from the effective end of Roman rule. Commonly known as the Dark Ages, it would only have seemed 'dark' to the inhabitants in relation to the continual uncertainty of war and piratical raids – the well-known legend of St Helier records one such raid, which, from the point of view of the invading Germanic or Norse 'pirates', went rather badly wrong.

Celtic society was maintained from the Iron Age throughout the period of Roman rule and for several centuries afterwards.

Although Jersey likes to look back on its Viking (or at least Norse) heritage, it is safer perhaps to say that these invaders, once they had settled in the Island, became the elite strata of Island life, with a strong understratum of Celtic inhabitants at the lower end of society.

Everything written in the previous chapter about drinks that the population would have known and enjoyed during the long centuries of prehistory would remain just as true in the so-called Dark Ages and throughout mediaeval times.

The countryside would have looked very bare to anyone time-travelling from modern Jersey: the original wildwood covering would have disappeared centuries before, although names such as St Jean des Chênes – St John of the Oaks – might suggest that the Island was not entirely treeless. But although the big open fields must have been windswept, there would have been a rich covering of plants and heather to attract bees and also thus for mead to be made from their honey.

As mentioned in the previous chapter, bees had been kept for their honey since at least Bronze Age times, if not earlier, and mead and metheglin enjoyed for centuries before the onset of the Middle Ages. It remained the principal drink in Jersey until the increasing popularity of ale, beer and the exploitation of the cider apple.

And it remained the favourite drink of those for whom wine was unknown, unavailable or too expensive. In northern Europe, Scandinavia and Anglo-Saxon England, kings and chieftains feasted their retainers in mead halls – such as the 'golden hall' of Heorot described in *Beowulf.* In this feasting, drinking mead made men feel like Gods, even though it might make them behave more like beasts. Rowdy Norsemen sitting on mead benches – it is a picture that anyone might readily imagine, especially if they have ever attended a Christmas Dinner of the Old Victorians Association.

The northern pagan conception of the afterlife – if only perhaps available for brave warriors – was Valhalla, a glorification of a mead hall, where they could feast and fight and drink mead for ever – until summoned by cockcrow and trumpet-blast to take part in the Last Battle at the end of the world.

What might it have tasted like, this drink of gods and heroes? Many readers – like the author – may have been lured in the past by mead brand packaging, such as labels in 'Olde Irish' script. Certainly once tried, there seems nothing to impel the purchase of a second bottle.

As Bee Wilson, the appropriately named author of *The Hive* puts it:

> 'You are expecting the nectar of the gods, but what you get is cough mixture (if you're lucky). It tastes like a mixture of Lucozade and the kind of cider that teenagers get drunk on and then make themselves sick.'

Writing in 1692, Jean Poingdestre in his *Caesarea*, says:

> 'In earlier centuries the people generally applyed themselves to the keeping of bees, which thrived there exceedingly and made a most excellent sort of honey than is seen ordinarily, which since by ye multiplying of apple trees hath by degrees been neglected… The honey was used to make a strong drink, mead, which was displaced by perry, which in turn gave way to cider.'

And from *A Picture of Jersey* (1809) by John Stead, we learn:

> 'There were formerly a great many Apiaries in the Island, before the Introduction of Cyder, the principal drink of the inhabitants being mead. The number of bees has decreased from the introduction of other sorts of beverage, perhaps less wholesome. The honey that is introduced here if of very superior quality to any other in Europe, and if the farmers properly understood the management, and

> would diligently attend to their bees, they would be amply rewarded for their trouble.'

The neglect of bees because of the rise of cider, was still being lamented by the Royal Jersey Agricultural and Horticultural Society in 1837, for in their report they state: '...in an island like this, abounding in bee food, the proper care of these insects ought to be more generally studied.'

But in 1837 there were no worthwhile apiaries.

In Jèrriais, the word *baechet* refers to a drink fermented from honey and *vitou* to metheglin – honey and water, with the addition of ginger and dried elderberry flowers.

Mead may have been superseded by other drinks, but Jersey honey has retained a reputation for excellence throughout history. Even in the 18th Century it was recorded that Jersey honey was famed for its flavour: in 1756 Thomas Le Maistre of St Saviour collected his honey three times during the summer months.

And bringing the story of honey up to modern times, Jersey honey is still famed for its flavour and Island beekeepers regularly win honey competitions in the UK with it.

But to quote Bee Wilson again: 'The victory of wine over mead is surely the passage to true civilisation.'

CASES brought before Jersey Assizes in 1299-1300 provide some interesting details of daily life of the time:

> 'Guillaume Alayn claims from Thomas Payn (the attorney of) the Abbot of Mont Saint Michel £12 tournois, left over from the sum which he owed him for three casks of wine which he unlawfully withheld...'

(It seems that not paying your wine merchant has historical antecedents).

Another case along similar lines:

> 'Guillaume le Petyt, attorney of Guillaume Aubaud, burgess of Saint Malo, claims from Guillaume de la Houge £16 tournois which he owes the burgess for wine bought from him. Le Petyt likewise claims from de la Hougue 60s. for wine and other things....

Drinking led to fighting, then as now:

> Raoul Perchard and Jourdain Perchard struck Philippe Payen in a tavern at night. And they came, and could not deny this, and so are fined.

The same Raoul:

> 'charged that he struck Pierre des Vaux in the King's market place, blood being shed, came and could not deny that offence, so is fined,'
>
> 'Jean Fillotte, Guillaume son of Nicholas, and Raoul le Norman, charged by an inquiry that they struck the son of Robert Le Fevre at night in a tavern and dragged him by his hair, which he burned in a candle flame, in breach of the peace. They could not deny the offence and so are fined.'

An Assize of 1309 shows that there were 148 taverners in the Island who were fined for various infractions of the law. It forbade the sale of ale until the liquid had become properly fermented by being allowed to stand in large barrels.

The record of the Assize shows that in 1309 there were 32 people in St Helier who were both taverners and bakers, while six were taverners only. In St Peter there were 12 taverners; in St Saviour 22 (another six were joint taverners and bakers); there were 18 in St Clement, eight in Grouville (jointly taverners and bakers); in St Martin, ten taverners; in St Brelade, seven.

Two cases were heard in which the defendants were accused of taking 'simple men' to the taverns and compelling them to pay for the defendants' food and drink. They were both heavily fined.

AN Assize in 1324 stated that four beer tasters in each parish should visit every tavern and sample every cask of beer, wine and cider; once, when it had been broached, once when it was half full and once when it was nearly empty. It must have been a much sought-after job.

WINE was made in southern England, northern France and Germany in the Middle Ages until the climate took a turn for the worse in the 14th Century. This area is about 300 miles farther north than the areas in France and Germany that grow grapes today and which do not now sustain commercial vineyards.

But although grape vines can grow successfully in Jersey, wine, so far as we know, was never made in the Island – at least commercially – until the later 20th Century. Road names such as Mont des Vignes refer to tomato vines, not grape vines.

Although wine would always have been needed regularly for the celebration of Mass in the Island's churches and chapels and priories, Jersey was very much in the same network of shipping and trading routes as it had been in Roman times, and so wine would have been easy to import. There was a considerable volume of trade between England and Aquitaine, Gascony and other wine producing areas, a trade that Jersey vessels did much to facilitate. There are many records of vessels going in and out of Guernsey and Jersey in the early mediaeval period carrying large cargoes of wine.

There is indirect evidence of contact between the Channel Islands and Gascony before 1204, which had already for centuries specialised in the production of wine. Because so much of their land was devoted to it, the Gascons needed to import food stuffs such as corn and fish. Here was an ideal trading arrangement for carriers such as merchant vessels from the Channel Islands.

In mediaeval London, for example, there were at least 56 types of French wine regularly available for sale and 30 varieties of Italian, Spanish and Canarian, as well as Greek and German wines among many others.

The loss by King John of his lands in Normandy in 1204 did nothing to impede Jersey's maritime trade.

In 1230, a time of war with France, a ship of Bayonne called *St Peter Le Buere*, which was laden with wines and other goods belonging to a merchant in Flanders, was arrested in Jersey. Six years later, Drogo de Barentin, Warden of the Isles, was told to seize all French wine that he could at sea and sell it for the King's benefit. This was a pattern that would be repeated again and again in future historical times, until the 18th Century and the era of privateering.

In 1294, when hostilities with France were renewed, the Bailiffs of Guernsey and Jersey were instructed to ensure that ships from Bayonne laden with wine and other merchandise were not shipping it to Normandy or any other part controlled by the King of France, but only to England.

In 1336 we hear of a ship from Jersey called *La Notre Dame* which had been freighted with wine at Bordeaux and had been plundered at sea by 'pirates' from Weymouth and Melcombe.

Jersey was particularly active in Bordeaux during the early 14th Century. At Bordeaux between 1303 and 1311 there might be 11 or 12 Channel Island ships a year picking up wine and of their 61 total departures during this period, 38 were by Jersey boats and 23 by Guernsey vessels.

The Mediaeval warm period that had helped vines to grow in northern Europe ended some time in the 14th Century. This turn for the worse brought with it the so-called 'Little Ice Age': harsher winters with reduced harvests. Food shortages and rapidly increasing prices were a fact of life as much as a century before the Black Death plague of the 1340s. Wheat, oats and barley – and consequently livestock – were all in short supply. Their scarcity resulted in malnutrition and increased susceptibility to infections due to weakened immunity.

From 1314, there were several years of cold summers and from 1315–1317, a catastrophic famine, known as the Great Famine, struck north-west Europe. Arguably this was the worst famine in European history and may have reduced the population by ten per cent. With the cooler climate, temperatures became too cold for grape production and the vineyards in southern England gradually declined. The climate stage was set for colder weather crops, such as barley and for drinks such as beer and cider.

Meanwhile, in Jersey, we get unrelated glimpses of daily life: a visitor to a fair at Mont Orgueil gets accosted by a drunken leper, for example. Fairs, such as the one at St John at midsummer, provided all too rare opportunities for rest and relaxation. In the accounts of midsummer bonfires at the fair and 'bacchanalian' dances around them, there is a strong whiff of not-yet totally obliterated paganism.

At St Martin's Tavern (not the building now known as 'the Royal') there was a fives court in the 15th Century. In 1461, John Hartford, an Englishman, played and got drunk on beer, and at St Lawrence Fair the same Englishman was found lying in a pig trough, where he ended up fighting with Colin Mauger (known as *Trigalleur*, the drunkard).

Two years later the Seigneur of Rozel and a friend 'went to drink (a beer)in the tavern of Colin Marguet near St Martin's Church.'

NO account of mediaeval Jersey would be complete without mentioning the exciting topics of shipwrecks and intentional wrecking.

In late mediaeval times, 'Wreckum Maris' was the right which the King or Lord of the Manor possessed to the debris that the sea flung upon the shores. The word '*Wrecq*' is the same as the more familiar word, '*vraic*', which, although now only applied to seaweed, is defined by Ducange in *Glossary of Feudal Terms* as 'all those things which the seas collect and hurl upon the shore.'

When this '*Wrecq*' consisted of barrels of wine, the Wreckum Maris was definitely a feudal right to be enjoyed.

Thus in the late 15th Century, when a storm brought ashore on the beach of a King's fief some barrels of Spanish wine, they were appropriated by the Bailiff, Clement Le Hardy, who sold them for a good profit. He had no right to this, so the Governor, Matthew Baker, clapped Le Hardy in prison, where he ultimately died 'full of lice and vermin'.

This story is linked with that of the great storm and the deliberate wrecking of a wine-laden boat. This incident was recalled a couple of generations later:

> 'At that time, a large Spanish ship laden with a cargo of sweet wine was shipwrecked by La Corbière. As a result the sands were saturated with wine, even the Hall of St Ouen's Manor lay almost filled with barrels of wine.'

This incident may be the fact behind the popular legend concerning the wreckers of Jersey's Wild West. This concerns five Spanish galleons inveigled on to the rocks; the surviving crew members and passengers were slain … and then, as if by divine vengeance, a sandstorm blew sand and gravel on to Quennevais, hitherto a rich and fertile area, converting the land into sandy desert and also burying the evil wreckers.

There may have been some wrecking – but such things are not normally written down in contemporary chronicles. In 1874, a Monsieur A G Cluveaux wrote a guidebook in which he told the story of how:

> 'the savage Islanders of the Quennevais made their cattle peregrinate on the uplands with lanterns fixed to their horns, while one of the forelegs would be fastened near their heads, thus making the animals limp. The up-and-down motion of the lanterns on the cattle, seen from afar, made vessels believe that they were the lights of ships sailing in an open sea.'

A ripping yarn.

Some mediaeval Jersey surnames derive from occupations or habits connected with drink. These include Le Boutillier (a maker of leather bottles), Le Cornier (a maker of horn cups), Malzard, (a round pot in which mulled cider was set among the embers) and Roucault, a leather bottle. Both the last two may refer, sarcastically, to waist measurements.

Boileau – meaning drink water – may have referred to an early teetotaller (or again, it might have been a sarcastic gibe). Of later date (early 18th Century) is the surname Tosdevin (Tostevin), from Old French *'toster'* to toast with *'vin'*. Originally this may have referred to someone who toasted bread at fairs for the purpose of dipping or soaking it in wine or it could have been a nickname for someone who enjoyed this fare too regularly. It is a Guernsey family name – members moved to Jersey in the early 19th Century.

~ 3 ~

Beer and Brewing in Jersey until the beginning of the 19th Century

The history of beer and its story in Jersey has been eclipsed by Jersey's 'Big Apple' and drowned in the sea of cider that was produced between the 17th and 19th Centuries. Historically, although Jersey is mostly associated with cider, it is possible that the production of beer predates the great expansion of cider orchards and cider production in late mediaeval and Tudor times. Ale would certainly have been produced since early times.

Beer, differentiated from ale, is simply ale boiled with dried, butter-tasting hop flowers. Hops (*Humulus lupulus*) are closely related to the nettle - and to the cannabis plant - and once they were a common wild plant in Jersey (the French name for them is '*du Houbillon*'). They were certainly common in the mid-19th Century, but by 1891 they were described as 'uncommon'; by 1903 they were 'rare'.

Some enterprising farmers turned their fields to hop-growing; in 1791 Abraham Aubin auctioned his three hop fields in Mont Millais. But early 19th Century attempts to found a Jersey hop-growing industry were unsuccessful. Today hops can still be found in hedgerows, according to the late Jersey naturalist Frances Le Sueur, but it is not exactly a common plant.

Hops are, in fact, native to Britain, southern Europe and western Asia. Its young shoots have been used for centuries as a spring vegetable - writers from Pliny to Cobbett have remarked on its excellence - and it also had medicinal uses. Hops give a special flavour to ale, making beer simply a more interesting and palatable drink.

To quote Samuel Johnson's Dictionary:

'Ale: A liquor made by infusing malt in hot water, and then fermenting;
Beer: Liquor made from malt and hops.'

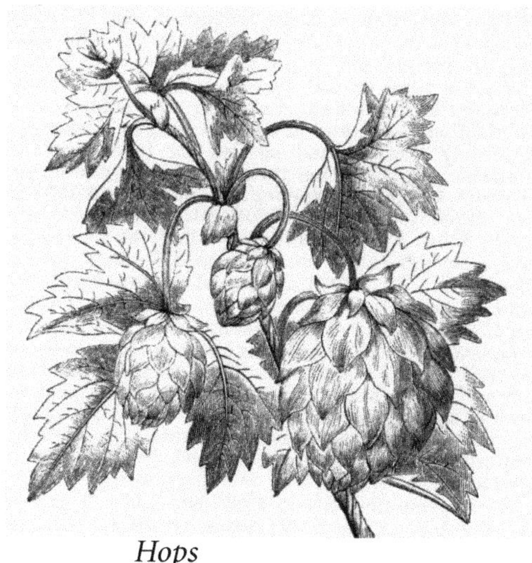
Hops

Hopped beer has been known about since early times – it is mentioned in the Finnish *Kalevala* in the 9th Century, and the word 'beer' comes from the Old English word *baere*.

But despite hops' use as an additive to ale being known in England from Anglo-Saxon times onwards – it seems never to have caught on until the 16th Century. It was initially popular in England's eastern counties – where Flemish settlers began growing hops and brewing beer.

The old rhyme: 'Hops, Reformation, Bays and Beer came into in England in one bad year' is not true to fact – but truer in spirit. All four were novel in Reformation England.

IT has been said magisterially by a previous writer that 'there is no documentary evidence available to show that beer was brewed locally during the 16th, 17th and 18th Centuries, and any speculation on the subject is useless.' In fact there is documentary evidence, as we shall see.

In the Middle Ages, Jersey's countryside would have been very different from what we now consider to be its traditional rural aspect: no steep banks, few trees, fewer small fields. Instead, there would have been big open fields growing wheat and barley – there are still traces of that in St Ouen.

The produce of these fields would have been taken to mills to be ground into bread – and also, in some cases, to make beer. There was enough produced for a small population of farmers and fishermen, but as soon as the population began to grow, there was less than a sufficiency, and records reveal that already by the mid-16th Century, beer needed to be imported, primarily for the garrisons at Mont Orgueil and later for Elizabeth Castle.

Although an increased population necessitated a local increase in production of alcoholic drinks – and this was cider – beer has always been brewed in the

Island throughout the centuries, using malt ground at local mills.

At one time or another between the 11th and 20th Centuries there were 17 windmills and 47 water mills in the Island, although they did not all exist simultaneously. The watermills were installed on the banks of the 14 principal streams or brooks and the windmills were usually built on high ground remote from the valleys. Some of the oldest inhabited sites in Jersey are those occupied by these mills. Waterworks Valley had seven mills on its course – the name of the lane is Chemin des Moulins. St Peter's Valley had eight mills. Grands Vaux and its tributaries had ten.

Their most important function was grinding grain into flour, but from time to time some of them, to meet a temporary demand, were engaged in fulling and grinding malt for making beer.

In the 14th Century it was commonplace for small breweries to augment their income by baking bread as well – both bread and beer need yeast and either malt or corn for grinding. In 1535 the States decided that bakers-taverners had either to bake bread or to brew beer, but not, under any circumstance, to do both.

It was cheaper to own your own malt mill than to pay a miller to grind your malt for you.

In about 1692 Jean Poingdestre wrote that there were '30 water mills beside four or five malt and fullers mills.'

Among the malt mills was Gigoulande Mill, St Mary, mentioned in 1528; Le Moulin de Loumel, L'Hommel or Chomel, in St Peter's Valley, also mentioned in 1528, and in 1790 as a malt mill, and Le Moulin à Bré at La Ferme in Grouville, mentioned in 1601 and again in 1649 as the 'malt mill bye or near the place called the Ferme'. This was bought by Philippe de Carteret from the Commissaries of King Charles II – the transaction was recorded in a Patente that was signed by Charles II at Elizabeth Castle, which now hangs at St Ouen's Manor. It was last mentioned in 1721 and has now quite vanished.

There were also two malting mills in the town area, which raises the interesting possibility that in the 17th Century there were two rival mills, just as there were two rival breweries in the 20th Century.

The first of these was Le Moulin de Débénaire or Moulin à Foulon et à Brée. Débénaire was a nickname that became a surname of a family that obtained land and influence through milling in the town area. Foulon means fulling. Brée, Brais or Bray means malt. It was thus a fulling and malt mill. It stood originally at the Faux Bié stream in future York Street, then called La Rue à la Planque Billot. It was owned in the early 1500s by a certain Guillaumine Débénaire and her husband, Jean Poingdestre.

Another mill, 'Moulin à Brays', is mentioned in 1607 as being positioned 'by the church yard' in Bond Street, near the mediaeval Chapelle de la Madeleine. In 1663 it belonged to the La Cloche family. In 1676 Jean Messervy owned or operated this 'Moulin à Brée et à Foulon' and he prosecuted Charles Hilgrove for operating a rival malt and beer-brewing mill, to his prejudice, since 1636 – i.e. for the past 40 years. Hilgrove's mill may have been the old Débénaire mill in York Street – and it is the last we hear of it – we don't know which side of this legal case was successful.

The Bond Street mill is last mentioned in 1786: it stood in the way of the new Conway Street and was already in ruins.

Beer and malt were also, of course, imported into the Island, probably mainly for the benefit of the English garrisons of Mont Orgueil and Elizabeth Castle. The 17th Century Jersey diarist, Jean Chevalier, records that a captured vessel, en route from England to Cherbourg, and loaded with malt for beer-making, was brought into Jersey in 1648. There must have been many more captures and many imports of malt and beer into the Island.

It was only in the 19th Century, however, that a multitude of small breweries opened for business, at a time that the town was expanding and of a much expanded local consumer market. Before then, however, we need to consider Jersey's 'big apple': its great cider industry.

~ 4 ~

Jersey's Big Apple

Once upon a time, there was an island in the west where apples grew. Not in the imagined world of Celtic or Greek mythology, but in a real island in the midst of the cold and salty waters of the English Channel. Jersey was an isle of apples.

Apple trees have, in fact, helped to shape Jersey's traditional landscape of little fields protected by hedges surmounting high banks. Maps of town in the early 19th Century, before it began to expand out of its historic confines, show that where there are now streets and houses were once hundreds and hundreds of apple trees.

An elderly lady – now deceased – once recollected to the author her visit to the Island in about 1925. She stepped off the mailboat and was met by her family on the pier with a pony and trap. They clip-clopped off home, into St Lawrence, and as they drove through the lanes the apple blossom in the orchards was so thick that the scent filled the air.

Those days are long past now. Even then, in 1925, there were far fewer orchards than there had been in a few decades before. Orchards had been grubbed up to make space, first for outside tomatoes, then for the Jersey Royal potato. The stone apple crushers once used in farms all over the Island have largely become decorative surrounds for flower beds.

Cider, of no great quality, continued to be made for Breton farm labourers for as long as they continued to work in the Island, but Portuguese workers, on the whole, prefer wine or beer and cider production diminished to almost zero.

But the important word there is 'almost', because cider production never quite stopped altogether, and now it looks as if something of a renaissance in cider apple growing is taking place.

With due respect to the Island's Jersey Royal growers, the sight of apple blossom, or of apple trees laden with fruit, has a picturesque quality to it that polythene sheeting over fields of young potato plants doesn't quite match.

The Jersey cider apple has had a distinguished past before its decline and fall;

now, in the 21st Century there have been more orchards grown and more cider made than for many a long year.

Could this trend continue – and could cider be Jersey's Once and Future crop?

(i) ORIGINS

> 'The inward parts of the Isle gently rise and swell up with pretty hills: under which lye pleasant vallies watered with riverets, and planted with fruit-full trees, but apple trees especially, of which they make a kind of drinke'
>
> William Camden, *Britannia* (1582)

Jersey lies in the middle of the great cider producing area of western Europe. To the north lie the English cider counties: Devon, Somerset and Dorset, with Hereford further north; to the east is Normandy, the home not only of cider but of calvados apple spirit; to the south and south-east lies Brittany.

The apple tree is suited to regions that do not particularly favour either corn growing or vineyards. The cider apple probably took root in Normandy first of all; crossed over to the Channel Islands and only later was it grown extensively in south-west England.

Cider may have been made in the Island from earliest times. There is no difficulty in growing apple or crab-apple trees in Jersey – and as mistletoe grows on apple trees, these were held to be sacred by the ancient Celts and their Druids. But although some cider may always have been made for domestic consumption, the recorded history of Jersey cider really starts in the mid-15th Century. Before then, most people drank hydromel (a mixture of mead and water) or ale. In 1469 cider is included in a list of payments to merchants in Caen by the quartermaster at Mont Orgueil; again in 1532 there are payments for 2½ pipes (about 250 gallons).

Cider was at first made for local consumption rather than as a commercial activity. According to the Rev Philippe Falle, writing in 1694:

> 'No longer ago than Queen Mary's Reign there was so little Cider made in this Island, that the Inhabitants were necessitated to apply to her for leave to import yearly from England Custom-free five hundred Tuns of Beer for their provision, besides one hundred and fifty Tuns more for the Garrison.'

However, production grew as cider merchants realised the untapped market for cider in England. For the first time, the Jersey smallholder found himself with a product that not only came from his own land but was also commercially profitable.

By the mid-16th Century onwards, apple orchards began to replace corn as a major crop in the Island and local cider production developed rapidly. Not only was it more profitable than corn, but also making (and consuming) cider had an intrinsic interest that cereal production simply lacked.

Soon every farm had one or more orchards and, apart from the town, most houses had one or more apple trees as the commercial potential of exporting to England was recognised.

As a source of cider for the English market, Jersey had a number of advantages. First, Jersey exporters did not have to pay duty on foods imported into England – it was not a foreign land. Secondly, incongruous as it might seem these days, it was easier for a merchant in one of the major English ports to collect cider from Jersey by boat than from an English farm. In other words, it was far easier to carry a heavy load of cider by boat from Jersey to an English port than have to send a horse and cart over the rough tracks that, until the late 18th Century, constituted the English road system, with all the attendant dangers of robbery and accident.

The increase in cider orchards in Jersey brought a considerable change to the landscape. The Jersey writer Jean Poingdestre, writing in 1682, wrote that the changes had happened in the previous hundred years.

The Island lay 'almost open' at the beginning of the period, but by 1673 so much land had been enclosed for orchards that fierce regulations governing the planting of trees were introduced by the States. Farmers had found there was more profit in apples than in the traditional corn, so had made orchards with huge hedges round them. The regulations forbade the planting of trees on agricultural land, 'the whole island was in danger of becoming, at last, a continued orchard, if care had not been taken to put a stop to that unlimited inclination of ye Inhabitants.'

The first arrival of cider orchards brought with it the planting of trees similar to that in Normandy. Hedges, usually of elm or hawthorn, would surround orchards. By 1670 every part of the Island had been planted with cider orchards. To protect these crops, hedges and small woods were planted. It was noted that in the 17th Century the Parish of St Lawrence was very beautiful with a forest-like appearance from high ground.

Elm was first recorded as being present in Jersey in 1533, though its pollen has been found in prehistoric peat beds. It is thought that in the 16th and 17th Centuries, elm was brought over from France along with the cider apple tree stocks and new varieties of cider apples, so as to grow the hedges bordering the orchards and to create shelter belts for them.

(ii) A SEA OF CIDER

> 'I do not think there is any Country in the World that (on the same Extent of Ground) produces so much Cider as Jersey does, not even Normandy itself... nor is there better, larger and more generous fruit than what grows in this Island.'
>
> *An Account of the Island of Jersey*, by the Rev Philippe Falle (1694, revised 1734)

JERSEY was being enclosed, but not in a way that enclosures of land were taking place in England in the 18th and 19th Centuries. There, the enclosures were led by the gentry and major land owners, backed by the law and parliamentary legislation. It resulted in the disappearance of common ground and in many cases, the displacement of rural communities and it contributed to the growth in towns and urban industry. In Jersey, on the other hand, the enclosure of land was undertaken by the smallholders themselves of their own desire and free will. Effectively, the so-called 'agricultural revolution' arrived in Jersey a century earlier than it did in mainland Britain and was demotic, not aristocratic .

The orchards needed shelter from high winds and protection from intruding animals and so they were enclosed by high banks, on the top of which blackthorn was planted. This made the small parish roads feel like paths in a maze. Cider apple trees were also planted on the top of these banks and as they were not on fields, they escaped the payment of tithes.

The Rev Philippe Falle, writing at the turn of the 17th and 18th Centuries, described Jersey's 'new look':

> 'One is not to imagine low fences here as in England. [They are] raised with much labour and expense, six and eight ft high, sometimes more, answerably thick and solid, planted with quicksets and timber-trees, many of them faced with stone to a competent height, as you see the outside of a rampart in a fortification. And for such they would serve against a prevailing enemy, to whom we might dispute every field. But still, I say, they are attended with this inconvenience, that they are too much multiplied, and take up too much ground, in a country where there is already little enough in proportion to the inhabitants.'

Nor were these enclosures welcomed by hunting people:

> 'These inclosures are great enemies to the Pleasure and Diversion of Gentlemen, who cannot well hunt, especially on horseback, unless about the seacoast, where a few of the worst lands remain open, or inclosed with low fences.'

Jean Poingdestre, the author of *Caesarea, A Picture of the Island of Jersey*, in 1682 wrote that husbandry was 'sore decayed' and that the people 'avoid tillage as a painful occupation.....

> 'There is hardly a house in the Island, except in St Helier, that did not have an orchard of from one to two vergées sufficient to produce an average of 24 hogsheads a year' (One hogshead of cider or beer = 54 galls).

And some years later Philippe Falle commented:

> 'This decay of tillage has sprung from a coalition of causes [including] the conversion of the best arable land into gardens and orchards for the growth of cider, a commodity with which we are now overstocked, whilst we want the more necessary support of life.'

By the end of the 17th Century Jersey was only growing half the corn it needed, but cider was being produced in vast quantities. Falle estimated an annual production of 6,000 tuns or 24,000 hogsheads a year, equivalent to one and a half million gallons a year.

Exports to England had developed into a major industry. By 1673 cider orchards occupied a quarter of all the arable land in the Island and the States ordered that no new orchards could be planted. Also, in the 1670s, the import of cider from Normandy was prohibited so as to protect the Island's cider industry.

During the 17th Century, a very common practice when making cider was to add a bucket of water for every hogshead. It was not a universal practice, but common enough to merit it being noted in contemporary accounts. The belief was that this improved the fermentation – it was said that that there was no cider at all upon the Island without some added water.

From Philippe Falle again:

> 'Many of our orchards are planted something in the imitation of the famous Quincunx and all of them in an order that gives them a Beauty beyond that which I have observed in Gloucester or Herefordshire, but we have had it in such plenty (some single trees have been known to produce a tun, or four hogsheads)...The common practise is to mingle all, sweet and sour too often, ripe and green confusedly together...'

He added that a quarter of the available land was occupied by cider apple orchards and that the Island was 'a sea of cider'.

Although cider was exported in significant quantities (the rate of £1.5s per hogshead is recorded in the late 17th Century), it was also the universal drink for domestic consumption in the Island. It was cheap (or free of cost if home-produced), effective in soothing a man's worries, and its consumption helped to pass the time, particularly in the winter when there was little else to do.

Importantly, at a time when the water supply was not good, drinking cider was the healthier option. As wine was drunk only by the wealthy and most beer was imported, cider was the only sound beverage that was easily or freely available.

The population of Jersey in the 17th Century has been estimated as being approximately 20,000. Supposing every man, woman and child drank on average one pint of cider a day, the local demand for what by then had become the Island's normal beverage could not have been much short of 1m gallons a year.

The normal utensil for drinking vessels was pewter – a robust and durable material for keeping, transporting and drinking this vast quantity of cider. The bulk of the vessels in the 17th Century and earlier may well have come from France, but there was also English pewter, either specifically imported or brought over, at the time of the Civil War, by Royalist refugees.

The typical 'local style' of flagon had a long incurved neck, which from just about between the base and lip swelled out in a flowing curve to form a bulbous belly.

There were six basic sizes of flagons. In descending order of capacity: *pot* (pronounced 'po' as in French); quart, pint, half-pint, noggin and half-noggin. 1 *pot* = 2 quarts = 4 pints = 8 half-pints = 16 Noggins = 32 half-noggins.

For commercial purposes, the basic capacity standard referred to in Jersey documents and used 'from time immemorial' was the *cabot*, applied to both dry and liquid measure and derived from France, most probably Normandy. 1 *cabot* = 10 *pots*.

Quantity and quality of the apple harvest varied considerably. In 1735 Pierre De Ste Croix wrote to Thomas Bandinel in Southampton to say he had consigned by Captain Luce two barrels of cider which he hoped would be satisfactory, but that the cider was '*méchant*' this year.

By 1795 just under 30% of all land was under orchard, the highest percentage being 26 per cent in St Saviour and the lowest 4 per cent in St Ouen.

Before moving forwards from this review of cider apple production in the 17th and 18th Centuries, it is instructive to conclude with this quote from the Rev James Playfair, Chaplain of the 83rd Regiment, which was stationed in

Jersey in 1781, the year of the Battle of Jersey. In a letter to his parents written in that year, he said:

> 'This island, like Guernsey, is all divided into small enclosures of two or three acres of ground and all surrounded with fail dykes or rather dykes of earth, which dykes are planted thick with trees so that from the roads you can scarcely see 30 yards about you anywhere, and the only view that one can have of the island is from the tops of steeples, from which it appears like a forest so you see nothing but wood.
>
> 'More than one fourth of the inclosures of the island are planted with apple trees under which the cows feed. The apple trees furnish them with cider which is all they drink, and the branches of the barren wood serve for fuel.
>
> 'There is nothing what may be called agriculture carried on here. Every man lives in his few acres, which are generally his own, he labours them with his own hands and keeps a horse and two cows. And his wife manages the matters of the house. Everybody has but little, but everybody is above want.'

(iii) APOGEE

THE first half of the 19th Century was really the apogee of the cider export industry.

By the late 1700s, one quarter of Jersey's arable land was taken up with apple orchards, most extensively in the parishes of St Martin, St Saviour, Grouville and St Clement.

In 1801, the Rev François Le Couteur, the Rector of St Martin and an expert on cider, estimated that the people of Jersey drank up to a million gallons of cider each year and that three-quarters of a million gallons were exported.

The quantity of cider exported to England varied from year to year, but the average amount during the late 18th to 19th Centuries remained between 65,000 and 150,000 gallons a year.

Jersey cider was renowned for its delicious flavour, which was achieved by the choice of fruit varieties. The farmers knew well how to create the bittersweet balance that was so popular.

The orchards were planted at 22 feet between the trees at 40 trees per vergée. Apples were picked when they were ripe into wicker hampers and taken by cart to the press house. The trees were long-lived but were replaced gradually in the orchards so that production was maintained. The new trees were grown from pips and grafted after three to four years.

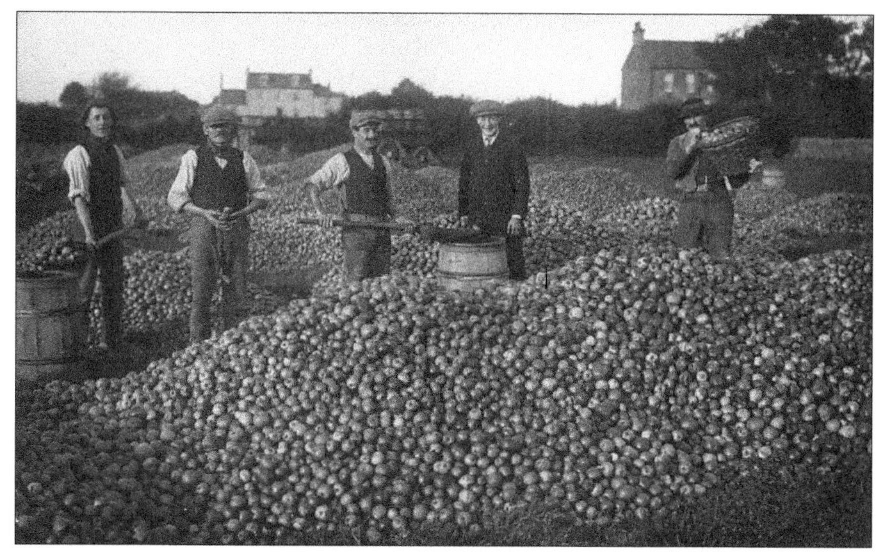

Two postcard views which recall Jersey's cider industry.
The one above, shows workers posing with the apple harvest for a photograph. It is postmarked 1911 by which time activity was already past its peak.
The card below is captioned as 'Old Jersey Cider Press', though it is more properly called an apple crusher. Such structures are massively built of granite in several curved sections and many examples may be spotted around the Island. When in use, a horse would have been harnessed to drag the wheel around the trough, a process which may be witnessed today at the annual Faîs'sie d'Cidre which takes place at Hamptonne Rural Life Museum.

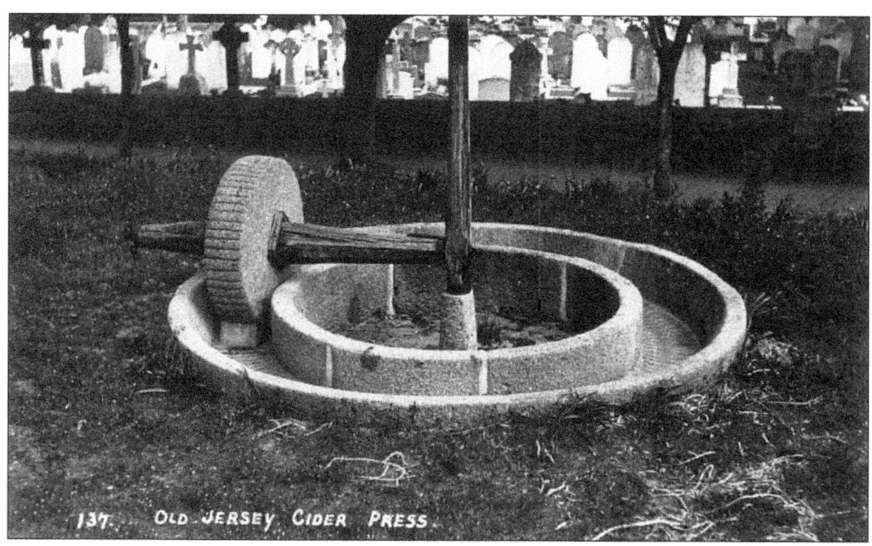

Cider not only changed the contours of the Jersey countryside but also contributed to the style of granite farmhouses as we know them today. The profits from cider helped many farmers to invest considerable sums of money in the circular granite apple crushers. Every farm had its cider press, crusher and equipment to make the year's supply of cider for the family and the labourers. Farmers went to the considerable expense of installing their own apple crushers and presses in purpose-built granite sheds, truly indicative of the smallholder character. They obviously preferred to be self-sufficient in business, and although two factories were built, both failed.

Much of the granite came from Chausey, as it was softer and easier to work than the harder Jersey granite. The combination of apple orchards, crushers and cider press houses led to the Island's countryside taking the shape we see today: granite farmsteads surrounded by small fields, set in a maze of lanes… Jersey's unique natural rural scene was created thanks to the cider industry.

At the time of the Richmond map (1795) over 20 per cent of the arable land was under orchard, or 15 per cent of the whole Island.

In 1801 the Rev Francis Le Couteur, the Rector of Grouville, published the first of several editions of his *Aperçcu sur le Cidre.* He estimated production in an average year at 30,000 to 35,000 barrels, of which 20,000 were consumed locally and the rest exported. His book included the names of some of the popular apple varieties of the period. In 1809, Stead wrote in *Picture of Jersey* that 35,000 hogsheads were made annually and 5,000 exported.

The biennial nature of an apple crop is evident from reports of harvests in the years following Waterloo: Plees, in *An Account of the Island of Jersey* (1817), estimated that 24,000 hogsheads were made annually, of which 1,800 were exported. But in the spring of 1818, when the orchards had all suffered during severe weather in the spring, nevertheless no fewer than 90,000 hogsheads of cider were made; the following year, 1819 was a bad year for the apple crop and, reports written from before the harvest, it was not supposed that more than 1,000 hogsheads would be made, although it was believed to be of excellent quality.

Thomas Quayle, writing in 1815, considered that a quarter of all arable land was under apples, particularly in the eastern parishes. In 1839 alone 268,199 gallons of Jersey cider arrived in English taverns.

There was even a Cider Society, which invited Jean Pipon of La Hague to dinner at La Motte House on 20 March 1845. On 1 Oct 1845 Philippe Marett wrote: 'Tenth day, making cider!'

In 1852, 142,240 gallons of cider were exported and 99,715 bushels of apples;

in 1853, 89,790 gallons of cider and 170,767 bushels of apples.

In 1856 *La Société Centrale d'Agriculture de la Seine Inférieure* was so dissatisfied with every aspect of cider production in that area that it sent two officers to study apple growing and cider making in Jersey. Their report gives full details of the process of cider-making as carried out in Jersey at that time. The best managed orchards and the heaviest crops of all that they saw were found at Mainland, St Lawrence, then farmed by Mr Moïse Gibaut. They declared that never, anywhere in Normandy, had they drunk cider as delicious as that made at Mainland.

Some Jersey place names connected with apples:

Le Clos Pomin, Trinity**; Pomme d'Or Hotel**
In St Lawrence: **Les Jardines Pommes, La Vallette à Pommiers**

Pommeraies – apple orchard (whence Pomeroy)
St Saviour, **Clos de la Pommeraie**

Pommier, apple trees

Pomona Rd occupies an area shown in old maps as a vale with orchards. However, the Jersey historian Philip Ahier says it was named after Pomona City, 33 miles east of Los Angeles, which was visited by a Jersey seaman prior to 1858.

Val Plaisant recalls a time when this now somewhat undistinguished road was once indeed a pleasant vale, lined by apple orchards.

Vigne – The Grape vine
Note that potato haulms and tomato plants are both known locally as 'vignes' or 'vines'

Vignette – a small vine – could be clematis, planted as decoration or ornament

Vinery –a glass house in which grapes or other dessert fruits were grown

(iv) DECLINE

IN the 19th Century, the Industrial Revolution was gathering pace. Especially from the 1830s onwards, there was a new emphasis on good road and canal building, combined with a realisation by farmers in the West Country and Hereford that conditions were favourable for apple growing and cider distribution. Consequently, the number of gallons of cider shipped from Jersey each year to the mainland decreased very quickly.

The quantity of cider exported from Jersey varied widely from year to year, presumably affected by the crop harvested, but the average remained fairly stable from the beginning of the 19th Century until about 1855, after which there is a steady fall until the 1870s, when it almost ceases. In 1804 it was, in round figures, only 65,000 galls (presumably a bad harvest); in 1806, 185,000 galls. For the years 1852-1855 it averaged 150,000 gallons but just over ten years later it had dropped to 35,000 galls. By 1874 it was only 4,000 gallons, and in 1875, the last year in which figures were recorded, it was 2,880 galls.

At the same time it is significant that the export of potatoes was growing steadily. By the year 1850, potatoes had taken first place as the main crop, although cider continued to be made on many farms. Potato exports rose from 4,000 tons in 1866 to 20,000 tons in 1874 and 28,000 tons in 1875.

For a while, the export of cider was replaced by the export of apples themselves, so huge quantities were sent to the new cider factories in England.

For some years after 1880, there was instead a vinegar export industry: 30–40,000 gallons of apple vinegar were exported annually.

But the ageing orchards were no longer replaced. Although exports had ceased, cider was still produced on the farms in good quantity, partly to supply the temporary workers who came from Brittany and who liked their cider.

For the first half of the 20th Century many farmers were still making cider for home consumption, but after the Second World War this domestic cider production also began to decline and by the 1970s very few orchards remained.

It was, perhaps, the decade of the 1970s that was the nadir of the fortunes of Jersey cider – as it was the nadir of much else. And although by then thought was being given to saving some of the historic Jersey apple varieties, the Great Storm of 1987 destroyed many of the apple trees that were left.

In 1978 an apple crusher was placed in King Street – a reminder of the town's economic history and an industry that, it seemed, had died. Things could not get much worse.

(v) REDIVIVUS

BY the later decades of the 20th Century, the loss of so many traditional Jersey apple varieties was causing concern. Several people began to think that an effort should be made to collect graft wood and plant an orchard, so that they could be saved. Jurat Henry Perrée, who was secretary of the National Trust of Jersey at the time, set about the task. He collected graft-wood from several known varieties and gave the wood to a nurseryman to be grafted on to rootstocks for standard trees. Unfortunately in the course of the work the labels became mixed, so that the trees had no certain names. These trees were planted first at the trust's headquarters at The Elms, St Mary, but were moved later to Morel Farm in St Lawrence.

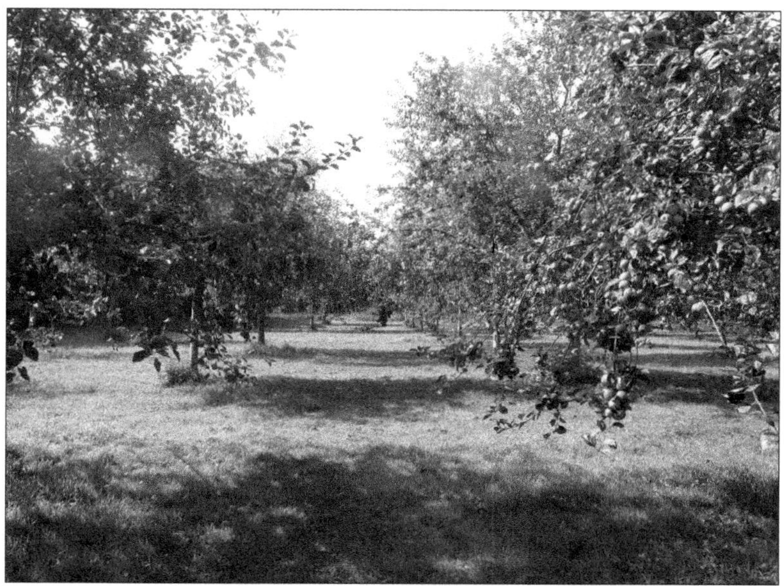

Trees laden with apples in the orchard at The Elms, September 2017

In spite of this effort, the continued decline in cider making meant that many of the ancient varieties of Jersey cider apple were near extinction and the Great Storm of 1987 brought concern about this to a head.

During 1988 to 1998, at least 350 trees were examined, of which 172 were officially numbered, tagged and recorded. The naming proved very difficult as even the experts were not familiar with more than a handful of the old varieties and historical records barely mentioned the names. Prominent figures in this project were Rosemary Bett and Brian Philipps – between them, they did much to save the Jersey cider apple from extinction.

Another 'saviour' of the Jersey cider apple was David Cashel of St Brelade who, helped by the parish gardener, Peter Pinglaux, helped to ensure that the cider-making tradition in St Brelade did not disappear altogether. Thanks to their interest and enthusiasm, in 1991 they planted 21 cider apple trees in a parish field next to the Parish Depot on La Rue Carrée. In March 1993, the trees were grafted with an old Jersey variety. Eighteen of them ended the century as healthy specimens, yielding good crops for making cider and black butter.

When the apple project began, the Country Life Museum at Hamptonne was being developed and it was agreed that a small traditional orchard of standard trees should be planted there. In 2002 it was decided that a formal trust should be set up to ensure the future status of the orchards and the continuity of management. The Jersey Cider Apple Trust was legally established on 11 November 2002 and the inaugural annual general meeting was held on 23 March 2003.

An orchard in Trinity, on States land that was made available by the Agriculture Department at Howard Davis Farm, was close planted with the aim of studying and assessing the qualities of probably unique Jersey cider and dual-

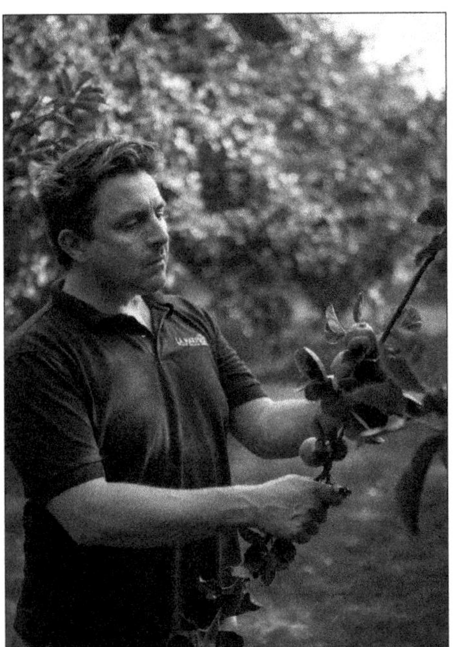

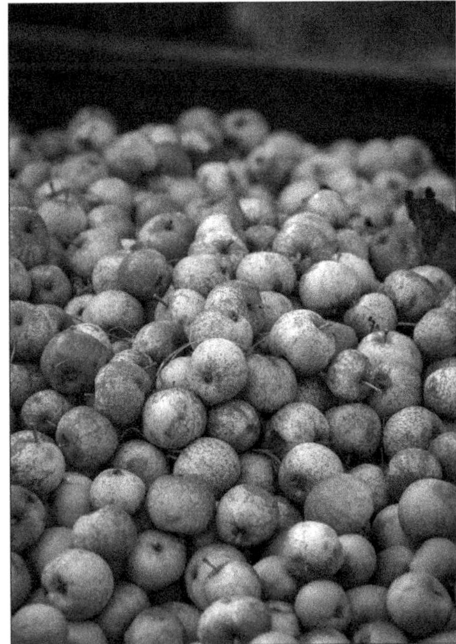

Apple harvest at La Mare: Pictured is their wine and cider maker, Daniel de Carteret (photo: Gary Grimshaw)

purpose varieties and to preserve them as a green bank. M25 rootstocks were established in this nursery.

But it was thought that a long-term orchard of standard trees should be developed, preferably on National Trust land. The trust was enthusiastic and after much discussion and soil testing, a part of Field 887 at The Elms was judged to be the best spot for the new orchard and work proceeded towards the aim of planting in November 2003.

A total of 108 trees were planted at the Elms – large standard trees, creating a traditional Jersey cider orchard in order to preserve the gene bank of those last remaining local cider apple trees. In total, these two orchards contained 52 different Jersey apple varieties.

There is now considerable interest in the Jersey cider apple, with several requests to the Jersey Cider Apple Trust for advice on planting orchards or small collections. It is, at least, a contributory factor to what could be a modest revival of the ancient cider industry in the Island.

In the winter of 2011–2012, the National Trust for Jersey's Lands team, assisted by Brian Philipps and Neil Molyneux, planted out a new cider orchard at Les Côtils Farm in Mont à l'Abbé, a property with a rich history of apple and cider production.

Over the past few years, hardened volunteers at various events have been undertaking the dutiful task of tasting ciders made by the Jersey Cider Apple Trust to identify the best flavoured apple varieties. This rigorous and thorough tasting has identified that 20 out of the 52 apple varieties saved now produce a good-tasting cider.

As a consequence of this process, the Les Côtils Farm orchard has been planted with 80 trees and contains just those 20 varieties. It is envisaged that shortly, when these trees are sufficiently mature to yield a good crop, that this orchard will once again deliver a good quality, pure Jersey cider.

A FIRM sign of renewal is when commercial concerns show an interest, so that Jersey cider ceases to be just a hobby for academics and antiquarians. At the time of writing there are two of these: La Mare Estate in St Mary and La Robeline in St Ouen.

The founders of La Mare, Robert ('Bob') and Ann Blayney, were very probably the first people in modern times to plant a commercial apple orchard at La Mare in the 1970s and to make cider, although it was always a minor product in comparison to their range of grape wines.

Bob Blayney said: 'Making local cider had almost disappeared. A few farmers made small quantities for their own family use and our gentle research was not impressed by the quality. Discussing the question with our ever-friendly farmer neighbour, Edgar Rolland, we found that he had the expertise and the generosity to teach us how to make real Jersey Cider.'

Since their retirement and departure from La Mare in 1997, the new management under Tim Crowley and wine maker Daniel de Carteret has continued with and expanded the cider production. New orchards were planted in St Lawrence and they continue to buy apples from the general public. They make a range of cider: draft for pubs, a sparkling cider ('*Branchage*') and a fine champagne style cider ('*Branchage Prestige*') in a corked bottle.

They also make, very successfully, a fine apple brandy which, to all intents and purposes, is calvados – although of course they are unable to call it that. Further details of their wine and spirit production are mentioned on pages 174-187 in the wine and spirit chapters of this book.

Richard and Sarah Matlock run their 'La Robeline Cider Company', from their old farmhouse in St Ouen. Richard is an engineer and was for 30 years the proprietor of a marine business that included the Channel Island dealership for Sunseeker Yachts.

He makes a traditional cidre bouché cider, '*Cidre d'Jèrri*', in medium and dry styles. This is made in the French way, using only apples, with no concentrates, no additives, no added carbon dioxide and is bottle fermented.

Richard had dreamt of making his own cider for a long time. In 2004 and then again in 2005 he spent several weeks in France learning how to make Normandy cider with local cider makers. He was also looking for a suitable cider press and eventually he found one in an old barn; he dismantled it and brought it back home to St Ouen.

The press turned out to be an 85-year-old piece of French history and included a beam of over 12ft. Being an engineer who loves old machinery, Richard restored the press and installed it in an out-building at their farmhouse.

Two cider orchards had been planted ready for the first harvest in autumn of 2005. In his words: 'La Robeline Cider started as a hobby business but has rather taken over our lives!'

With the help of friends, Richard pressed several tonnes of apples that first year and produced an authentic 'Champagne' style cider, which resulted in 1,200 bottles. The new cider was launched at Bienvenue Farm in St Lawrence on 21 July 2006 and sold out in six weeks. He said: 'Our initial success that first summer convinced us both that there was a market for our cider. However, at that stage, and for the next nine years, the business had to remain small and manageable as we still had our marine business.'

A further three orchards were planted that year. Richard and Sarah entered the cider in the Royal Bath and West Show in 2007 and won a 'Highly Commended' award; in May 2009, the cider won first prize in the International class. In 2015, the medium cider won the coveted 'Two Gold Stars' in the Great Taste Awards, with which they were particularly pleased, as it was the first year they had entered.

The cider is widely available in the Island through farm shops, wine merchants and supermarkets. He also makes a flat cider for draught sales; since 2009, kegged and 'bag in box' cider has been selling very successfully through the Liberation Group in several local pubs. It can also be tasted at many of the country shows and markets and 'Genuine Jersey' events at which La Robeline has a stall to sell their own cider and home-made sausages, cordials and cakes.

Richard and Sarah subsequently planted many more orchards and continue to plant bespoke orchards every winter. In the autumn of 2016, La Robeline Cider harvested 26 orchards, the majority of which they had planted over the past ten years.

La Robeline Cider is an 'organic' product. No chemicals are used in any of the orchards that are harvested for La Robeline cider. Some orchard owners have flocks of sheep which graze under the trees; others have beehives or cut the grass for hay and some just enjoy their orchards and allow La Robeline to harvest the apples each year.

In Richard's words: 'Each year we plant more orchards and as they reach maturity, we are able to harvest more apples. So as the annual crop increases, so will our production. We have produced up to 20,000 litres of cider each year but will be producing more as our harvest increases. Approximately 1kg of apples go into a pint of cider. We source all our apples locally form orchards around Jersey. Currently we sell everything we produce in the Island and sell out by Christmas with the new season's product being available from the early spring.'

Asked how important provenance and freshness were to La Robeline, Richard replied: 'Crucial! We are passionate about our product and the fact that it is made from local apples and nothing else. Over the years we have planted many orchards that not only enhance the countryside but bring diversity to the environment. 'It just wouldn't feel right to bring apples in from elsewhere.'

Jersey cider apple varieties are planted in the nursery orchard belonging to Hans van Oordt in St John, who at the time of writing has made apple juice from traditional Jersey apple varieties for the past few years and is now making cider from those same varieties. A sparkling apple juice is now being made by Jenni Liddiard of Field Farm in St Lawrence.

OVER the past few years there has indeed been a great re-planting of apple trees and apple orchards. Many of these are not commercial orchards, nor do they provide many apples for the commercial makers. Their main point, in all honesty, is to provide something to fill an empty field and – especially – to provide a screen to a property to block out the curious and intrusive gaze of passers-by.

Certainly, if there is any redundant land, a good answer to the question of what to do with it is to put it under apple trees, as so much of the Island's land was in the past. It is good for the environment, it certainly does not harm the land, and if at any time the land was needed for something else showing a more immediate return, it could be almost immediately available.

If the trees are high enough and protected sufficiently, livestock can be kept underneath the trees: cows, sheep, pigs or poultry.

If enough trees were planted, the produce need not necessarily be limited to cider. A single juicing plant could be established and run on a co-operative basis, or – like the old mills in the Island to which the farmer took his grain for milling – the juice could be returned to the apple grower to make whatever he felt was profitable with it: such as marketable fruit juice or cider vinegar.

In short, it would be a way of letting any surplus land rest until it was needed again, and a way of keeping everything tidy and productive, and looking beautiful.

One might surmise that visitors would come to see an Island covered with apple blossom; the ecology would benefit and it could encourage more people to try their hand at farming on a small-scale. And what could be more attractive than an Island covered with apple orchards?

The Jersey Heritage Trust was the inspiration of a popular modern festival at Hamptonne Country Life Museum in October: *La Faîs'sie d'Cidre*. This celebrates Jersey's rich heritage of growing apples and making cider. There are apple games, displays, stalls, arts and crafts, local food and music and cider. The event highlight is the traditional cider making. The public throngs there to enjoy the sight of a horse walking round the Chausey granite crusher crushing apples and the apple pulp layered with hessian on the twin-screw wooden press to extract the juice that will then be put into barrels and turned into cider.

Also there are cabbage loaves and Jersey wonders, apple juicing, a Jèrriais language education stall, La Robeline Cider selling its cider and home-made sausages, the Jersey Cider Apple Trust, a Genuine Jersey market and Jersey beekeepers judging their honey.

It makes a pleasant day out, especially if it is a warm and sunny October day, and an opportunity to remind the public about the history of cider-making.

But the Big Apple in Jersey is not only a crop of the past but a potential crop of the future as well: Jersey's once and future crop?

(vi) BLACK BUTTER, CUSTOMS AND FOLKLORE

IT would be hardly surprising if some half a millennium of cider making had not resulted in apple-related customs and folklore – and that indeed is the case. The best known aspect of this social history is the making of the concentrated apple preserve called 'black butter' (*nièr beurre*). It is flavoured with spices originally imported from the New World.

In cider production's 'glory days', Jersey was also a shipbuilding and cod fishing Island. Many Islanders would farm for part of the year, and then go fishing for cod off Newfoundland and Canada. Their catches would be salted, and then transported to the Catholic countries of South America. There, the Jersey fishermen would exchange their catch for exotic spices for which there was a good market in Britain.

In the cider season, making Black Butter was a convenient way of using up a seasonal glut of apples, which could be flavoured by those 'exotic' spices brought back from American fishing and trading voyages. The practice of making Black Butter is thus likely to have started in the 17th Century, at the same time as cod fishing began being a major economic activity for Islanders,

Traditionally, it was made in small quantities at home over a hearth fire, but it could also be a huge communal effort with families or whole neighbourhoods getting together to make 250 or 300 pounds at a time.

Two to three days would be spent peeling as many as 42 hundredweight barrels of apples, which at the same time gave a wonderful opportunity for catching up on all the gossip and news and singing of the traditional songs.

Then, on the big day, the hearth in one of the outhouses would be lit with small branches and long, black logs to produce a fierce heat. A large brass *bachin* with 20 gallons of cider would be put on the trivet in the late afternoon and the liquor would be reduced by half. Apples would then be added, up to 22 half-cwt barrels of sweet peeled apples (and two of Bramleys) throughout the night and during the following day. Two men would stir the mixture the whole time to prevent it from sticking to the bottom and burning.

The accordionist would have played and much singing and dancing would have taken place with lots of recently home-brewed cider to quench the thirst of these industrious people. *Bouchies* were eaten and *Chaudé* drunk (hot cider with beaten eggs). At 6pm the party returned to stir the mixture with the long-handled *moueux* or a *rabot* by the light of the *crâsset.*

When all the apples had been absorbed into a thick creamy brown mixture, 21 pounds of sugar, 24 chopped lemons, 1 pound of grated nutmeg 1 pound of cinnamon and 3 pounds of mixed spice were added along with sticks of liquorice. All was tasted and stirred well together. Then the *bachin* was lifted off the hearth by many strong men and the lovely aromatic mixture potted up to make some 300 pounds of *nièr-beurre*, stored in earthenware glazed pots of all sizes for use during the winter months.

Fast food it certainly is not – more like slow food with attitude.

It tastes very good on bread as an apple spread (traditional), as a flavour for sausage (non-traditional), as a cool side-dish with a hot curry (definitely non-traditional) or as an ice-cream flavour (cool, hip, modern).

This very old and traditional farmhouse delicacy is important as one of the elements of Jersey's traditional rural culture. Lots of labour was needed to make it – so it was a co-operative project that brought together family and friends. Refreshment would be needed for the apple choppers and apple peelers, and for the stirrers at the cauldron – so it made for quite a party atmosphere.

Lots of time was needed to make the black butter, and lots of stamina to keep awake during the night hours. So, music and songs helped to make the time pass quicker, and for those awaiting their turn to stir there might be dancing and cards and storytelling – it comprised what is called, in Jèrriais, '*Un Séthée de Nièr Beurre*' (*Un soir de beurre noir*).

They provided a rare opportunity for hard-working farming people to get together and have a bit of fun.

During the Occupation years, Black Butter continued to be made whenever possible in the autumn. It was not quite the traditional recipe: no sugar, lemons or spices were available but liquorice and saccharine for sweetening could be bought from chemists such as La Croix de Lorraine and Stones' in St Helier. The preserving quality was not good, but it did not have to last long and it was eaten quickly. With the curfew in force, everyone involved stayed on site and *eune sethée de nièr Beurre* must have lifted the spirits for many days afterwards during those unhappy times.

Black Butter continues to be made, but more by clubs and societies for fund-raising purposes, such as by the National Trust, St Martin Methodist Church and Young Farmers Club. A major producer and organiser of Black Butter evenings for the past few years has been the National Trust for Jersey.

Director of operations at the trust's annual Black Butter-making event has been Neil Mourant. For him, Black Butter making is a regular occurrence going back to his childhood days in the 1950s.

The recipe he uses comes from his grandmother's family; they made black butter for generations past, and the recipe has not changed over time. He recalls:

> 'We made two or three batches of black butter a year on the farm when I was a child,' he said. 'It was part of the farm income. The apples came from our own orchard, and to clean them we carried out an old zinc bathtub and filled it with water, and dunked the apples in it. The apples we didn't use for black butter went to make cider for the Breton labourers.
>
> 'My grandfather would come at 5am to light the fire, and by the time I went off to school the apples were being placed in the big *bachin*. The day before, lots of aunts and great-aunts would come and peel the apples, carrying on all day, with breaks for lunch and tea. It was very much part of my life.'

It was not a folklore session and there was no special party atmosphere – but it was an opportunity for the extended family to come together.

Black Butter's labour-intensive and lengthy making process does not lend itself exactly to commercial production, but one commercial outlet, La Mare Estate, produces it for sale. It uses modern equipment and a mere five-hour stirring period. La Mare exports it to the UK and Europe – their product intermittently gets 'discovered' by food writers, and is stocked by trendy delicatessens around the country.

But there are not too many *Séthées de Beurre Nièr* these days: for one thing, it is difficult to find the premises with hearths sufficiently big enough to accommodate the *bachin* – too many old farmhouses have been converted to expensive rural residences.

The glow of the fire that keeps the mixture bubbling is, increasingly, the soft warm glow of nostalgia for the past.

Recipe for Du Chaûdé

Warm, in separate pans, a glassful of cider and ¾ glass of milk, beat 2 eggs and stir into the warm milk, then add the cider, very hot.

It is said that this was the favourite drink of country people for warming themselves when they came in from the cold.

The proportion of cider and milk and the number of eggs may be varied to taste. The main thing is to drink it hot.

(From *Buon Appétit*, published by the Jersey Island Federation of Women's Institutes.)

THE custom of bell-ringing at St Mary's Church from Christmas Eve to midnight in Christmas Day had – historically – a lot to do with the enthusiastic consumption of cider which made the bell-ringers get out of hand.

In 1866 the Rector, Rev Le Couteur Balleine, decided to put a stop to the noise and the nuisance: he crept up to the Belfry, removed the bell clappers, then the bell rope, and finally the ladder to the belfry itself. He then changed the locks on the church doors.

As can be imagined, the bell-ringers were furious. A hand-bill was written and circulated telling the Parish: '*Enfants de Ste Marie, vos droits sont envahis.*' Then under the leadership of the Church Warden the bell ringers took retaliatory action. They kicked down the church door; one of them dashed to St Helier to fetch a rope and another dashed to the blacksmith for him to hammer out a rough and ready bell-clapper.

Once again, the Rector had to listen to ten church bells from 10am on Christmas Eve to 4a.m on Christmas morning. The church was also in a disgusting state after a mammoth drinking session.

The Rector got no sympathy from a Parish Assembly when he brought a complaint to it. He was told: 'If there were any disturbances, it was entirely due to the pig-headed behaviour of the Rector who wished to deprive the inhabitants of a right which was dear to them.'

IN the 1870s and 1880s, it was the custom on the first Sunday in May for the young people of the town – '*Les Vilaises*' (the townees) to get up at sunrise and walk to the farms on the town's outskirts. There they would drink milk still warm from the cows they had watched the farmer milk. One of the favourite haunts was Vallée des Vaux, where there used to be a house called 'Milk Punch House'. It was so-called because some of the young people would drink milk punch near there. To make this refreshing drink, they needed three-quarters of a glass of fresh milk, two teaspoons of sugar, one wine glass of brandy and one pinch of cinnamon.

Recipe for Milk-é-Pan'tch

Sweeten half a gallon of milk to taste, add a pinch of grated nutmeg or ground cinnamon. Half a cupful of rum and 6 beaten eggs.
The punch was traditionally drunk on Midsummer's Day.

For a single glass of wine:
¾ of a large cupful of milk
2 teaspoons sugar
Wine glass of finest brandy
A pinch of cinnamon. Mix well

Youngsters got up just after midnight on 23 June and would milk two or three of the neighbours' cows and robbed eggs, then went back to bed. Later they added rum to the milk, poured it on to the beaten eggs and added nutmeg or cinnamon.

(From *Buon Appétit*, published by the
Jersey Island Federation of Women's Institutes.)

JERSEY'S CIDER APPLE VARIETIES

As collected by the late Frank Le Maistre. Originally this appeared in the *Bulletin of the Assembliée d'Jèrriais* and was reprinted in the *Bulletin of the Société Jersiaise* for the year 1970, following the article titled 'Pommage' by J G Speer, 'to preserve for posterity the Jersey names, characteristics and times of ripening of many of the apples that were once so great a part of Island life'.

Du Doux Am'thé Sweet, soft, yellow; very juicy and makes good quality cider.

Du Vert Am'thé Bitter-sweet, green, hard and late. Fruit well shaped but poor in quality.

Des Pommes d'Avouetage Apples ripening in August (*en Avoût*) Yellow, small, sweet and soft. Good eating but do not keep.

Des Pommes d'Avranches Very sweet, green and soft. October. Good for cider and very good for baking.

Du Nièr Binnet A very good all-purpose apple. Makes excellent cider when really ripe. December.

Des Pommes dé Brétangne (du Gros Brétangne) Sweet, flat in shape and streaked with red. Good for baking. February. If the apples are really ripe, the cider bottles well. A strong tree.

Des Pommes dé Cabot Sweet, soft, reddish colour. Good for cider. October. Tree bears well.

Des Cadelinnes Rîlyies Sour, streaked with red and of good quality. Good cooker and bears well. October.

Des Vèrtes Cadelinnes Cooker. Formerly there were 12 to 15 other varieties of Cadelinne known in Jersey!

Des Pommes dé Cannelle Small, bitter-sweet yellowish fruit. Makes good cider. November.

Du Caplyi Streaked with red. October. Cider of good flavour.

Du Gris Caplyi Sweet, small fruit, greyish-red. February to March. Makes a nice sweet cider with good flavour. The tree bears well in alternate years.

Du Gros Caplyi Sweet, green, November. Good cider that bottles well. This apple may be mixed with any other.

Du Su Caplyi Sour. November. Good cider that keeps well and doesn't turn to vinegar. The tree bears a very heavy crop.

Du Vèrt Caplyi Small fruit, bitter-sweet, grey-green. January. Good cropper.

Des Pommes à Chucre Small, sweet, yellow fruit. A strong tree that bears well.

Des Pommes dé Cire Sour and green, well flushed with red on one side. January.

Du Côtard Green and sour. December. It makes only a small tree but bears well.

Du Court-Pendu A bitter-sweet, very green fruit, good for cider. But this tree does not bear well and the branches die back at the tips.

Des Douoches Danmes Very sweet and early. The cider does not keep well after March.

Des Pommes d'Empereur Alexandre Sour, soft. September. A good all-purpose apple.

Du Jaune Ernet (or d'l'Ernette Dorée) 'Golden Russet'. Good keeping apple, late April and useful for all purposes.

D'l'Ernette de Bâtard Hard green sour apples, good for cooking. November.

D'la Grise Ernette Sour, very grey colour, ruddy skin, good cooker. December.

Du Blianc Fieillu Sour, green, medium size but smaller than the next. Fairly good apple.

Du Rouoge Fieillu Sour and hard, red colour and medium size. January. Exceptionally good keeper.

Des Belles Fil'yes Early, sweet and green. A good all-purpose apple. The tree bears well.

Des P'tites Fil'yes A very good old apple, sweet, very small, striped with red. November. The best apple to mix with Caplyi for cider but also makes very good cider by itself.

Du Fôsset A soft green apple, a little sour but good eating. August to September. A very useful early apple.

Du Gros France A large, sweet green apple, good for all purposes.

Du P'tit France A medium size sweet apple, hard and very green. December-January. One of the best, that makes cider with a special taste (and for bottling) and keeps well.

Du Gros Frêtchian A red, sweet apple, large and soft and shiny. Considered the best of all for cider making.

Du P 'tit Frêtchian A reddish grey apple of beautiful appearance; before 1914 it was much in demand for table decoration. No use for anything except cider and not even that if used alone. But from five to eight per cent added to almost any other apples improves the quality of the cider made. Two or three trees were planted in every cider orchard.

Du Frisé A good cider apple, soft, striped red. October.

Des Gare d'Angliéterre Very large soft green, sour apples that do not keep well but make a good dry cider. October.

Des Pommes d'lvraie (or Su France) Sour, bitter apples good for jelly and for cooking. Makes a long-keeping dry cider. Tree bears well.

Du P'tit Jean A useful all-purpose apple, sour and streaked with red; keeps well.

Des Pommes dé Juin A little sour, soft and yellow. Good for cooking and eating but does not keep well. June.

Des Pommes dé Limon Very hard, sour, green and late. March. Good for baking. Tree does not crop well and the branches die back.

Du Loumé (or Lonmé) Very good, green and sweet. Makes sweet, dark cider. December.

Du Maugi Sour to bitter, hard, of medium size; keeps well and the tree bears well. A good apple for making jelly. Makes a very good dry cider, clear and of a yellow-brown colour. Can be mixed with any other cider apple.

Des Mère du Ménage Sour apples, good for keeping.

Du Musé d'Boeu Sour, soft, striped red; a good early all-purpose apple. The tree bears well.

Du Musé d'Brebis Bitter sweet apples, small and green. November. Makes good cider.

Du Pépin Bâtard For cider only. Small and green, bitter-sweet. November.

Du Pépin Billot For cider. Sweet, green and good. November.

Du Pépin au Bro For cider. Sweet, green and good. November.

Du Pépin d'Fliandres Hard, green and sour. Cooks well and keeps well.

Du Pépin J'valyi (Chevalier) Fruit is soft and a bit sour, grey and striped red. Very good to eat and for cooking. September. The tree grows quickly and bears well but is short-lived.

Du Pépin Orange Large, sweet, flat-shaped apples with yellow skin. Good apple. Tree has the same characteristics as the last-named.

Du Vèrt Pépin Sweet, green and medium size, cider only. Makes good flavoured cider that bottles well. November.

Du Pigeonnet Very much the same as *Rouoge Fieillu.*

Des Pommes dé Pontis Fruit a little sour, soft, green and of medium size. Very juicy, good for eating and cooking. August.

Du Doux Rom'thi (Romeril) Fruit flattish, green and sweet. One of the best sweet apples and one that can confidently be used for any purpose. When other kinds are spoiled by excessive heat in September or cold in October this apple is not affected. It is best mixed with '*du Maugi*' to make cider for bottling.

Du Gros Rom'thi A sweet, soft green apple, the poorest known to cider makers. Lacking in colour and taste, it is also weak in alcohol and tannin. November.

Du Su Rom'thi (or Sueur Rom 'thi) Shape and colour of fruit like the '*Doux Rom'thi*' but the tree does not bear well.

Des Pommes dé Rosée Fruit sourish, soft and greenish yellow. Good for eating and cooking, but doesn't keep for very long. Good strong trees. August–September.

Du P'tit Rouoget A sweet, red, hard apple that keeps well and makes good cider. January–February.

Du Rouoget Late. Acid but a good keeper.

Des Pommes dé Saule Bitter-sweet and yellowish. Cider only. December.

Des Pommes dé Suzanne Sour, soft, striped and red. An August apple that doesn't keep but useful. Bears well.

Du Têtard Cider only. Bitter-sweet, green. December.

Des Tête dé Cat A keeping apple. Sour.

Du Doux au Vêque A little apple which makes a yellow cider, one of the best for bottling. November. Bears fairly well.

Des Pommes dé Vin Sour, soft, with flesh red right through. August. Good for baking in the oven.

LE QUESNE & Co.

Wine and Spirit Merchants

SPARKLING JERSEY CIDER

(Blue and White Label)

Warranted Absolutely Pure

Awarded Bronze Medal, Allied Trades Exhibition, London, 1908

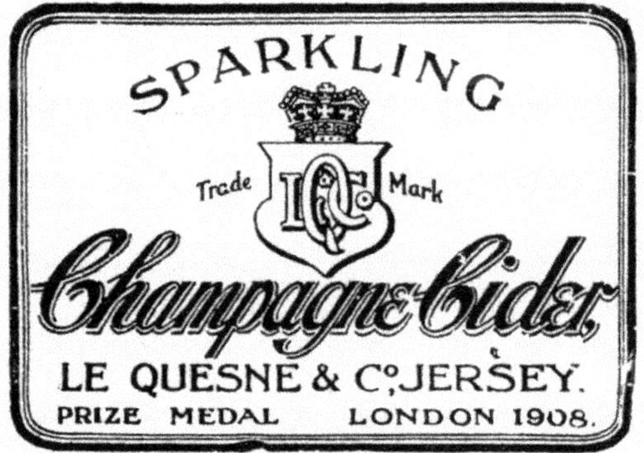

Sole Agents for Robertson's Celebrated "Yellow Label" Scotch Whisky. Eldridge Pope & Co.'s Famous Dorchester Ales. *Speciality*: Crystal Ale at 2/9 per doz. Choice Old Wines in the Cellars

All the Leading Liqueurs kept in stock

---

9 & 11 Burrard St. and 77 Halkett Place

Telephone—No. 95 **JERSEY** Telephone—No. 95

~ 5 ~

Drinking in the 16th to 18th Centuries

'[Channel Islanders] speake French: yet disdaine they to be reputed or named French; and can very well be content to be called English'

William Camden (1561–1623) *Britannia*

For much of the three centuries covered in this chapter it was a time when religion was uppermost in the public discourse: religious Reformation and Counter Reformation; Protestantism, Calvinist and Huguenot Puritanism; Methodism. In Jersey, the mediaeval Catholic churches became 'temples' and the colourful vestments of Catholic priests became the black and white monochrome clothing of earnest Protestant divines.

Considering how popular were the mediaeval fairs and the jolly celebration of various Holy Days, one wonders why Islanders were quite so quick to jettison an annual calendar of feasts and fairs for an unsmiling Protestantism; to forsake the apparently 'bacchanalian' dancing round maypoles on midsummer's day for the pious rendition of metrical psalms. Whatever the reason, Jersey embraced Reformation with enthusiasm – but Reformation came not from an English source but rather inspired by the teachings of Jean Calvin of Geneva.

But although Jersey people became, by and large, a Puritanical society, beer – and especially cider – continued to be safer as everyday drinks than water; the religious Reformation was not a Temperance Reformation.

The beverages common in the 16th and 17 Centuries were cider, beer, '*cervoise*' (barley beer), French wines and a locally made article called '*Vittoe*', a kind of mead of which honey was the principal ingredient. It was very strong and could make the unwary drinker drunk: a phrase then in use was '*vous êtes envittoé*'.

The sales prices were regulated by the discretion of the Court.

However, occasions where the consumption of alcohol might inspire inappropriate behaviour – especially between the sexes – were looked on askance. Such occasions were the popular pastime of sand-eeling: a night-time jaunt on a beach by lantern-light to dig for sand-eels; probably most hilarious affairs and certainly with the element of hilarity enhanced by the consumption of cider.

Thus, on 6 September 1589 the Royal Court passed an ordinance in regard to sand-eeling parties: women and girls were prohibited from taking part in these excursions, unless accompanied by a husband or parent. And in October 1619, Catherine Le Sauteur was convicted of having dressed and masqueraded as a man: she was condemned to be placed in the stocks, with the breeches she had worn were to be exhibited beside her.

On 11 October 1589, playing the game of '*jeu de quilles*' was prohibited on Sundays, and on 25 March 1597 all games on Sundays were prohibited. On 14 May 1603 similar ordinances were proclaimed in the Place du Marché, with the addition that all Taverns were to be closed on Sundays:

> 'Whereas heretofore many Acts which have been passed for the suppression of vice have fallen into desuetude through the negligence of our officials with the result that drunkenness, blasphemy and the profanation of the Sabbath have continued to increase, to the great scandal of the righteous. To remedy this the States have found it expedient to ordain that the orders of this subject should be duly enforced by the officials, especially as many abuse the Sabbath by frequenting taverns after service to the great scandal of the righteous and disregard of the said Actes. For this reason innkeepers are forbidden to open their taverns and inhabitants of this island also are forbidden to visit the same throughout the whole of Sunday and the night thereof, on pain of a fine of ten francs in the cases of innkeepers and of three groats for each person found on the premises.'

In 1608 an Ordinance was passed to compel taverners in the town to keep at least two beds available for travellers. From this time onwards, the Court records make constant reference limiting the number of tavern and taverner licences in town. In 1572 there were only 14 Taverners in St Helier; by the winter of 1594-95 taverns had been reduced to six in number.

In June 1597 the States complained of the misery which existed through the common people flocking to Town to attend the Court, and once in town, spending their time in the taverns and '*cabarets*' and consequently neglecting their families. There were fines for drunkenness and the person fined was also prohibited from frequenting taverns.

On 27 September 1595 it was enacted that no taverner could sell wine until it had been first sampled by the Bailiff, assisted by the Jurats – nor beer, unless it had been tasted by the Constable or a Centenier – duties that must have done something to ameliorate the cares of public office.

Remedies from the late 16th Century involved treatment with alcohol; evidence that drinking was encouraged for medicinal reasons – as it had been since time immemorial.

A collection of folk remedies for minor ailments from Guernsey, dated 1589, mentions, for example:

> 'Bad breath: 'To remove bad smells from the mouth, it is good to wash the mouth with wine in which has been boiled aniseed and cloves, or to chew either the root of the yellow iris or a lump of putty for a sufficient length of time.'

At least chewing gum has an historical precedent, it seems.

> 'For those unfortunate or misguided enough to swallow a serpent: 'drink a mixture of vervain with wine is something to be tried.'

THE strong commercial connections and trading links between Jersey, France and England that had existed already since before the Middle Ages continued in Tudor and Stuart times. In 1599, for example, three Guernsey vessels and two Jersey vessels entered London with wine from Saint Malo and Bordeaux.

The Channel Islanders were middlemen in cross-Channel Anglo-French trade, with particular emphasis on taking French wines to England. From 1508 to 1520 at least four or five Jersey vessels and one Guernsey vessel carried wine from Bordeaux to London, one of which, the *Henry* from Jersey, made repeated voyages in 1512, 1514, 1515 and 1519. In the year following Michaelmas 1570, the *Star* and the *St John*, both of Jersey, entered Bristol with wines from St Malo; and we read of the *Star* (20 tons) entering Minehead in Somerset with a cargo of wine from Oporto.

In 1599, three Guernsey and two Jersey vessels entered London with wine from St Malo and Bordeaux; by the later 17th Century French and Spanish brandies also formed a part of this trade.

In the year following Michaelmas 1600, another two Jersey vessels entered

Bristol with wines and sack from Calais; in 1630 and 1631 at least five Jersey vessels entered Southampton with Sack and Malaga wine from Saint Malo, three of which made more than two voyages.

Wine shipments into Ireland were also an important part of Jersey's wine trade. Customs records of 1614 and 1615 suggest that Channel Island vessels, especially those of Jersey, were active carriers in that trade: eight Jersey and two Guernsey vessels (three of which made two separate voyages) entered Irish ports with shipments of wine. Eight of the vessels came from Saint Malo, one from Calais and one from La Rochelle. Most of the wine was Sack, carried in small amounts ranging from 6 to 32 tuns, chiefly for Irish merchants.

In 1646 we have records of the *Philip*, sent out by John Brocq and his brother on a triangular voyage from Saint Malo to Malaga and back to Jersey with freight.

SIR Walter Raleigh was Governor of Jersey from 1600 to 1603. The Bristol Hotel – which until shortly before the time of writing this book stood at the corner of Kensington Place and the Esplanade, was claimed to stand on the location of a hostelry that existed in his day. As likely as not this was a legend invented by the Bristol Hotel itself, but it is possible that a tavern did stand in what were then the sand dunes west of town and that this provided a halfway house for traffic between St Helier and Elizabeth Castle.

And so we revert once again to the subject of taverns and the attempts by the Royal Court to manage the number, or at least to raise some income by taxing them. An Ordnance for the Isle of Jersey, dated 29 July 1619 and signed by James I, declared:

> 'We were pleased to grant them power to levy wine to be sold in taverns, we do now signify our further pleasure that the said grant shall be passed to our Bailiff and Jurats, as a body capable of such a grant, to levy it expresse ordered, that the benefit thereof be farmed out yearly, to such as will give most.
>
> 'The money raised should be used for the assuaging of the poorer sort of our subjects, to provide powder and ammunition for them, to pay them for repairing sea-banks and landing places, and lastly… [a hospital and a house of correction].'

In 1635, Charles I was on the throne and nothing had yet been done to build that hospital and house of correction. 'It was thought fit and ordered that a House of Correction should be provided there for the punishment of rogues, vagabonds and idle persons.' But there was no mention of a hospital for 'poor and impotent persons'.

The Governor, Bailiff and Jurats were also told to reduce the number of taverns and alehouses and that each of these had to have a licence to retail wine, spirits and cider.

The 'House of Correction' remained unbuilt, especially with the turmoil of civil war that was about to descend on Jersey and the importance of other ventures, such as the building of a pier at St Aubin, which seemed more pressing (and more profitable).

An Order in Council of 12 June 1635, which was registered by the Royal Court on 24 September, related to the 'reformation of abuses of and in taverns, cider houses and alehouses. It is thought fit and ordered that the Governor, Bailiffs, and Jurats should refuse and bring them to a convenient number and that they punish drunkards and also alehouse-keepers breaking the assize and that are permitted to retail wine, beer or cider without licence'.

On 28 April 1648 the number of taverns in St Helier was reduced to six.

The project for funding a hospital and 'house of correction' was not entirely forgotten: on 13 January 1647, heads of families were assembled to see if they would help in paying to construct a 'house of correction' in the town for casual drunkards and the work-shy. It was quickly concluded that 'if all the drunkards came to be housed there the place would find itself well-provided with guests'. Requests for funding at parish meetings met with a cold reception.

On 19 March 1649 Sir George Carteret, the defender of Jersey for the King during the Civil Wars, convoked the States to show them letters he had received from Charles II. One was a thank you letter – and a gift of 500 *pistoles* to help them build a pier. The other was an order that a tax should be levied on wine. The States said that this revenue should be left in their hands as a public fund for the purchase of arms to be issued to men who were themselves too poor to provide them (and, of course, for the building and maintenance of a House of Correction).

The tax took effect from 26 Apr 1649 (Easter Monday). Wine that had cost 8 *sous* the *pot* (half-gallon) was raised to 9 *sous* the *pot*, with a tax of 1 *sou a pot* levied in accordance with the King's letter and Act of the States.

The Island only got round to building a Hospital 108 years later, in 1755.

FOR recording the Civil War period, we have to thank the contemporary resident of the Place du Marché, Jean Chevalier, who kept a diary which contains many of the details that make that eventful period of the Island's history come alive.

We learn, for example, of the extent of imported wine and beer from France, for use both at Elizabeth Castle and the besieged Castle Cornet in Guernsey.

Thus in 1646 Sir George victualled Elizabeth Castle: 'Hardly a week passed without some commodities for the provision of the Castle being imported, such as peas, bacon, oats, cider, beer – in addition to what the local brewers furnished him weekly – wines of Spain and Bordeaux, quantities of rice and barrels of beef.'

On 7 April 1647 a 'beer boat' that had been sent for by Sir George Carteret arrived from St Malo. She had in her 15 casks of beer for use in Elizabeth Castle. The 'brewers of St Helier' brewed for him 12 barrels every week – and he had them carried across to the castle.

And on 17 July a boat was sent to Guernsey by Sir George to Castle Cornet, laden with beer: nine casks, three barrels of powder, a new pair of cannon wheels and some casks of peas. The breeze failed, and the vessel was unable to reach the Castle that night. A frigate gave chase, attacked the boat, but when the castle discharged a gun at the frigate, it drew off and allowed the boat to land and be unloaded. She sailed for Jersey the next morning.

Much of the alcohol in the Island at this time came from captured shipping, such as demonstrated by these entries from Chevalier's dairy in the mid-1640s:

> 'The Royal Frigate named the *Hart*, left Jersey on 4 May but returned four days later having captured a London ship of some 90 tons, armed with five guns and two perries [siege weapons] and a crew of 10. She was on her way from London to Topsham laden with cargo for the grocers of Exeter. She was brought back to Jersey; her cargo was transferred to cellars in St Aubin. In the cargo were 16 casks of Malaga wine, bales of hops, a case full of crystal glasses and general merchandise. An auction will be held on 15 May at St Aubin. It will be the first prize to be auctioned here....
>
> 'Captain Barnet, who had left Jersey in his frigate on 13 March, returned to Jersey on Wednesday 21 March with a captured Flemish ship, laden with Bordeaux wines, belonging to Southampton merchants. The prize was of four score or one hundred tons and had four score casks of wine in her and was adjudged a lawful prize and unloaded partly at Elizabeth Castle, partly in the town and partly at St Aubin.
>
> 'Sir George bought all the cargo from Captain Barnet and partners and after keeping his own and the King's shares, sent two boat-loads of wine to be sold at Saint Malo and one load to England in a Norman boat. In this boat he sent a Jerseyman to see what price the wine fetched. She left on 25 March and returned on 13 April laden with slates for the Castle. She also brought eight Englishmen from Fowey.'

On 26 July there arrived a hoy of 30 tons loaded with malt for making beer –

a vessel captured on its way from Belgium to Topsham. Another captured boat contained ten barrels of cider.'

At this time, supplies for Elizabeth Castle were pouring in, and it is said that the cellars there were overflowing with wine, cider and beer. The crypt of the old Priory church were used for this storage, so when a lucky shot hit the church in 1651, bringing the defiance of Elizabeth Castle to an end, the alcohol stored there added to the flames and fury of the fire. The stores of beef, peas, biscuits, fish, wine, cider and beer were two-thirds destroyed; together with 16 of the castle's defending soldiers and many more wounded. Sir George Carteret had no option but to surrender the castle.

ON 7 December 1647 we hear of a murder committed outside one of St Aubin's inns. There were two Englishmen involved: one was Manuel Clement, the Lieutenant of St Aubin's Tower, 'a gentleman by birth', the other Michael Jenkinson, the master owner of a ship.

During the Civil War, Jenkinson had lost all his wealth, possibly while engaged in privateering. So he came to Jersey, whereupon Sir George Carteret gave him one of his galleys to go privateering. It came about that they were drinking together with some other Englishmen in a tavern at St Aubin where Clement frequently lodged. When he was about to take his departure there arose a dispute over the payment of the bill. On this, Jenkinson flung his money on the table, left the premises and made off in the direction of town, where he had lodgings. Clement ran after him and found him on the point of leaving for St Helier; he wanted Jenkinson to come back to the hostelry, but the latter declined – he had paid his share of the bill; it was getting dark and he wanted to go home.

Seeing that he could not persuade Jenkinson to return with him, Clement drew his sword out of its scabbard, and in one stroke thrust it through Jenkinson's intestines – the latter fell dead on the spot. Clement came back to the tavern and told the others that he had slain a man and boasted also that he had killed many – but this one he had done while intoxicated.

The others left the tavern to see what had happened and found the dead man. They sent for the Constable and the officers of the Parish of St Brelade to arrest him. If he had not blabbed that it was he who had done the deed, and urged that there were no witnesses to the deed, he might have been released.

He was apprehended for murder and sent to Gorey Castle for trial.

He disappeared on 16 March 1648, in spite of the ports being watched. He escaped from Mont Orgueil at dead of night and was never seen again.

ONE of the world's earliest datable wine bottles was found during excavation at Mont Orgueil during the 1920s.

The bottle, now on display at Mont Orgueil, bears a seal bearing the arms of the Jermyn family – a crescent between two stars. It must refer to Henry Jermyn, who was governor of Jersey between 1644 and 1649 and again from 1660 to 1666 and it was one of a number of bottles made especially for him.

If the bottle was from his first governorship, this would be the earliest known datable bottle. Even if it dated from his second governorship, it would still be among the earliest known wine bottles – perhaps the fourth or fifth oldest bottle.

AFTER the successful invasion of Jersey by the forces of Parliament and Cromwell in 1651, the troops were billeted around Jersey. When they had eaten up the host's provisions, 'they made a round of the houses and stole foodstuffs, such as bread, butter, bacon and such sheep and poultry as was left. Rich and poor suffered alike. A terrible waste of cider too – for an infinity was drunk in 3 or 4 months, The year had been a great one for corn and cider in Jersey, and it was all consumed in a short time.'

IN December 1648 the States had yet again tried to reduce the number of taverns in St Helier to six – unavailingly. By 1676 the incidence of disorderly behaviour on Saturday nights, partly caused by the lack of an effective police force, resulted in the institution of a curfew bell. In July 1676, an Ordinance was passed ordering all persons at the sound of the Curfew at dusk on Saturdays to repair to their homes and stay there, 'under pains and penalties at the discretion of the Court.'

But with the development of the Town and increases in population the number of taverns constantly grew until in 1771 it had reached 60 in St Helier alone. In 1777 the number was reduced to 40, but between 1777 and 1797 it had increased to 100 – thanks to the great wave of émigré immigrants fleeing from the French Revolution. When this great wave had dissipated, the number was reduced to 80 and then to 61 in 1801.

FINALLY, in 1755, the long discussed hospital was built – although its daily regime was more like that of a workhouse. Drunkards were not admitted to the dining room; no one was allowed to bring in strong liquor. The rules placed in the hospital were read aloud once a month by the Master.

Misdemeanours were few. Anybody who was absent for longer than expected had his cider ration stopped. One such trouble maker was John Le Masurier from St Saviour: he had his cider ration stopped but after five days without cider, he declared he was a reformed character, and the cider ration was reinstated. But further infringements and awkwardness followed: he was put into solitary confinement, was deprived of his cider yet again – and as soon as he was free went out and got drunk, when he 'swore, blasphemed and was insolent.'

THE Martel family had lived in Jersey for many generations (the first record of the surname in Jersey is in 1299). Jean Martel (1694–1753) brought undying fame to his family name – anglicised as Martell – by founding the famous Martell cognac house.

The Martel family had lived in St Brelade since 1525, when Brelade Martel bought '*Les Terres de la Sergenté*'. A relation, Nicholas Martel was the fortunate owner of three dogs – until 1536, when he was fined for exceeding the dog limit; in his station of life he was legally permitted only one dog. There was the equivalent of a parish hall enquiry into the circumstances.

It is believed that Brelade demolished the old house and built a new one on the present site. The initials of François Martel and the date 1681 suggest it was further restored at that date.

Brelade's only son, Philippe, married Catherine Balleine of St Peter. They had six children, including the Philippe who married Marie Gobat, whose son, François, seems to have renovated La Sergenté. One of Philippe's other sons, Thomas (1652–1698), married Martha Hérault in 1768 at St Saviour's Church. He was a Deacon of St Brelade, but is primarily remembered as a trader – his ship was called *La Fidelité*. The Martel family had become one of the leading commercial families in the Island, treading a fine line between legal commerce and smuggling – or at least, knowingly supplying smugglers.

Their seventh son was called Jean and he provided the cognac connection. Jean worked for seven years in Guernsey and then in 1715 he and a friend, Jean Fiot, set up in business as English merchants at Bordeaux. This proved a failure, and in 1727 they had to come to terms with their creditors. However he had also founded, in his own name, a brandy brokerage company, and he moved to Cognac with two Jersey friends, surnamed Kastel and Maret, all three of whom decided to double the last letter in their names to prove their British nationality.

He was known as a man of principle, honesty and fairness and was described at the time as '*un fort honeste garçon*'. Through his own dynamism and energy, business quickly expanded. He was often to be seen on the river bank of the Charente, below Cognac, supervising the loading and departure of his merchandise. He developed a large export trade to the Channel Islands, where the Jersey and Guernsey smugglers were his best customers, and carried his brandy to England and America. He also traded with Rotterdam and the Hanseatic ports of Lübeck and Hamburg.

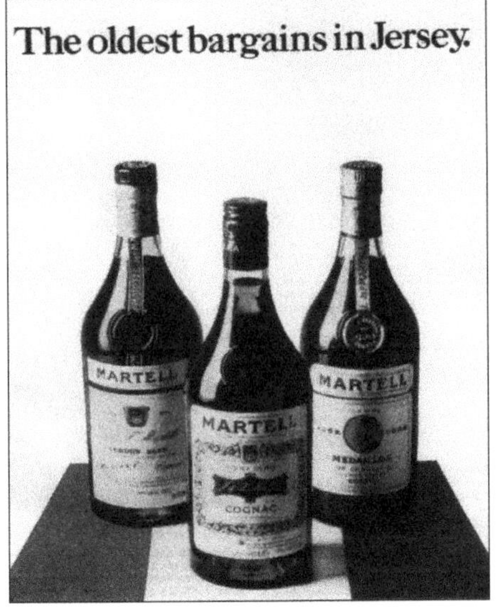

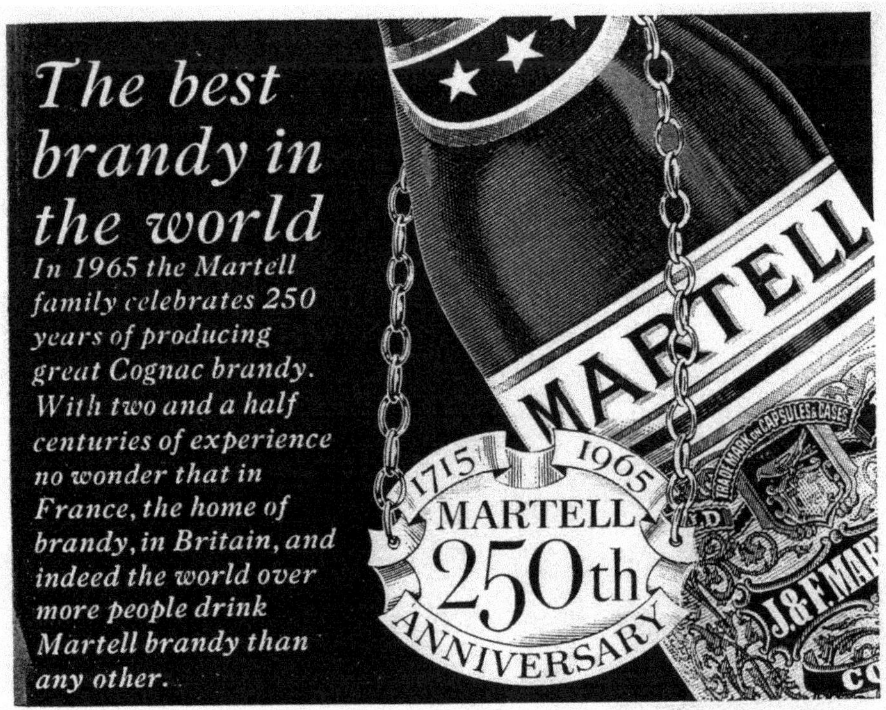

As a sideline he imported into France Jersey-knitted stockings, collected for him by his mother. He also dealt in tulip bulbs, tea and linen and a host of other commodities, as well as importing Guernsey butter for his own enjoyment.

He loved horses, books and travelling and until the end of his life he was noted locally for the fluent – but rather 'strange' way he pronounced his French. It seems he never forgot his *Jèrriais*. A Jersey stamp issue celebrating the career of Jean Martell was issued on 7 September 1982.

There are letters between Edouard Marett of La Haule – a connection by marriage of Jean Martel, in the course of which Marett ordered brandy and red and white bordeaux but complained that the Grande Borderie wines were not liked, 'being subject to yellowing'. One bill was paid in Spanish gold pieces.

BY the end of the 18th Century, increased mobility began to have an impact on daily life, and consequently on drinking culture

The first horse bus service was started on 15th November 1788. It travelled every Saturday between the Bunch of Grapes tavern on St Saviour's Road and The Swan tavern in St Aubin. The fare was ten sous. This increased mobility, of course, would only increase in the ensuing 19th and 20th Centuries and into modern times.

~ 6 ~

Smugglers' Tales

'Five and twenty ponies,
Trotting through the dark –
Brandy for the Parson, 'Baccy for the Clerk.
Them that asks no questions isn't told a lie -
Watch the wall my darling while the Gentlemen go by'

Rudyard Kipling

Smuggling has always had a whiff of adventure and romance about it. However much that reputation may be deserved or undeserved (most probably the latter) in Jersey, because of its median position between two countries quite often at war with one another, smuggling was very much a major economic activity.

Already in the Middle Ages smuggling was prevalent: in 1248, for example, during the reign of Henry III, an inquiry laid down when conger could be dried and salted because the 'fishermen were secretly carrying their fish to the enemies of the Lord the King.'

And so smuggling would continue down the centuries, reaching a high tide during the 18th Century, when high customs duty on imported spirits made smuggling highly profitable.

The 'handling of illicit goods' is perhaps a more correct terminology, since the goods were not smuggled into Jersey for home consumption; instead, they were landed and stored in the Island ready to be sent on to France or England. In Jersey, local traders would buy tons of tobacco and gallons of brandy and Geneva (gin) from France and sell it to the smugglers. These illegal cargoes were then landed in creeks or on lonely beaches along the English coast.

Jersey ships brought cod from Newfoundland and tobacco leaf from Virginia and wines and brandy from France, for export (or smuggling) not only to England, buy also America, Brazil and the West Indies.

Jersey was effectively a huge warehouse, with tobacco or woollen wear hidden away ready to be sent to France, and tea, brandy, rum, tobacco, soap, cloth and wine stored ready to be taken to England.

Such a volume of tobacco leaf was smuggled into France that the French revenue collectors in Brittany and Normandy were in despair. Big profits could be made by smuggling tobacco into England as well as into France.

To give some idea of the size and scope of the Island's involvement in *la fraude*, in 1698 the French authorities estimated that 50,000 tons of tobacco was shipped to Brittany alone.

As HM government employed only one Customs officer in Jersey to register goods as they landed, it was easy enough to bring contraband into any number of bays away from his prying eyes. Such was the audacity of entrepreneurs that in 1694 John Button of Jersey stored goods from Saint Malo in Elizabeth Castle, ready to be smuggled on to England.

In any case, the 'Customer' was not above taking part in smuggling activities himself: in 1693 a vessel took brandy and wine from Guernsey to Plymouth, with the connivance of William Hely, the Customer in Jersey, who had also sent lead to France illegally.

The isolated bays and harbourages along Jersey's north coast made excellent sites for smuggling activity. Hence the well-known story of the spectral 'Dog of Bouley Bay' with eyes like saucers, which could be met at night-time by unwary travellers in the lanes near the bay … a good story to encourage people to stay away from the area. Grève de Lecq and Ouaisné Bay were also frequented by smugglers.

Again, there are stories and purported sightings of spectral marriage and funeral processions on Jersey roads during the hours of night. What better way to make sure that the curious and the officious stayed away from contraband goods being transported along the Island's roads, than to stage such a 'spectral' procession, with the goods concealed, for example, in the spectral coffin?

From such isolated and lonely bays the contraband was taken out to small, fast sailing ships and then on to their mainland destination. With Normandy and all the south coast of England to supply, the volume of goods stored in Jersey at this time must have been tremendous.

Jersey privateers continued taking ships throughout the 18th Century and masters made fortunes from auctioning off the cargo of the captured prizes. Captain Fiott and the *Charming Betty* for example, captured a number of prizes in the late 1750s. In 1758 they captured a French brigantine, loaded with sugar – a valuable commodity.

In the same year Fiott and his crew, along with a second ship, *Le Burnett,* came across the *Adventurer* of London. She had been taken by a French privateer on a voyage from Jamaica. The prize became Fiott's and the cargo – sugar, spice, logwood, mahogany, rum, coffee and cottons – fetched a great deal of money.

On the return journey, despite being shorthanded as they had put a prize crew aboard the English ship, the *Charming Betty* also took a Dutch ship carrying 200 tuns of wine from Bordeaux to Saint Malo. The total value of the two cargoes is not listed, but on 3 March 1759, Fiott captured two more ships, which were sold along with the unspecified cargoes, for 30,000 livres.

Smuggling continued throughout the Napoleonic Wars and reached a peak in the first part of the 19th Century.

For example, in October 1806, a large quantity of spirits was discovered on board the sloop *Active* of Jersey (Philip de Heaume master), shortly before the vessel left St Helier on a voyage to Scotland. The *Active*'s lawful cargo was 504 bushels of apples, but hidden behind a double bulkhead were found 110 casks of brandy and Geneva gin, totalling 634 gallons of spirits. The vessel and the contraband were seized by Customs, but it is not known whether the vessel's owner, Jacob Voisin, was prosecuted.

Some 200,000 gallons of spirits were imported legally into Jersey in the year 1805–1806, but the equivalent of one-eighth of that amount was reckoned to have been smuggled in.

Another example of a typical smuggling operation: in October 1814, Peter Sogier and John Alexander hid about 85 casks of brandy and Geneva gin aboard their cutter *Ann*. Clearance was then obtained from the Customs stating that the *Ann* was bound for Saint Malo in ballast. But once at sea, her master, Charles du Feu, took the vessel to Plymouth and told the authorities that he had been driven there by bad weather. The casks were unloaded at Stone House Mill Bay, near Plymouth, where a reception party was waiting to collect them.

A Customs report on 17 March 1823 stated: A Cawsand boat loaded in St Brelade's Bay 300 ankers of brandy.' And on 31 March: 'A Plymouth cutter in the same bay took on 600 ankers of brandy and gin.' An East Looe cutter on 19 June also loaded in St Brelade's Bay 690 casks of brandy.

Smuggling had diminished by the mid-19th Century, when the lowering of excise duty rates made smuggling less profitable. But even in 1863, the statement of a crew member of the *Eliza,* a Jersey-owned vessel, recorded that she loaded at Bonne Nuit Bay 2½ tons of tobacco, snuff, spirits and 'segars'. After a long chase of several hours by a Customs cutter, this cargo was landed on the coast near Fishguard.

‘We must not think ill of our forebears for their smuggling activities. Smuggling – *faire la fraude* as it was called – was an entirely honourable occupation, and I remember that in my youth my respect for the old parish stalwarts was greatly increased if I learned, as I often did, that in the old days they had been fraudeurs. It showed, for one thing, that they were men who were prepared to take active measures against the established authority, and as you know, opposition to the established authority is still one of the qualities which a Jerseyman most admires’

Sir Arthur de la Mare, addressing the Jersey Society in London,1956

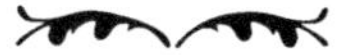

~ 7 ~

The 19th Century

(i) DRINKING AND DRUNKENESS

Those Islanders whose memories of Jersey extend back over a few decades are often heard to comment on the unwelcome changes in Jersey that they have experienced and are usually all too visible: seemingly endless building development, a fair proportion of it inappropriate, uninspired or downright ugly.

But the differences experienced in modern times were certainly paralleled in the 19th Century which, for example, saw St Helier expand from a small village in the vicinity of the parish church to a busy town that extended far inland over an area that had previously been marsh or dunes, water meadow or cider orchard.

It seems sensible to extend the account of this century by a decade or so at each end, from the time in the early 1790s that *émigrés* fleeing from the French Revolution poured into the Island and Jersey really first encountered the modern world beyond its own confines, to 1914, when the start of the Great War created another punctuation point – a tragic marker – in Jersey's history.

As the terror of the French Revolution caused a mass exodus of refugees to arrive in Jersey there was, it seems, only one hotel in St Helier capable of offering comfortable accommodation to guests (as opposed to taverns or drinking houses, of which there were, generally speaking, more than a sufficiency). This hotel would become, in the next century, the British Hotel and is now Barclays Bank on the corner of Broad Street and Library Place. The owner of the hotel made so much money from the French refugees looking for accommodation that he was later able to add two more storeys to his premises.

The impact of all these arrivals from France had a transforming effect on Jersey and Jersey life. Before the early 1790s, St Helier had only 400 houses. Many of the inhabitants hired out their homes as refugee accommodation while they stayed with relatives elsewhere. Such was the pressure of refugees that emergency accommodation had to be built and the population of the town doubled almost overnight. Suddenly there were about a hundred taverns – although many of these would have been no more than private houses that sold drink. As the wave of refugees diminished, the number of taverns fell by 1796 to 80 licenses, 71 in 1799, 65 in 1800 and 60 by 1800. But as much as the States restricted the number, more always opened up. There were, of course, plenty of British soldiers and sailors in the Island to help keep the drink flowing – and to encourage the availability of places for off-duty drinking.

At the end of the Napoleonic Wars in 1815, the Governor reduced the number of taverns to 80 in St Helier (and also reduced the number in other Parishes).

Seven years later, on 9 February 1822, at an Assembly of the Governor, Bailiff and Jurats, a total of 78 licenses were recommended by the St Helier Parish Assembly, plus a further two recommended by the Seigneur de la Motte completing the number allowed by the Reglément to St Helier.

A further Act was read by the Attorney General, requesting that the Governor, Bailiff and Jurats extend the number to 90.

Jurat Anley objected and suggested that the number of taverns be reduced to 60. He produced an Act of the Court of 1655 when the Assembly had met to discuss the number of taverns and reduced the number to 35 for the whole Island.

The result of the 1822 voting was that the number of taverns remained at 80 in St Helier in agreement with the Reglément of 1815. The total number of licenses granted in 1822 were:

St Helier	78 plus 2 recommended by the Seigneur de la Motte
St Peter	12
St Clement	12
St Saviour	12
Trinity	13
St Brelade	12
St Martin	22
St Lawrence	12
Grouville	26
St John	12
St Mary	5 (the Reglément allowed 8)
St Ouen	(the taverns of this parish received their licences from the Seigneur of St Ouen)

The figures throughout the next century continued to ebb and flow. In 1844 there were upwards of 400 alehouses in St Helier, producing a revenue of £2,000 a year – a good reason not to be too severe when it came to licensing pubs. Ten years later the total had sunk again to 114 taverns in St Helier.

During the first half of the 19th Century, only the name of the licensee or the street address was recorded when recommendations were made at a Parish Assembly for the granting of licenses. It was only after 1859 that the distinctive names of the inns were (sometimes) recorded by the Constable's secretary.

The St Helier Parish Assembly met on 22 December 1859 to vote £500 as extra assistance for the poor during the winter, a proposition that was passed unanimously. The Constable brought to the attention of the meeting that it had been 'his painful duty to fine several publicans during the past year'. Wives, he said, were coming to him daily to complain of their husbands' late hours at the public houses while they and their families were starving at home. This did not prevent the Assembly from allowing 131 licences to be recommended with an extra seven licences for beer and cider houses in the town.

In 1896, the *Jersey Times Almanac* listed 73 inn-keepers, 26 wine and spirit merchants and four breweries in the town. By 1957, the number had risen to 221 licensed houses, excluding off-licenses.

JERSEY in the early 19th Century was not a healthy place to live for those on a low income.

Guidebooks of the 1820s emphasised the cheapness of food, wine, tobacco and rent and wine and spirits were so inexpensive they would keep the most addicted inebriate content for £15. Wages paid to labourers were low, and with deflation rather than inflation, did not change for years. A skilled workman might earn 3s a day without drinks – and earned in the region of 18s a week. However, most working families lived on 10s.6d to 12s.6d a week.

In 1832 there was a cholera epidemic, which hit especially the poor, who often went hungry and were more likely to be seriously addicted to spirits. English and Irish labourers, who enjoyed the cheap spirits available in Jersey, were especially susceptible to illness because of heavy drinking.

Based on 1860s prices, a family with four children would have nothing left from the weekly wage having spent money on rent (2s) beer, tea, sugar and salt (9d), and bread – 12 lbs at 3d a pound (3s).

Many families were able to live respectably on 12s.6d a week, but if consumption of beer or spirits became excessive, then they stepped below the poverty line into the category that did not deserve help of any kind.

An unusual death is mentioned on 8 August 1824, when Isaac Coutanche of St Martin killed himself by gluttony. He ate 18 raw eggs, and drank 10 glasses of gin; he followed that with a quantity of raw pork and two glasses of brandy. Not surprisingly it made him very ill – he died two days later and it is difficult to avoid a certain lack of sympathy for the deceased. The coroner's verdict was suicide.

This might be a bad way to start one's visit to Jersey:

> 'On Wednesday last on the arrival of the Saumarez a most disgraceful scene took place on the pier. Two porters, both in a state of inebriation, were fighting for a Gentleman's trunk, when one fell into the water, carrying with him the cause of consternation, which had it not been for one of the bystanders, would have sunk and occasioned considerable loss to the owner.'
>
> 14 October 1837

IN the 1840s, Jersey experienced a new immigration explosion, as workers, mainly escaping from the 'Hungry Years' of the Irish famine, came to the Island in search of work on the massive public works then being undertaken at the Town Harbour, Fort Regent and, especially, what would prove to be the abortive construction of a new harbour at St Catherine's Bay.

The immigrants came both directly from Ireland and from England, where the construction of the railway system was beginning to slow down. The local press reported in 1851 on 'imported pauperism'. If the workers were discharged from the works, there was nowhere for them to move on to; they were trapped in Jersey without money for buying a fare away from the Island. And so they robbed.

Any accommodation close to St Catherine was inadequate for families, so many wives and families were compelled to live in town with their menfolk returning home at weekend. Left to their own devices, the men would behave badly – going on drinking sprees and generally getting up to mischief in groups. Thus there were many petty robberies, prompted by simple hunger, and crops stolen from local farmers' fields. At one time the inhabitants petitioned the Lieut-Governor to provide detachments of soldiers to assist the parish police, especially in the eastern parishes of St Martin, St Saviour and Trinity. The *Jersey Times* campaigned for 'Night Police'.

It was not only hunger that led to disturbances and serious wounds. There was a traditional animosity between the locals and the imported workmen which sometimes flared into dangerous incidents under the influence of alcohol. Gangs of half-drunken fellows – always, it was claimed, from the St Catherine works – rolling round the town throughout the night were commonplace.

Such incidents were not always the fault of the Irish workmen, of course. In the mid-19th Century St Helier was a port, with international trading links. So there were brothels and taverns and drunkenness – the interests of the sailor on shore leave throughout the ages.

Violent incidents fuelled by drunkenness also happened in the country, such as what took place at Mrs Mollet's pub in St Martin: a few Jerseymen were quietly enjoying their ale 'when five or six workmen entered and commenced an attack on the Jerseymen. The landlady's nephew was roused from his bed to assist in quelling the fracas – for his pain he was hit in the mouth with a stone and broke five teeth.'

A drunken quarrel occurred at St Catherine which ended with one of the oystermen drawing his knife and stabbing a workman of St Catherine within an inch or two of his heart.'

The problems caused by off-duty soldiers of the Jersey garrison drinking too much was discussed by the ADC to Queen Victoria and prominent Jerseyman, Sir John Le Couteur.

In a letter, written in the 1840s, he said of a regiment about to be stationed in Jersey:

> 'When composed of young recruits, as the second battalion is, it should not be sent to Jersey, where spirits are so cheap, and where numbers of low women lead the inexperienced into constant troubles. None but only well-trained corps should be sent here. It causes the British army to be a by-word in France for drunkenness. During four months that I was at Pau, I think I saw only one French soldier intoxicated.
>
> 'Only a few days ago the Governor received a letter from the C.O, Colonel Chapman, complaining that his men were maddened from debauchery and intoxication. But liquor was obtained at the Devonshire Arms Tavern in Hill Street and the Bull Tavern corner of Wharf Street. I got samples of brandy and gin from both these disreputable houses.'

Sir John was right to be concerned about the effect of so many taverns and cheap alcohol on young British soldiers posted to Jersey.

Especially in Pier Road and Hilgrove Street there were plenty of establishments that were inns on the ground floor and brothels above.

So long as a landlord paid his taverner's licence, he could also be, without too much official interest being taken of his premises, landlord of what might euphemistically be called 'a disorderly house'.

Such houses were certainly there in the back streets of town behind the market, before the 'New' Market was started in 1882 and when many surrounding slum properties were cleared away.

The reputation of 'French Lane' was legendary. According to Mary Robin, who wrote a history of Halkett Street: 'Within living memory there were elderly Jersey people who could repeat tales of soldiers being carried out of the inns on barrows, drunk,' and she mentions the 'ladies of the night' who frequented the back rooms in and around Hilgrove Street; ladies whose services were much in demand by off duty soldiers.

On 3 April 1863, John James Hoare, 23, a printer, died in hospital in consequence of a glass being thrown at him by Mr Ormsby 'to wake him up' as he was sleeping on the counter of Mr Baker's public house in Colomberie. The glass was supposed to have been thrown at his head but some say it was thrown on the counter. This took place on 7 March when he should have been in his bed. The Forresters carried him and a large number of them attended his funeral on Good Friday.

from the 'Index of Records 'of Sinnatt's Funeral Directors.

ALMOST a century after the Hospital was established, the *Chronique* reported in 1850 on the number of people passing through the Hospital the previous year. This came to 1,444 (although not all of these were there at the same time). The number included 509 drunkards, as well as vagabonds, disturbers of the peace and prostitutes.

(ii) THE RAILWAY AGE

VIOLENCE, fuelled by alcohol; is not a new phenomenon on public transport,

As recounted by Peter Paye in his book, *The Jersey Eastern Railway* (JER), on 17 May 1884 two seamen from HMS *Dasher*, the Gorey protection vessel, were charged at the Court of Correctional Police with intemperance and fighting in a coach of a Jersey Eastern Railway train and breaking a piece of glass in one compartment. The two men were placed under the control of the guard and arrested on arrival at St Helier. One of them, William Marlow, judged to be the aggressor, was charged 10/- for breach of the peace and a further 10/- costs for breakage of glass.

Concern was expressed about dubious characters travelling on the JER services, especially in the evening. The railway company assured passengers that any person causing annoyance would be harshly dealt with. Two months later a £2 was levied against a man charged with being drunk on the 8.30 p.m. Gorey to St Helier train on Tuesday 28 July. The accused had joined the train at La Roque and during the journey annoyed women passengers after the train departed Le Hocq. At Georgetown the guard was called and he took the offender into his brake van before handing him over to the custody of the station master on arrival at Snow Hill.

Gorey was a popular destination, especially during the summer months, and gangs of youths invariably finished the day in high spirits after heavy drinking in the local pubs. On Sunday 16 June 1889 a group of youths gathered at Gorey Station well before the train to St Helier was due to depart and generally made a nuisance of themselves. After staff had warned them on several occasions to desist, station master Biggins ordered the group off the premises, only to be met with verbal abuse. A porter was assaulted by one of the youths, named Stevens. The group quickly dispersed and walked to Grouville Station, where Stevens was arrested by the Grouville station master. At the Court of Correctional Police he was fined 10/- for attacking the porter.

(iii) HOME-MADE DRINKS

JERSEY'S mild climate means that anything appropriate to the temperature zone can be grown easily. In the 19th Century especially, all sorts of vegetables were grown and fruits – both hard and soft – flourished, including figs, grapes and melons. There were many different varieties, particularly apples and pears, which were often trained against walls.

In 1838 Nurseryman Langellier stocked 500 varieties of pear and in the same year Mr E Nicolle established a vineyard at his house, Bellozanne, on the present location of the sewage works.

Vines were grown fairly profusely, but it seems as if little or no wine was made.

However, like any rural community, all sorts of home-made drinks were made, using both the products of the domestic fruit trees and the wild fruit that could be easily found in local hedgerows, such as blackberries, sloes and elderberries.

In 1820 Philippe Marett gave his recipe for blackcurrant brandy: 1 *pot* of gin 1 *pot* of brandy, 8lbs currants and some syrup pinks – good by February 1821.

Sloes, the fruit of the blackthorn, are native to Jersey's cliffs and hillsides. They were also used extensively in the hedging and enclosures of cider orchard in the 17th Century, together with hawthorn and willow.

Sloe gin – *Du Gin de Prunelles*

2lbs sloes

8-10 Oz sugar

'Wash the berries, remove the stalks and prick the sloes all over with a sharp needle. Pack the fruit into airtight jars, alternative layers of sloes and sugar. Crush a few of the stones to give that characteristic almond flavour and fill the jars with gin. Ensure the lids are tightly closed and leave in a tight place for 3 months, shaking the jars occasionally. Drain through a muslin cloth, bottle and keep till required'.

Tastes of the Channel Islands, by Amanda Closs

Collecting sloes for making sloe gin remains a very popular Jersey pastime and those who have access to a ready supply of sloes are often not too keen to share the information with all and sundry about where the sloes can be found.

~ 8 ~

The Breweries

(i) BEER AND BREWING IN THE 19TH CENTURY

THE beginning of the 19th Century saw a steep increase in the number of Jersey's population and for the first time 'incomers' were exceeding the numbers of the indigenous population.

There was, of course, a considerable army garrison – and new industries derived from shipbuilding and the expansion of the town harbour: soldiers, stevedores, sailors, shipyard builders, oyster trade workers... all of which led to an increase in beer production, importation, and taverns. By 1809 there were several breweries in existence in the Island.

Gradually, the making of cider dwindled and the consumption of beer increased. The failure of the apple crops in 1826 and again in 1831 no doubt helped to accelerate the change and local breweries began operating in increased numbers.

H D Inglis in *The Channel Islands* (1834) gives statistics for the import and export of ale, beer and porter for the years 1829 to 1832 inclusive: 'Imported 4 pipes, 100 hogsheads, 24 casks, 222 barrels, 8 firkins, 12 half-hogsheads, 149 half-barrels, 37 quarter casks, 33,636 gallons and 250 dozens.' During the same period, 8,805 dozen and 350 gallons were exported as Jersey manufacture. During the same period, 28,051 lbs of hops were imported, which were used, no doubt, for the Island manufacture of ale and porter.

ON 21 August 1819, Thomas Turner opened the New Market Brewery, in what is now Beresford Street. This is one of the roots of the present day Randalls Ltd; its history is detailed later in this chapter.

Between 1833 and 1847 there were six breweries operating in the Island:

- Blandy & Co	the Castlebridge Brewery, Esplanade;
- Brown & Co	Beresford Street (probably using Turner's old premises;
- F de la Taste	Old James Street
- C Matthews	Parade Place
- J B Quick	Old James Street
- T Turner	7 and 9 Gloucester Street

According to the British Press *Almanac* for 1847, the following breweries were working at that time:

- W Andrews	Springfield Brewery, Trinity Road
- A Blandy	Castlebridge Brewery, Esplanade
- J Brown	Cannon Brewery, Cannon Street
- F De La Taste	Brewery, Wesley Street
- Le Vesconte	Parade
- S G Nott	St James Street
- J B Quick	Old James Street
- Simon	Albion Brewery, Colomberie
- Turner	Clare St Brewery

By 1858 the number of local breweries had decreased to five. These were:

- Andrews	Springfield Brewery
- Brown	Cannon Brewery, Cannon Street
- De la Taste	Wesley Street
- J B Quick	Minden Place
- R Randall	Clare St Brewery

Of these, only the Springfield Brewery survived with Randall's and the Ann Street Brewery (established 1871) into the 20th Century. Randall's and Ann Street are still with us – the latter now known as the Liberation Brewery and part of the Liberation Group. Their fuller histories are contained under separate sections. The remainder – small operations of the type now known as micro-breweries – have only left the bare details of their proprietors and address.

We have a few more details about Kine's Old Springfield Brewery. A number of bottles with the label of Kine's Brewing Co Ltd were found in the roof space of a wash house at Les Ruettes, St Saviour. One of these bottles is now in the Jersey Museum.

Originally Andrews' Springfield Brewery premises were at 7 Springfield

Terrace, Trinity Road. The business of Kine's Old Springfield Brewery was established there in 1857 by Thomas Kine, who, with his brother, William, bought the premises in 1872 from the Andrews Brothers.

The *Jersey Express Almanac* for 1865 shows Thomas Kine as a brewer carrying on business in Trinity Road and also shows Z Banks as carrying on business at the New Springfield Brewery, 3 Trinity Road, and this is probably why the Kine's brewery took the name of 'The Old Springfield Brewery'.

The Kines feature in *Hill's Historical Almanac of the Channel Islands*, from which it seems that Thomas Kine was also a manufacturer of soda water, lemonade and ginger beer, as well as a billiard room proprietor. His addresses are given as 37 La Motte Street and 8 Charing Cross.

In 1877 Thomas sold his half share of the brewery premises to William, and in 1891 William sold out to François Le Sueur. Though the Kines disappeared from the scene, their name was retained when the premises were leased under the name of Kine's Old Springfield Brewery in 1909. The lease, for 14 years, was under a newly-formed company, Kine's Brewing Company Ltd.

The venture did not last long; a composition with the creditors was made in 1912 and the business was taken over by a new company, Kine's Brewing Company (1912), of which Fred Clarke of C Le Masurier Ltd was a founding member. The lease of 7 Springfield Terrace was cancelled in 1913, and printed labels on the bottles show that they came to be used for Hills and Underwood's table vinegar.

The name had disappeared by 1917.

8 (ii) ANN STREET BREWERY and its successor businesses

THE first record of beer being brewed in Ann Street is generally quoted as being 1871, when J S Palmer began his brewing operation there.

However, there is some reason to believe that he may have taken over a going concern, or reconstructed an existing brewery building, as some sources detail brewing on the Ann Street site in or around 1857.

We know that Mr Palmer had been employed as a brewer at William Kine's Old Springfield Brewery before he set up on his own. But who his immediate successors as owners were, or their relationship to Jersey or what had been their prior or subsequent history – that is information that has been lost in the passage of time.

The first reference to what became the Ann Street Brewery is in the *British Press Almanac* for 1872 (compiled, of course, the previous year), when it is mentioned in an advertisement:

> 'Ann Street Brewery, Mr. J.S. Palmer, Brewer and Malster (sic), having lately erected the above spacious and commodious premises, is now prepared to supply Ales and Porter of superior quality, equal to the best English brewed. The above Prime Ales may be had in Bottles, Pint or Quart. A trial is solicited, Orders punctually attended to. Note the address: Ann Street Brewery.'

The *British Press Almanacs* for the years 1873 to 1877 report J S Palmer as being the owner of the Ann Street Brewery, but in the 1878 issue of the almanac a change in ownership is recorded to 'McKay and Co.'

By 1881 this had become McKay, Vade & Co. In the same almanac for the following two years (1882-3) no mention is made of any brewery in Ann Street – perhaps the premises were not occupied.

However, in the 1884 issue, the brewery is owned by Messrs Pinel and Le Masurier and in the following year (1885) there appears the following advert:

> 'Pinel and Le Masurier, Export and family Pale Ale and Stout Brewed on the English Principle, from the very best Malt and Hops procurable. Guaranteed absolutely Pure, and Warranted to keep sound on draught. Supplied in casks of all sizes and Bottled in Barrett's Patent Screw Stoppered Bottles. Pinel and Le Masurier also bottle Bass's Ale, Guinness's Stout etc. In Barrett's Screw stoppered Bottles, which is the most convenient arrangement ever brought before the public, Price lists on application. Liberal terms to the trade,'

A similar advert appeared in the *BP Almanac* for 1886.

In 1887 the Ann Street Brewery is listed as belonging to Messrs Le Masurier and Groizard. From 1888 until 1891 Mr H Le Masurier appeared to be in sole charge of the brewery; in 1891 he was also advertising Aerated Waters.

The *Jersey Times Almanac* for the year 1892 records new proprietors for the Ann Street Brewery. They were Messrs R and J Gordon – but in 1893 and 1894 the *JT Almanac* records the owners of the brewery as Messrs Gordon and Gilbey – both names are well known in the English spirit and wine trades. But it is impossible to make any definite connection between the English and Jersey names, or whether they were just coincidental.

It would appear that Mr Inverness John Bathe and Mr James Reginald Hole acquired the Ann Street Brewery sometime during 1894, and on 23 September 1895 they formed the Ann Street Brewery Ltd. Mr Hole retired to Nottingham but retained a considerable share of the capital in the company. After his death and that of his wife his shares were disposed of, opening up ownership of a share in the company to a number of Islanders.

Mr I J Bathe was the first managing director and also the chief brewer for the firm until his death in 1927. A portion of the capital owned by him was passed to his son, Mr Greville Inverness Bathe, who retained his interest in the company until his death in 1964. His shares were left to charitable trusts.

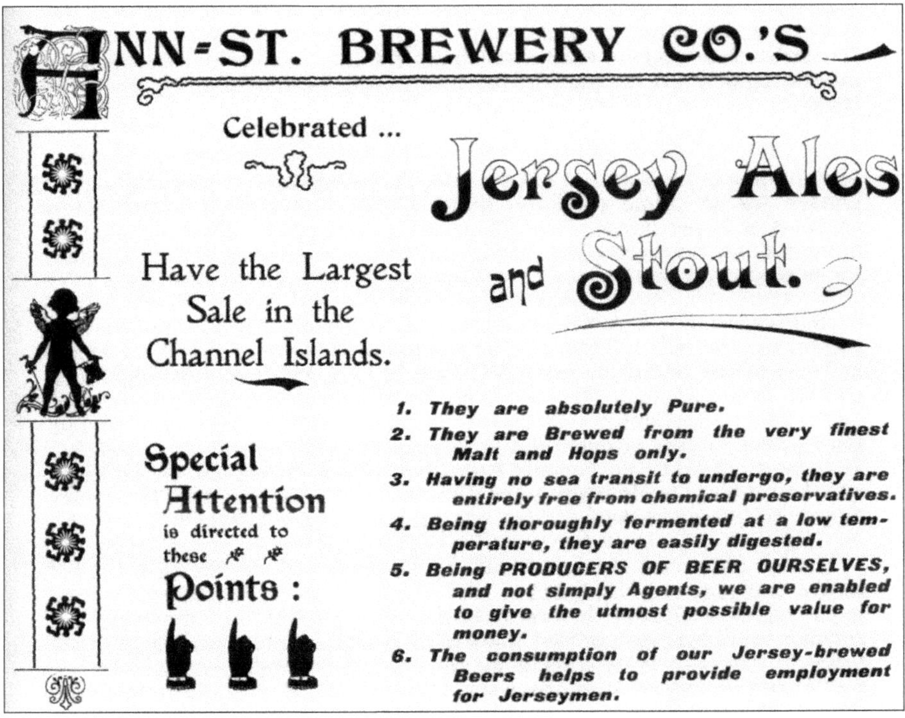

From 1895 the *Almanac* mentions the Ann Street Brewery Co under their lists of brewers and ten years later, on 23 September 1905, it was registered as a limited company. Among the original members of the Board formed in 1904 were F J Bois, Deputy for St Saviour, and father of a future Deputy Bailiff, F de Lisle Bois OBE MA and W H Dickinson, the engineer manager of the defunct Jersey Railways and Tramways Company. The first secretary of the company was P P Payn, who eventually became managing director.

Kelly's Directory of the Channel Islands in 1911 states that the brewery had branches at 45 Hill Street and 45½ Great Union Road, St Helier.

It is believed that the first mention of the 'Mary Ann' brand also dates from around this time, although it was not registered as a brand in the Royal Court until the late 1920s.

THERE are many theories about how the name Mary Ann originated.

There was, for example, a popular music hall song published by Francis Day and Hunter in 1911, titled: 'Mary Ann, she's after me'. The chorus went:

> 'Mary Ann, she's after me,
> Full of love she seems to be
> My Mother says it's plain to see
> She wants me for her young man.'

The tune was very popular among the various concert parties who came to Jersey in the first decades of the 20th Century to give their performances at the Tin Hut – the building that later made way for the West Park Pavilion – and the pubs of Jersey. It had a very catchy tune.

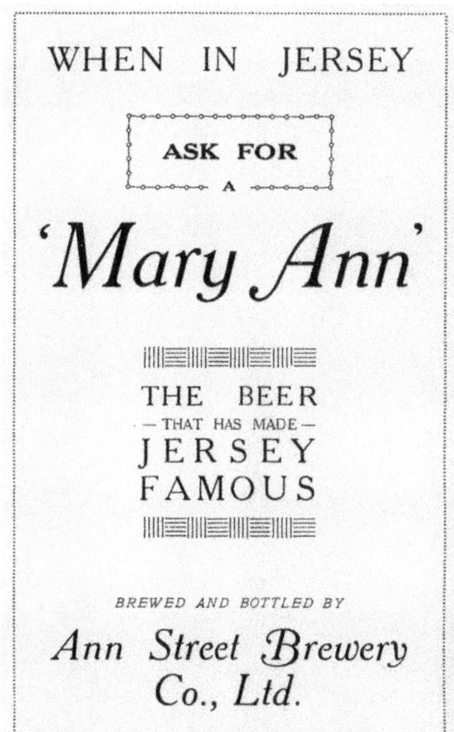

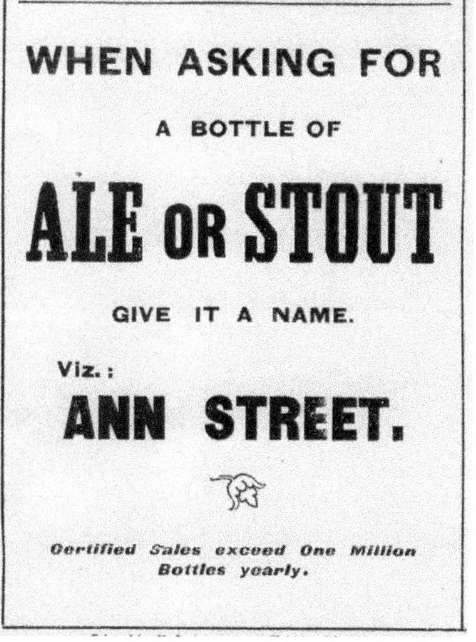

The origin of the name obviously has a lot to do with the brewery's address and the name of the company. Ann Street was originally known as Rue ès Helles. The Helle family was an old Jersey one, now extinct, who owned Le Fief ès Helles in St John as well as much property in town. There was a considerable Anglicisation of street names in the early 19th Century and the obvious translation of La Rue ès Helles would have been Hell Street – not too appropriate at the best of times, and certainly offensive to Victorian susceptibilities.

The whole area was developed by Clement Hemery, who called Ann Street after his daughter and the adjoining Charles Street after his son.

Mary Ann was also a common Jersey girls' name. The French name, 'Marianne', has also been popular as the personification of the spirit of the French Republic – a rather more flighty equivalent of Britannia, the spirit of Britain - and it has been supposed that there is a link with the Jersey name, Mary Ann.

There was also a family surnamed Beer, who lived from 1917 to 1939 at 1, Gaudin Villas, Ann Street. The first names of Mrs Beer were Mary Ann; she died at some point in the 1930s. The coincidence of a person called Mary Ann Beer living so close to the brewery may have helped – or at least contributed to – the naming of the brand.

In 1923 Mr Payn purchased no less than 15 hotels and inns from Frederick Middleton, who traded as wine merchants de Veulle and Co at 4 Hill Street and owned many licensed properties. This formed the basis of the company's diversification into ownership of bars and public houses.

The first recorded mention of a slogan that remained popular until recent times occurred in 1926, in an advertisement in the *Jersey Directory and Express Almanac*: 'Ann Street Brewery – The Beer that has made Jersey famous. Telephone No 61.'

The year 1929 had front page advertisements in the *Jersey Morning News*: 'Ask for Mary Ann. The beer that has made Jersey famous, guaranteed to be brewed from the same materials as the best imported English Ales.' The beer was called 'Mary Ann' by James Woodman, the secretary of the brewery at the time and its future managing director.

For a further theory as to the origin of the name 'Mary Ann', the late Henry Kempster wrote to the *JEP* in 1977 recalling that the owner of the Seymour Inn between the wars was a shareholder of the Ann Street Brewery. Her name was Mary Ann Jane Le Vesconte. A meeting of shareholders was held at the brewery to decide on the name of the new beer, and Mrs Le Vesconte was late. As the meeting was mulling over possible names, someone by the door, seeing her at the end of the corridor, called out: 'Here's Mary Ann coming along now'– and that was that. The shareholders had the name for their new product.

In 2008, the late Fayette Jackson, daughter of the then company secretary, J. R. Woodman, wrote:

> 'About 84 years ago (when I was two) my father had the name registered in the Royal Court after being told by several publicans that in the summer months,

visitors, after ordering the beer, would stand at the bar singing the old music hall song of that time, "Mary Ann". He thought it would be a good idea to use the name for the beer. The board agreed and the rest is history.'

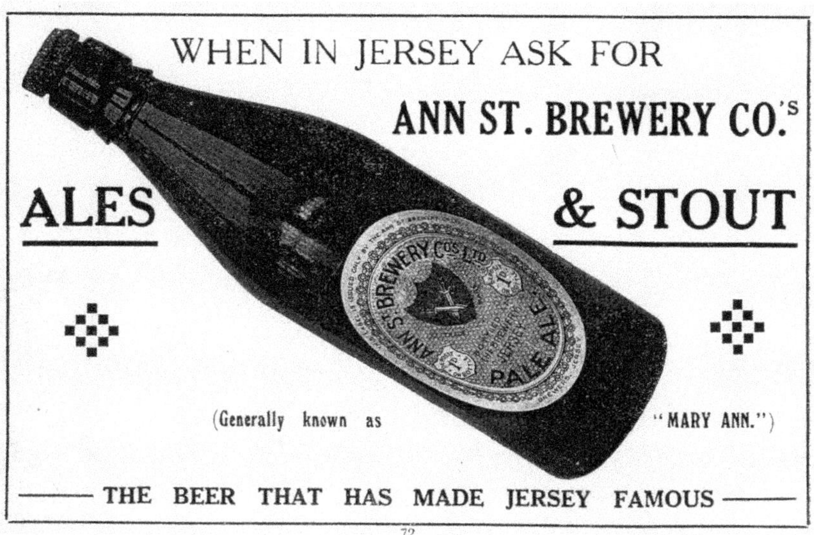

ON Tuesday 21 June 1927, the *Evening Post* recorded the death of Mr I J Bathe: 'The death occurred suddenly, yesterday, at his residence, 1 Westbourne Terrace, of Mr Inverness John Bathe, who for many years has been Manager of the Ann Street Brewery. The deceased, who was 68 years of age, was very highly respected by a large circle of friends.'

After his death the Board was reconstituted; Mr J R Woodman became its secretary in the place of Mr Payn, who died in 1940.

The German Occupation during the War had considerable effect on every aspect of Jersey life. For the Ann Street Brewery Company, the consequences were summed up by the chairman during his address at the company's 36th annual general meeting: 'There is no doubt that if it had not been for the Occupation of the Island and the consequent cutting off of our supplies from the mainland, we would have carried on at a profit.' He added: 'We hope the time is not far distant when we shall be able to make a fresh start and you can rest assured that everything will be done to keep the plant and premises in good order, so that we can take full advantage when the time comes.'

The only interruption to brewing was a short period in the war. Between 1942 and 1944 it had to brew for the Occupation forces from ingredients purchased in France. About 40,000 gallons of a lager-type beer were produced during that time.

Shortly after the war, work started on the construction of a new brewery in Ann Street. The building, and an additional brewhouse, was completed in 1950 at a cost of £500,000. Beer cost the equivalent of 4p a pint.

It was built on the traditional tower system whereby the raw materials were kept on the top floor and the various processes were carried out on descending floors finishing up with the bottling and kegging on the ground floor. The main value of this system was the elimination of pumping up.

There were 12 fermenting vessels, each of which could hold up to 3,600 gallons of wort, and capacity for 40,000 barrels.

After Mr Payn's death, Mr Woodman became the managing director, and Mr W J Ralph, an original shareholder, was Chairman. Mr Woodman died in 1947.

THE post-war years saw continued expansion: the company acquired the license to manufacture and distribute Coca-Cola in the Channel Islands in 1952. In 1954 the company was licensed by Allied Breweries to brew and market Skol Lager – up until then the new company had only brewed ale. In 1958 the company acquired the distribution license for Bollinger champagne for the Islands.

From the 1950s production was mainly keg beer under the Mary Ann brand.

The memory of some of those who worked at Ann Street in the post-war period was passed on to some of the present generation of employees or newly-retired employees when they first started work there, such as the legendary 'Sailor Lee', who, as the name suggests, was a former sailor. A very large and strong man, in the days before automation he was able to climb to the top floor of the brewery bearing two 75-kilo containers, one on each shoulder.

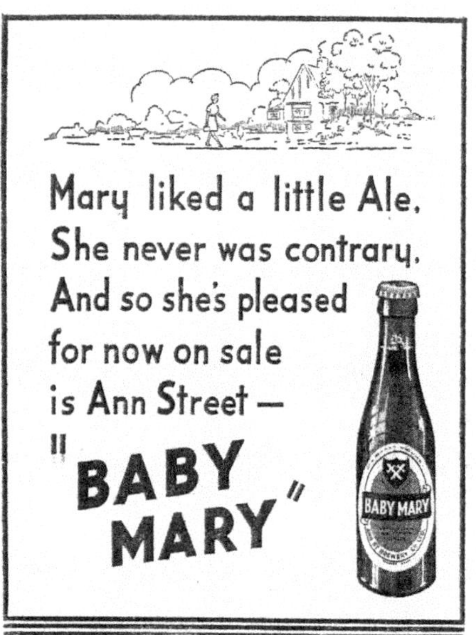

A legendary figure of the time was Philip McElwee, (known as 'Mr Mac') the head brewer, who first joined Ann Street in 1937 as assistant brewer. Apart from the Occupation years, he continued to work there for the rest of his career and was appointed to the board in 1959. A man with an ample figure, he was an excellent walking advertisement for the brew. He brewed Mary Ann and saw his beer win many international competitions, including the Brewer's Guardian Trophy of 1972, where Mary Ann was voted the best keg beer.

Ann Street remained a modest-sized business into the early 1970s. A turning point for the group came in 1971, when Ian Steven took over as the company's managing director. Chairman was H F Le Gresley, head brewer was P C McElwee and the other directors were P G Blampied, C A Nicolle, R B Hartley and R A Falle. Secretary and Company Accountant was D A Williams

Under Mr Steven's lead, Ann Street began developing its pub estate holdings, which grew to more than 100 across the Channel Islands. The company also entered the French market, acquiring L'Abeille, a French leading supplier of private-label soft drinks for the French supermarket sector.

In 1972 Ann Street Brewery entered the Brewers Exhibition and won the Brewers Guardian Cup for the best keg pale ale in the British Isles against nearly 100 other entries. It was Ann Street's first attempt at this competition, and the ale, Mary Ann Special Keg, had to be brewed down to a gravity of 1042, as opposed to the usual commercial gravity of 1045, so as to qualify for entry. At the World Exhibition (Brussels, 1973), it won a gold medal for Mary Ann special and a silver medal for the best bitter. In 1976 bottled Mary Ann won a gold medal, and a gold medal for the best stout in the British Isles. The two medals were won in the face of stiff competition from no less than 272 rivals.

Brands imported in 1974 and bottled at the brewery were Manns, Mackeson, Guinness, Double Diamond and Worthington E. By then the kegging process had become virtually automatic, and the filling machine was the most modern of its kind in the Channel Islands.

When Randall Vautier stopped brewing, it became the sole remaining commercial brewer in the Island. Local draught beers were marketed under the 'Jersey Best' and the award-winning 'Jersey Special' labels.

In Jersey pubs during the 1970s and 1980s, a popular beer mixture was a 'Brown Boiler', a creation made from a mixture of bottled and draught beer.

A range of national and local soft drinks were manufactured and distributed by A E Smith & Sons, a subsidiary that had been founded in 1894. Popular brands include Pepsi Cola, Britvic, Iron Bru as well as the company's own brand of drinks marketed under the name of 'Quencher'.

The public house chain in Jersey included some 57 managed and tenanted houses, the largest operation of its kind in the Island.

Victor Hugo Wines Ltd was founded in 1981 as the group's wine and spirits arm. The business of the Guernsey Brewery was merged with Ann Street and brewing ceased in Guernsey in 1988.

Visitors used to go on tours of the whole building in Ann Street up until about 1992.The women would receive a memento of a small beer bottle filled with perfume. Open days took place, such as the one on 20 May 1994, which was held in conjunction with the second Good Food Festival. A total of 500 people did tours of the brewery and outside there was a street party with meals prepared and sold by the brewery staff: chilli con carne with a dash of Mary Ann. A total of 1,200 Jersey Wonders were sold and there were two bands and some Scottish pipers and dancers from the Italian fair in Halkett Place.

In 1995 the name of the company was changed to the Jersey Brewery and that was the first of many changes to come.

MIRRORING the changes in the ownership of the brewery was a change in the licensed trade in Jersey, mainly thanks to the decrease of tourism and the effect that had on the Island's economy. Bass Charrington unloaded its pubs and Le Masurier sold its 28 outlets. Randalls Vautier bought up the Le Masurier outlets and Ann Street took over the Bass Charrington outlets. Country pubs, such as the Windmill in St Peter, were closing due to a downturn of trade and the breathalyser.

The Jersey Brewery, which had been listed on the London Stock Exchange's main board, began to seek an extension on to the English mainland, building up a pub estate in southern England. In 2000 the company bought the Brubeckers restaurant chain. The changing economic climate in the Islands encouraged the brewery to increase their scale at the end of the 20th Century.

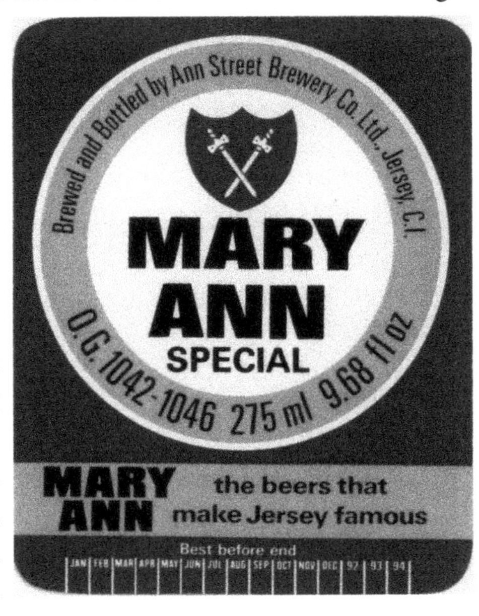

It is unnecessary in a book that attempts primarily to chronicle drink and drinking in Jersey to go too deeply into the commercial buy-ins and buy-outs, amalgamations and name changes that have punctuated the modern history of what was Ann

Street Brewery in the 21st Century.

Suffice it to say that due to Tom Scott, an English businessman who had relocated to the Island in the mid-1980s and who had soon grown into a leading figure on the Channel Islands business scene, Ann Street became part of a new business, CI Traders. By then the new group employed more than 2,000 people, and had extensive interests in the brewing, bottling, manufacturing and sales of beers, wines, spirits and soft drinks plus a growing portfolio of hotels, restaurants and licensed premises.

The company's real ale operation, the Star and Tipsy Toad Brewery, was bought in 1997. It was based at St Peter; it had been founded independently by brewer Steve Skinner, as 'real ale' had become a commercial proposition. This helped to compensate for the decision, taken in 1998, to abandon the brand name of Mary Ann and replace it with 'Jersey Best'. Tony Russell, sales director at the time, recalled that when the name was changed, he had been upset and disappointed – as indeed were many in the local community who felt that the particular local character of Jersey had been further diminished.

Jersey Brewery and Tipsy Toad were relocated to the current site in Longueville in 2004. The brewing of beer was now much reduced in quantity since the heyday in the 1960s and 1970s because of a marked change of taste of consumers away from beer and into other alcoholic drinks. The new Longueville Road was much smaller. Its new address, Tregear House, was formerly the site of the soft drinks company, A E Smith and Sons, and it is ironic that it is named after the founder of that company, John Tregear, a leading local supporter of the Temperance movement.

The Ann Street Brewery site in Ann Street is currently (2017) in the throes of redevelopment, and developers are turning the historic brew-house into flats – a process impeded by the prevalence of asbestos in the old building. It has been estimated that it will take at least £150,000 to make the building safe. The façade is listed, which might suggest that it will not disappear, but at the time of writing its future remains unclear. However, considerable damage has been done to the interior through neglect and casual vandalism.

From relatively large production capacity (it had been a 40,000 barrel brewery that used to brew large brands such as Skol under licence), the site relocated and downsized to a very modest 40-barrel plant in its new premises.

The changes continued; the brewery was syphoned off to Sandpiper CI Ltd by then, through a management buy-out, became part of a new Liberation Group in 2008, with the present (2017) chief executive, Mark Crowther, appointed. The acquisition was led by Mr Crowther, with the intention of growing and developing all areas of the business that had suffered from a lack of significant capital investment.

It now forms the largest pub, restaurant and drinks business in the Channel Islands. The group also includes the Liberation Brewery (renamed in 2011) and Victor Hugo wine company and Bucktrout's in Guernsey, plus associated wholesale and retail outlets. The 'Liberation Brewery' still uses the previously known brand names. The group continues to expand.

Paul Hurley, the now retired chief brewer at the Liberation Brewery, discussed the eventful period of the past decade or so: 'At some stages there was almost no production of cask ale in Jersey. At one point we even stepped away from it completely and were purely keg – it was only Steve Skinner at the Tipsy Toad who was producing it'. (The Tipsy Toad microbrewery now sits within the larger Liberation brewery, and the small eight-barrel plant is still providing real ale. He continued: 'As brewers, we've always fought for cask but different owners have had different ideas. We also had the opposite problem of too much real ale – at one point we had 40 or 50 different ales on the Island, produced here and imported, and the quality just dipped.'

The brewery may have passed between owners but he is optimistic about the future: 'We've been owned by property companies, retail groups, people who were running hotels, laundries and petrol stations. I remember going from working in a brewery, which was the only business, to being part of a group where we were a long way down the list of interests. Now we're back to the sort of company I joined 25 years ago. It's got a family feel and you feel the brewery is at the centre of it all.'

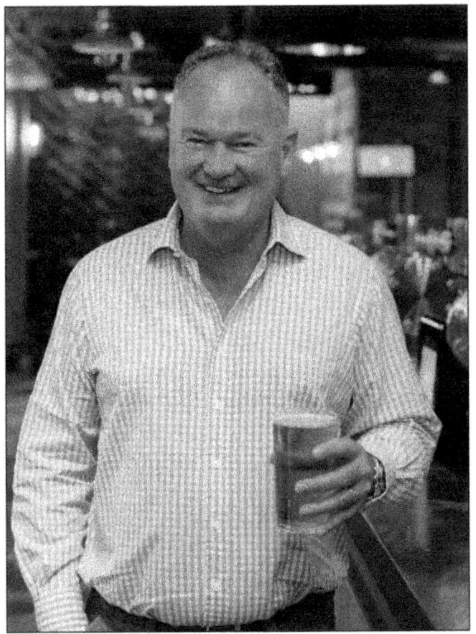

Mark Crowther

Mark Crowther, formerly a senior manager at Carlsberg UK, has made sure that the company was just about pubs and brewing: 'At a low point we were producing no cask ale at all, even quite recently only five per cent of our production was cask, the rest was all keg, and now we are up to 50 per cent cask beer production, which is really pleasing for us as brewers.

Where once the Jersey Brewery, in its various guises, was seen as only active in closing pubs, the Liberation Group is opening and refurbishing them.

The Brewery concentrates on seasonal ales, such as Christmas Ale, which features Black Butter. Its range includes Liberation Ale, Blonde, Ambrée, Noire, Rouge and the Mary Ann brand, which was reinstated in 2008 because of the decline in beer sales which was reinstated in 2008 because of the decline in beer sales. On reading the news in the *JEP*, the daughter of Mr Woodman, Fayette Jackson, then aged 86, wrote a letter to the editor for publication, welcoming the news of the reinstatement. She was invited to the brewery, where she enjoyed her first taste of beer for 20 years as she toasted the return of Mary Ann. She recalled her pre-war memories of the brewery: 'It was a great company. I remember being four years old and my father taking me to the brewery to meet everyone. After that day, they all knew me and whenever I went there someone would hold me up to the vats to breathe in the lovely smell of the hops.'

When, as a girl, she became ill, doctors told her father to give her Mary Ann and she recalled: 'it pulled me up and made me feel much better.' She added: 'Mary Ann for ever!'

Liberation Ale debuted at the Great British Beer Festival in 2009.

The brewery's flagship cask ale, Liberation Ale, has picked up a raft of awards including Gold at the International Brewing Awards in 2013 and 2012. In 2013 the bottled version won Bronze at the prestigious International Beer Challenge, and in the same year, Liberation 140, brewed especially to celebrate the brewery's 140 years of brewing in the Channel Islands, also won bronze at the International Brewing Awards.

In July 2014, the brewery struck gold when it won three awards at the British Bottlers' Institute 2014 Awards, picking up a gold medal for its Liberation IPA.

In December 2014, Liberation Group acquired the Butcombe Brewery and pubs business, located near Bristol, as a platform for expansion in the UK. The group currently has 120 pub outlets, including 44 pubs in Jersey, 22 in Guernsey and two in Alderney.

The most recent chapter in the history of this long-established company is its sale for £118 million to Caledonia Investments PLC. It has pledged to provide an additional £40 million of funding for investment.

It is a long way, both in time and conceptually, from Mr J S Palmer brewing beer in St Helier 1871.

(iii) RANDALLS LTD.
(formerly Randalls Vautier Ltd.)

THE origin of Randalls Ltd. is a coalescence of a number of small town breweries.

In 1819, on 21 August, Thomas Turner announced the opening of the New Market Brewery, in what is now Beresford Street. By 1833 he had removed to Nos. 7 and 9 Gloucester Street and by 1847 had installed himself at the Clare Street Brewery, at 10 Clare Street.

A second strand introduces the name Randall: Robert Randall (1811–1898) came as a boy to Jersey from Yeovil in Somerset with his father.

As a young man, he joined one of the fluctuating numbers of breweries in town: the Minden Place Brewery and became the maltster there.

Originally there were two breweries in the one street, one of them run by F de la Taste between the years 1833 and 1837, the other by J B Quick. Later, Mr de la Taste removed his own brewery to Wesley Street, calling it the Brewery.

The years rolled on and in 1847, shortly after Thomas Turner had moved his own brewery to Clare Street, Robert Randall took over the brewery.

It was some 40 years later, between 1875 and 1880, on the death of Mr Quick, that Robert Randall bought the Minden Place Brewery for his second son, Charles Walter Randall (1850–1919).

The two breweries were then run as one concern.

Charles Randall often travelled to Normandy to buy barley for malting, while he would sell both malt and hops to the smaller Jersey breweries, of which there were several in mid-19th Century St Helier. The cargo would be imported by schooner and, when discharged, the captain of the vessel would be paid in golden sovereigns to take back to Normandy.

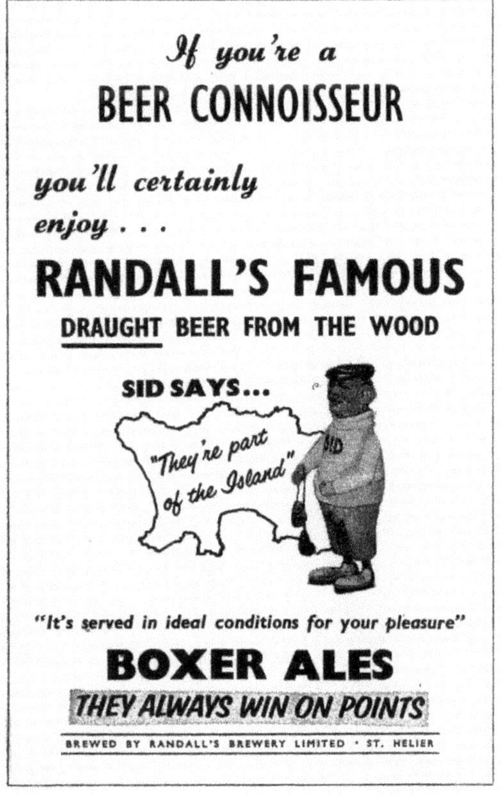

His brother, W A (Albert) Randall was brewing at Clare Street in 1900 and by the following year the business at Clare Street and Minden Place was being operated as Randall Bros.

The Minden Place Brewery was located at the top of James Street, and it was also the location of the bottling department and the stables for the horses and delivery waggons. The bottling for the Clare Street Brewery was carried out at 6 Peirson Road, where the seed shop belonging to Le Marquand Bros later stood (now the pet shop, Pet Paradise) and this location also provided the malting facility for the Clare Street brewery.

Albert Randall died in 1912, when his son, Harry Aubin Randall (1884–1935) took over both breweries.

During the First World War, the whole of the brewing operation was carried out at Clare Street in order to economise on labour, but following the war the Minden Place Brewery was re-opened. Charles Randall died the following year, 1919.

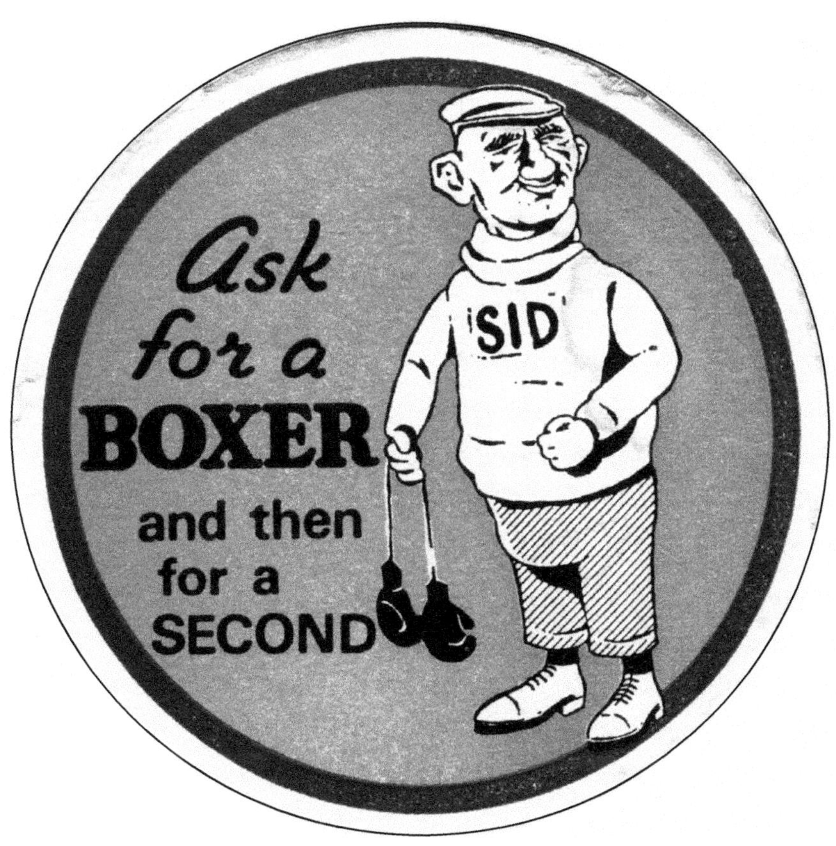

The business was carried on by Harry Randall until his death in 1935. In 1936 the business became a limited company under the style of Randalls Brewery Ltd and it was owned by Harry Randall's widow, Violet, and his sister, Kathleen. Violet re-married, and both she and her second husband, Melville Walker, died in 1964.

The business was bought in 1964 by the Hon Edward Greenall of the Warrington brewers, Greenall Whitley and Co Ltd. The Greenall influence was seen in the brewing in Jersey of their 'Grunhalle' Lager. A new bottling plant was installed and the brewery was extended.

The wine and spirits merchants, J F Vautier Ltd., were acquired in 1976 and in 1983 the company was split into two, Randalls Vautier Ltd and Randalls Properties.

A specialist wine company – Merchant Vintners – was bought in 1986.

Brewing ceased in September 1992 and the company operates today as the owners of 49 pubs in Jersey.

These include The Admiral and Chambers (1994), the Earl Gray (1998) and refurbishments at country pubs; Les Fontaines. Pembroke and La Pulente as well as the Old Portelet and the Goose on the Green (now called 'The Goose'. A retail cash and carry, Vins Direct has been opened and the former St Peter's Country Inn was refurbished under a new name, the Sir George de Carteret. The brewery premises on the north side of Clare Street were redeveloped in 2005 and now form the company's offices.

In 2011 the two companies were merged together once again and the company is now known as Randalls Ltd.

(iv) MODERN AND MICRO

ONE of the great – and most promising – trends in modern drinking culture in Britain has been the rise and rise of real ale. Beer, brewed often in small breweries, or in converted garages, or on the premises of pubs is a welcome development that illustrates modern consumers' preoccupation with produce that is local and made in a traditional way.

It is certainly a sea change from what was on sale in the post-war decades until the 1970s – the world of Double Diamond, Mackeson and that ilk.

STAR & TIPSY TOAD BREWERY

This was Jersey's first micro-brewery. It was founded by a Jersey couple, Steven and Sarah Skinner, who had lived in London and there experienced the sudden and fashionable vogue of pub breweries that developed in the 1970s and 80s. They thought it would be just the thing for Jersey. The local breweries did not make anything then, other than keg bitter, and very little cask conditioned ale found its way into the Island. This was the opportunity for Mr and Mrs Skinner's 'Tipsy Toad' brewery to hop on to the scene in 1992.

At the time he was the Ann Street licensee of what was then called the British Union pub in St Lawrence, near the parish church. He had been in discussion with the Ann Street managing director to refurbish the former small town brewery site that became the Victoria in Minden Place – the traces of the brewery are still discernible behind the fabric of the present pub. It appeared to be the obvious and very appropriate site for a new microbrewery and would be the 'real ale' arm of Ann Street.

An understanding was reached with Mr Skinner about the creation of a microbrewery at the Victoria, but at the same time, Ann Street bought and refurbished the Saint Pierre Park Hotel in Guernsey. Suddenly there was no budget to proceed with the Victoria Brewery plan. In view of the fact that Mr Skinner's plans had been let down by this new corporate development, he was assisted financially in his own alternative plan of buying the 'Star' in St Peter, which its previous owner had agreed to sell to him free of tie. There thus existed the incongruous situation in which a brewery helped to establish a microbrewery which would sell beer in competition to its own beer. Mr Skinner's first thought was to base it on the name 'crapaud' – but he realised that this might lead to unfortunate puns or misunderstandings. So instead he opted to translate the word into English – Toad. The word 'tipsy' was frowned upon at first – in some quarters it was thought it might encourage inebriation.

The Tipsy Toad Brewery, which opened in 1994 with a 9 barrel plant, brewed eight to ten barrels a week, selling mainly in the Star but also to one other local pub and a few private bars, including the Rugby Club.

In 1995 the Town House in New Street was added in premises that had belonged to the J F Vautier wine company. This had a 20 barrel capacity.

The company ceased brewing during the latter months of 1997 and was then taken over by Ann Street; Mr Skinner left Jersey to run a small real ale brewery in Cornwall, Skinner's Ales.

The Tipsy Toad in its time trained and employed a woman brewer, Liz Mitchell – in mediaeval times women brewers were more of a rule than an exception and were known as brewsters.

The beers brewed were Star Dropper (1060); Horny Toad (1050); Jimmy's

Bitter (1040) and Agile Frog (1038).

On the departure of the Skinners to Cornwall, the Star was taken over by Ann Street, which also took on the then Tipsy Toad brewer, Patrick Dean. In 2004 the brewing equipment was taken over for use in the Jersey Brewery at Longueville; the equipment at The Town House was sold to the Isle of Arran brewery – which currently produces award-winning beers.

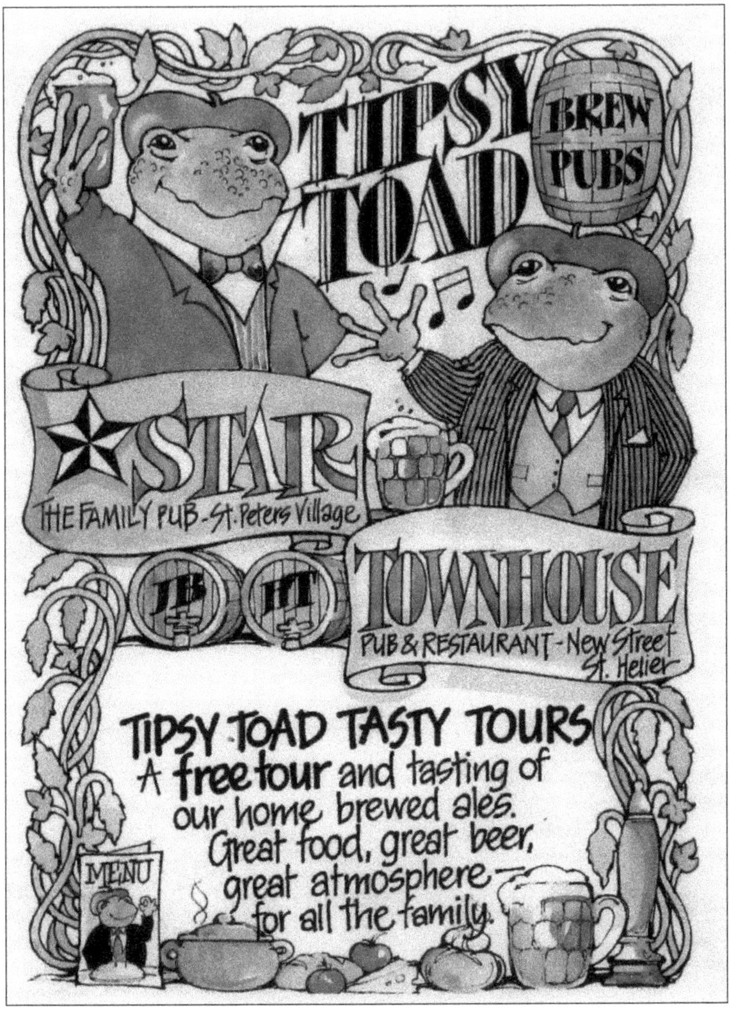

Imaginative advert for the Tipsy Toad brewery and pubs

~ 9 ~

The pub in Jersey 19th and 20th Centuries

I fly from pomp, I fly from state,
I fly from falsehood's specious grin,
Freedom I love and form I hate,
And choose my lodging at an inn.

Lines quoted in *A Stranger's Guide to Jersey* (1833)

The brave new world of the 19th Century also brought a new invasion of Jersey: people travelling for pleasure. The first tourists were already visiting Jersey at the time of the Napoleonic Wars and, for tourists in the first third of the 19th Century, a number of guidebooks were published. We have mentioned some of them in the preceding chapters.

Included in their number is *A Stroll through the Island of Jersey* (1811), which mentions in town: 'three good inns, the Royal Hotel, Union Hotel and Deal's Hotel, where a stranger will always find comfort in recommendation, until he can procure private lodging which are here let from between 9s and 18s per week.'

By the 1830s there were many different trades and shops, but only three eating houses as such, six banks, and 'a café': **Bertault's**, at 4 Halkett Place. **Kent's Coffee Shop** in Market Place was also in existence shortly afterwards.

The Strangers Guide To The Island Of Jersey (1833) included a commercial directory. Extracted from the directory and other tourist guides of the time is this listing of inns and hotels in town, together with the surname of the licensee and address:

Establishment	Licensee	Location
Albion	Thompson	Mulcaster Street
Britannia	Brée	32 Hill Street
British Hotel	Almond	Broad Street
Caledonia	Le Cornu	Pier
Commercial	Gregory	Pier Road
Commercial Hotel	Mrs Paton	Don Street
Deal's Hotel		Pier Road
Le Sueur's	Mauger	Hill Street
London & Royal Yacht Club	Miller	Pier
Market Inn	Brabin	Halkett Street
Nelson's	Nelson	13 Bond Street
Old London Hotel	Mrs Collins	North Pier
Union Inn	Le Veslet	Royal Square
York Hotel	Mrs Le Gros	Royal Square

At the British Hotel, the Union Inn and Rout's Hotel (possibly the previous business of an owners of the Union Inn), the author, W Plees, states that 'the prices of the necessaries for luxuries of life may be enjoyed at one half the expenses attending upon a residence in England.'

The 1858 guidebook: *The Channel Islands Pictorial, Legendary and Descriptive*, by Octavius Rooke, lists the principal hotels in town at that time: 'The British, the Yacht Club, the Royal, the Union, the York. Plenty of good boarding houses: Bree's in Bath Street. Tozer's, Whindley's etc. The charges for board and for lodging are usually about 25 shillings a week.'

Such listings, combined with subsequent listings in guidebooks and almanacs, have provided the primary source material for the details of the 19th Century hotels and pubs in this section of the book.

Why some hotels were selected for special mention and others were not shows at least the writer's personal preference, and perhaps it is not too cynical to see in these descriptions and other similar ones of the period an early flowering of that fine literary genre, the 'advertorial'.

(i) HOTELS AND PUBS IN ST HELIER – A 19th CENTURY DIRECTORY

THIS is necessarily an incomplete list. To track down every hotel, licensed guest house, tavern, pub, hotel and other drinking place in Jersey that has existed in the past or still exists would almost be a life's work in itself.

Bear in mind that some of the listed pubs of the Victorian era would have been little more than a private house with a front room in which drinks were served – although some of these establishments might have offered further amenities upstairs.

There is scope for such a directory and it could be a worthwhile project to undertake, but it would be a sizeable volume, and in the context of the long story of 'drinking in Jersey' through the ages, it would be the tail that wagged the dog.

Included in this necessarily incomplete directory are those establishments that, whatever their origin, have grown into the major hotel names we know today. The 'Royal Yacht', for example, might be quite taken aback by being included in the same alphabetical list as the 'Red Lamp' and vice versa, but irrespective of the quality or social standing of the establishment, an alphabetical list is the easiest way to guide the reader through the forest of names.

Also at the end of this chapter are listed names that are later than the 19th Century and do not have a long history as a pub or hotel, even though the premises themselves may be centuries old and familiar in former times as, for example, farmhouses.

It is hoped that the information in this following list, if in many ways incomplete or deficient, will go some way to cataloguing the many places that have offered hospitality to Islanders and visitors in the past and whose names do not deserve to sink into total oblivion.

NOTES

The names of the survivors – those establishments that have survived into the 21st Century - are written in bold type.

The names of those establishments – and one or two later ones – who between now and then have succumbed to the vicissitudes of time, are written in italics. Where there is little or nothing to record apart from an address, the name is recorded separately in a section at the end of this list.

ADELPHI, The Parade

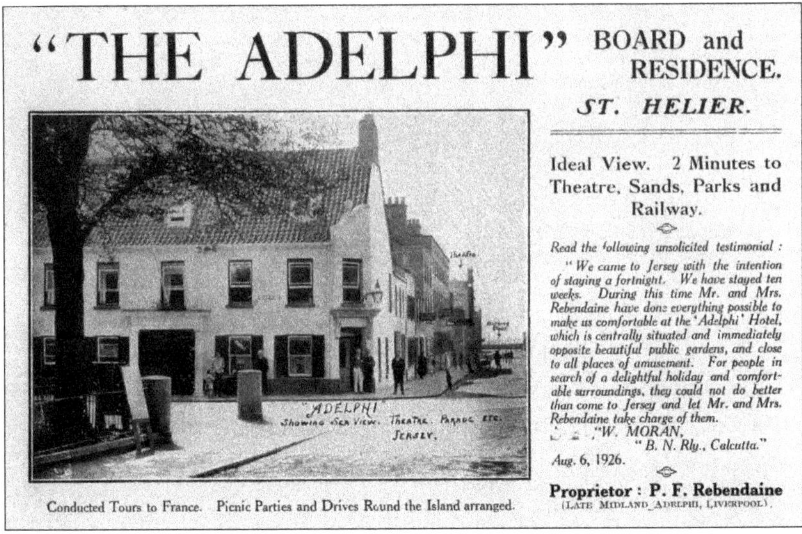

Advertisement for the Adelphi from a late 1920s guidebook. The proprietor is stated as P. F. Rebedaine (Late Midland Adelphi, Liverpool). The Liverpool Adelphi is a huge and impressive hotel and which opened in 1914. Might Mr Rebendaine have named the Jersey Adelphi after its Liverpool namesake?

ALBION HOTEL, 7 Mulcaster Street
Mentioned in 1820s. It had been 'Mr Le Sueur's wine shop'; this either became part of the Albion or was succeeded by it.

AURORA, Cattle Street
The name is said to be a shortening of the 'Aurora Borealis' – the Northern Lights – but the Latin name meant little to the authorities and was too long, so it was registered simply as 'the Aurora'. It is mentioned in 1858 as providing the catering for a banquet at the Queen's Assembly Hall to celebrate the inauguration of the telegraph cable from England to Jersey and it seems to have preserved a reputation for the quality of its food.

It was advertised in 1889 as being not only a pub (with accommodation) but also as 'wholesale and spirit merchants.' Horses and carriages were on hire and 'table d'hote every day at one o'clock – price 1 shilling.' The building was re-built in 1907, and existed throughout the 20th Century. It was converted in recent years to a café – bar and shop attracting Portuguese-speaking customers. Next door is the Caesarea; the two pubs are both owned by the Liberation Group.

BATH HOTEL now the **AFRICA HOUSE**, 90 Bath Street

The hotel was established there in 1922 by Hilda Blanche Ford-Hacking, who leased the property. The house had been built by Jean Le Gros and then handed down through family and into Renouf family by marriage. It was sold in 1895 by Charles Renouf to Charles Randall, when it was described as Chicago House and also known as 40 Bath Street. Randall was the owner of the Minden Place Brewery. The family have retained ownership ever since.

The hotel flourished under Hilda Ford-Hacking's tenancy. It was particularly renowned for its gardens, which were designed on a Viennese theme and where live music was held regularly in the summer months. Later it was part of Le Masurier car park. It ceased to operate as an hotel during the Occupation, although Hilda managed to stop the German forces commandeering the hotel on two occasions and even refused to serve German soldiers behind the bar. Following the Occupation, the hotel did not reopen, but Hilda and her daughter, Florence, continued to run the property as a public house – it was well frequented by gas workers!

Its location was beside the premises of Le Masurier's, which were destroyed by fire. The Bath Hotel was sold to that company afterwards and the property still belongs to them.

BOND HOTEL, now **LEBLON,** Bond Street

In 1869 it was known as *The Mariners Inn* and in 1886 as *The Birmingham*. However, it kept that name for only two years before the name was changed again to the Bond Hotel. (In the same year a *Birmingham Hotel* was opened in Broad Street. Whether the pub took its name from being originally a bonded warehouse or just from the street name is unknown. It was bought by C Le Masurier Ltd in the 1970s.

BOULE D'OR – Hotel de la Boule d'Or, Conway Street

Established c 1885 or earlier – it existed until 1937, the centenary year of the neighbouring Pomme d'Or Hotel, when it was bought by the owners of the Pomme d'Or.

BRISTOL HOTEL, Esplanade, on the corner of Kensington Place.

This claimed that it was the successor pub to a tavern on the same site, which had existed since the 16th Century. In its later days it had become a cabaret but was demolished very recently and the site is now taken by a small part of the new mammoth headquarters in Jersey of the Royal Bank of Canada.

BRITISH HOTEL

An hotel on this site was established by 1789 and was likely to have been the only hotel (as opposed to tavern) in town at the time. The proprietor made so much money from French émigrés at the time of the Revolution – arriving in Jersey rather hurriedly with very limited accommodation available for them – that he was able to afford to extend his hotel by a further storey.

The hotel building that took its place was established in 1810 by Richard Rout, although there seems to have been little interruption in service: a Mrs Le Toublin is mentioned the year before, 1809, as the proprietor.

The known proprietors in the 19th Century were:

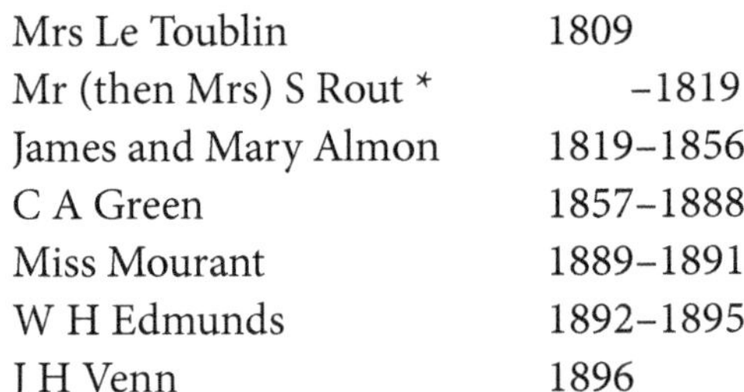
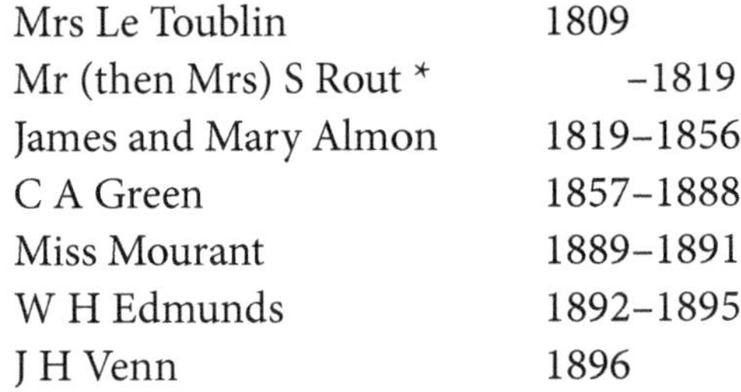

Mrs Le Toublin	1809
Mr (then Mrs) S Rout *	–1819
James and Mary Almon	1819–1856
C A Green	1857–1888
Miss Mourant	1889–1891
W H Edmunds	1892–1895
J H Venn	1896

*The name *Rout's Hotel* may refer to a former establishment kept by the Rout family.

It was the location of many municipal functions and at various times housed many distinguished visitors, including one of Napoleon's favourite Marshals, the Marquis Emmanuel de Grouchy, the veteran of Waterloo, who, accompanied by his wife, visited Jersey in 1836.

It was used as a hotel for visiting high-ranking personnel during the Occupation and was also one of the five German Soldiers' Homes (*Soldatenheime*) in the Island. In more modern times, the Beatles stayed there during their performance at Springfield in 1963. It is now a part of Barclays Bank.

BUNCH OF GRAPES, Dumaresq Street
Landlord in 1859 was Henry Church, who was involved in an incident at The Halfway House, Millbrook (q.v. below)

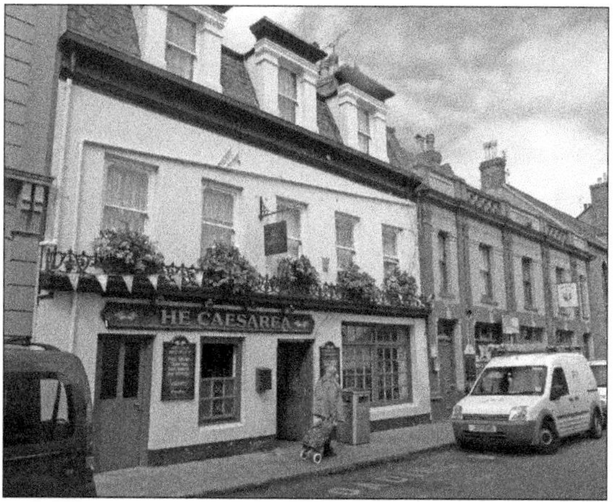

CAESAREA, Cattle Street
Stands next door to the Aurora, the Caesarea is the older of the two. It is one of the four oldest public houses in the town, established at least in 1834 if not earlier.

CHANNEL ISLANDS HOTEL, Corner of Mulcaster Street and Weighbridge.
Proprietor, c 1867 was a Mr Gribble). This was one of a cluster of pubs and hotels around the new harbours, which, like the Pomme d'Or, catered for visitors arriving or leaving by steam packet. Other names in this area of Mulcaster Street in the 1840s were the Café des Italiens, the Royal George, the Grasshopper and the Navy Arms.

CHARING CROSS TAVERN, 8 Charing Cross
Now Bellagio's Restaurant

CIGAR DIVAN, 3 Beresford Street

> 'This establishment has an excellent Coffee Room, where Wines, Spirits and Coffee of the best quality are supplied. It affords that comfort which has long been wished for, and undoubtedly must meet the support of a discerning and liberal public. Dinner and supper parties accommodated. Superior draught Ale, bottled porter and rich cordials, Havannah and other cigars. Superior peppermint cordial for relieving Cramps and Spasms.' (1820s)

CLARENDON HOTEL now **LIDO'S**, Market Street

The hotel was commenced in 1865 and for six generations was in the same family. It is a Free House. The first member of the family to own it was Edward Ainsley who moved there and took over the premises then known as the Old Kent Coffee House, ran by a Mr Whale.

Two generations down the line the pub was inherited by his grand-daughter, Elizabeth Jane Ainsley, who married Mr C Ashelford in 1912. She held the licence for 55 years; her regulars nicknamed her 'Lido', hence the present name of the establishment.

Until very recently the licensee was her granddaughter, Jane Ashelford who has since sold the premises to the Jersey Pottery, and is undergoing extensive redevelopment.

ALWAYS A WELCOME AT

THE CLARENDON HOTEL

(Prop.: Mr. Ronald Charles Ashelford)

A FREE HOUSE

MARKET STREET, ST. HELIER

Telephone: 22358

COCK AND BOTTLE, Royal Square

The pub was first mentioned by this name in guide books of the middle of the 19th Century. The original meaning was that draught and bottled beers were available on the premises – the 'cock' meant the tap. There is also a suggestion that the name might be an anglicisation of the French '*Le Cocq en Bataille*' – a reference to cock fighting, although this is doubtful, according to the historian, Philip Ahier.

The name 'Cock and Bottle' may have been too suggestive for Victorian susceptibilities, and it was changed to the *CENTRAL HOTEL.* It then became known as the COSY CORNER before reverting to its original name – the middle pub between the Peirson and a hotel which once stood on the site of the building later occupied by the Chamber of Commerce and now the offices of the Liberation Group. As quoted by historian Philip Ahier:

> 'At the time of the Battle of Jersey in 1891, a Jersey man, watching its progress from the pub and feeling that he had 'to do his bit' stalked out with a pitch fork and proceeded down King Street (*La Rue de Derrière*) and was prepared to slay any Frenchman attempting to escape or to prevent any desertion on the part of any Jerseyman who feared that after Major Peirson had been killed, "*tout était perdu*" – all was lost.'

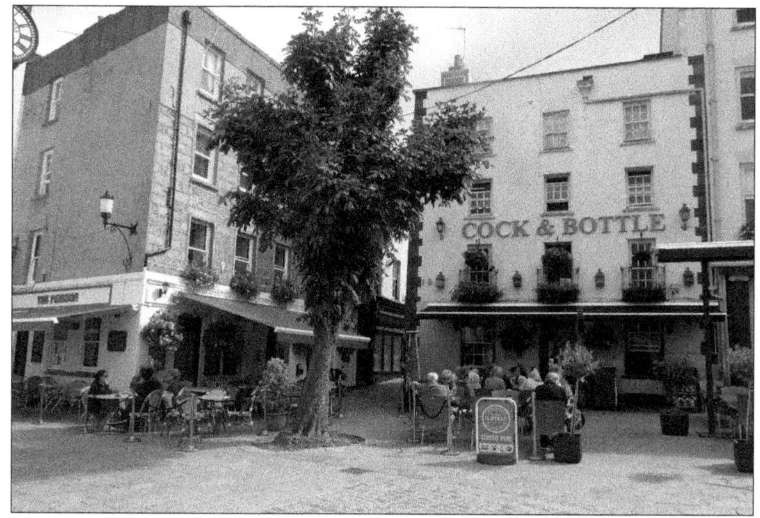

The Cock and Bottle facing the Peirson, in the Royal Square

COMMERCIAL HOTEL
On the corner of Conway and Commercial Streets; now the Bento Sushi Bar.

CRICKETERS ARMS now **SEATON BAR,** 14 Seaton Place
In 1870 the building was a bakers; in 1874 a pawnbrokers. A year later it had become a tavern and in 1880 the licensee, Mr T E Jeune, had named the pub 'The Cricketers Arms'. In the 1950s there was a display by the doorway of an arrangement of stumps, bat and ball, but how long they had been there, and whether they were responsible for the name of the pub or vice versa, is not known.

The pub (a free house) was inherited by his son, T J Jeune, who also hired out tents and marquees for events around the Island. He sold it in 1935 and since then there have been various changes of ownership.

CROWN AND PUNCHBOWL, Havre des Pas
May have been the forerunner of the *PRINCE'S HOTEL* (q.v) kept, reputedly, by 'a bonny widow named Coutanche'. It is described in the pages of *Le Crapaud* (1835): 'The inn has a spacious balcony overlooking the widow's little garden, commanding a beautiful prospect of the sea and the promontory of La Collette where the newly-erected Tower seems to fling defiance to the billows of the sea.'

It was the meeting place of the 'Hodge-Podge Club' a social club with similar rules and objectives as the modern Rotary movement.

CUSTOMS HOTEL, 10 The Esplanade

The property was owned from 1869 by Charles McAllen; by 1873 the Jersey Railways Company had opened their offices at this address and in 1874 they were taken over by a Mrs Blake, who ran a restaurant from there named Blake's Jersey Railway Hotel and Restaurant. After her departure in 1881 Mr McAllen resumed possession, opened it as an hotel and called it The Customs – the customs office was next door at No 14. There were various changes of ownership until Randall's purchased the hotel in 1969. The building has since been demolished and replaced by one of the many large financial and legal offices that have moved into the area.

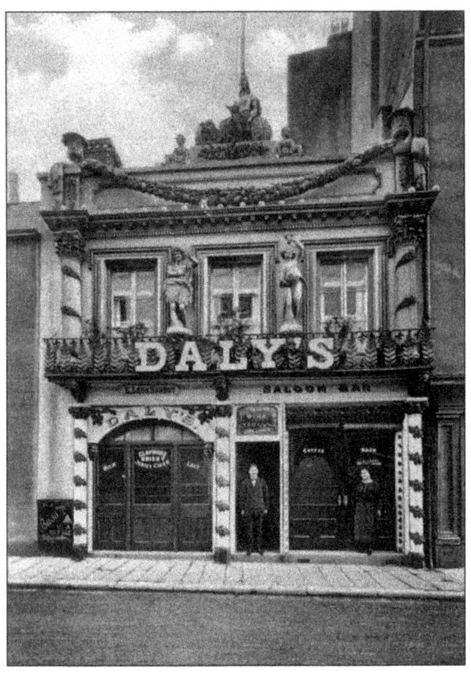

DALY'S HOTEL, now the **LAMPLIGHTER,** 9 Mulcaster Street

There was a cluster of pubs and hotels built around the new harbours of the 1840s, catering for visitors arriving or leaving by steam packet.

By 1871 there were joined by the opening of *Daly's Hotel*, with D Daly as proprietor. Unlike some of the other Mulcaster Street premises, Daly's small hotel survived for over 100 years, and it wasn't until 1960 that it changed its name to *The Grapes* and then again to **The Lamplighter** in 1983.

Former landlords of Daly's Hotel have not enjoyed the best of luck. Monsieur Barbot, for example, was murdered in France and his body thrown into the River Seine. Mr Ferrand, who walked out of the pub on the evening of 10 June 1940, was killed by a bomb from a German plane in the air raid that preceded the Occupation.

The current name, 'Lamplighter', refers to the old gas lamps in the inn and is also a tribute to the old 'lighters', the sailing ships that could be found in the Harbour in the 19th Century.

The façade of the pub is highly decorative, but is nevertheless a diminution of what it looked like before alterations made in 1960.

DEAL'S HOTEL

This consisted of three houses on the west side of Pier Road, at Numbers 29, 31 and 33. (Its original number was 6). It had a stucco front rather elaborately ornamented with stone figures. At one time it was known as the *Hotel de l'Ocean*. The French political figure, General Georges Boulanger, lived in one of these houses for a short time before travelling to Brussels and committing suicide on the grave of his mistress.

In the early years of the 19th Century, the hotel was kept by Mr Deal and in 1834 by 'Mrs Deal', doubtless his widow. It was one of a number of hotels and inns that provided room for Masonic functions in the early 19th Century.

Writing in 1809, the writer William Plees mentions *The King's Arms* kept by Mr Deal, which might have been his business before buying Deal's Hotel or a previous name for the hotel. The book says of The King's Arms:

> 'The best conducted and principal hotel in St Helier is the King's Arms kept by Mr Deal, where Assemblies are held every fortnight during the winter months, and on all public occasions; this house is capable of accommodating families as well as individuals, in the most comfortable style; good hack horses are kept by the proprietor, who has convenient stables and coach house.'

It is not certain where the King's Arms was located.

DEVON AND SOMERSET, Halkett Street

The '**DOG AND SAUSAGE**' was always the pub's nickname, and it was officially re-named that in the late 20th Century.

DEVONSHIRE BARS, Route de St Aubin

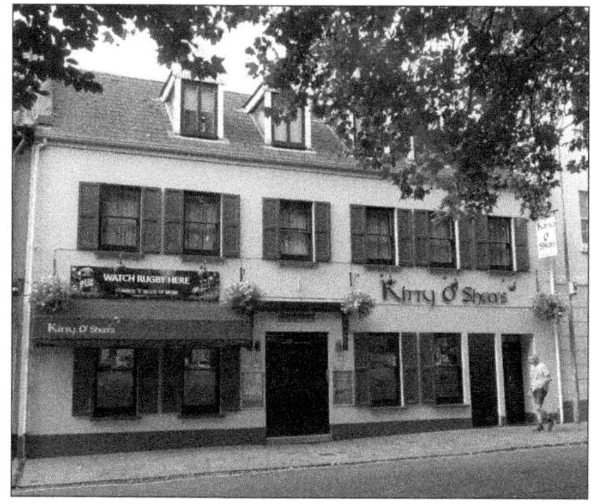

DON HOTEL, The Parade

Formerly the **Golden Anchor**, managed in the 1820s by a Mr Le Gros. It is now known as **KITTY O'SHEA'S.**

DON INN, Don Road

Both the *DON HOTEL* and the *DON INN* derive their names from Lieut-General Don (1756-1832), Lieut-Governor of Jersey between 1896-1809, and then again from 1810-1814, the famous builder of the main roads in the Island.

The first road he undertook to construct was from St Helier to Grouville Church via Longueville… past where the Don Inn now stands.

There is a stone butting against the left hand side of the Inn which is believed to have had some connection with the original road planned by General Don. At one point in the post-war years it was removed, but had to be replaced and restored to its original position, as it was a landmark. The pub is currently closed as no licensee has been found for it.

EAGLE TAVERN, Lemprière Street

Begun in the 19th Century; a number of different licensees found the pub difficult to make profitable. It survived until the turn of the 20th and 21st Centuries but is now demolished.

The magnificent golden eagle inn sign stood on the wall of the building, representing the coat of arms of the Lemprière family, who owned property in town and gave their name to Lemprière Road.

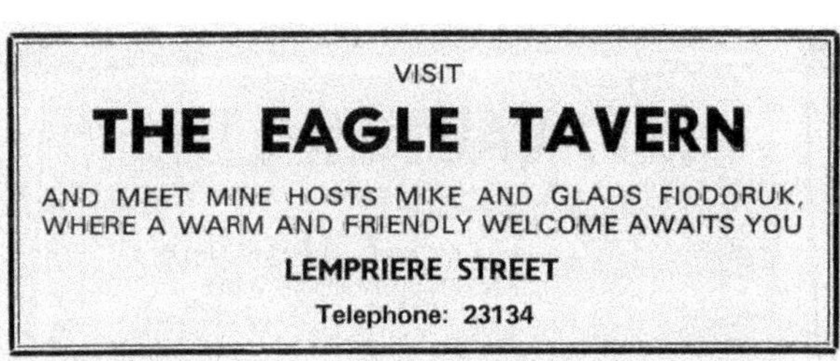

EASTERN, Snow Hill

Originally the *Jersey Eastern Railway Terminus Hotel* – the railway operated at Snow Hill from 1874. It was bought by Fred Clarke of C Le Masurier Ltd and remained the company's property. It became the Eastern Railway Terminus Wine Bar in 1974 and in recent years (before 2017) became the **LOVIN' SPOONFUL** café.

EDWARD CLARK'S HOTEL and *PHIL BREE'S HOTEL*, Rue de Derrière (King Street)

It is possible that both these names refer to the same building, with Clark's becoming Bree's. Phil Bree was the father of Elias Bree – a noted local freemason – who founded the hotel on the corner of Stopford Rd and David Place that became known as Bree's Hotel - now the **ROYAL HOTEL**, David Place.

EUROPE, Hotel de l'Europe, now known as **CHAMBERS,** 4 Mulcaster Street
Established in 1868. The first name of these premises was the *CAFÉ DES ITALIENS* circa 1840s); in 1862 this hotel seems to have been known as *BENTLEY'S HOTEL.*

Between the years 1858-1867 the Hotel de l'Europe was in Don Street. The name of Mme Délépine is recorded as a landlady of the time. The guidebook, *Souvenirs de Jersey* by Auguste Luchet, describes the hotel as an 'old house kept by Madame Favell à la Française'.

Karl Marx stayed at the hotel in 1879, having moved from the **Trafalgar Hotel**, St Aubin (q.v.), out of disgust at their monotonous menu. He certainly approved of this hotel: 'It is excellent and one day we must go here together, toute la famille', he wrote in a letter home.

It was popular with French tourists - hence its name - and also popular with the agricultural sector. It was near the harbour and convenient for potato merchants (who held annual dinners there in 1905 and 1906) and with the Royal Jersey Agricultural and Horticultural Society, whose premises were very close by. During the First World War it was owned by a M Tremel, and used by officers of the French army whilst on leave.

There were a number of changes of ownership throughout the 20th Century; in 1966 it was taken over by Mr Carlston; the attached restaurant, 'Pedro's', was well-known, especially for its fine seafood. In the 1990s it was acquired by Leslie de la Haye and converted by him into the extensive pub, **Chambers**.

EXETER, Queen Street
One of the Island's oldest taverns. Horse-drawn omnibuses started from there to go to Gorey, operated by Bus Company.

In 1849, it was managed by Mr Clark, who made the place so comfortable that that the Yarborough Masonic Lodge preferred to meet there than at the newly constricted Masonic Temple.

The business was managed by the related Picot and Le Cocq families from the 1880s for just under a century.

FIRST AND LAST, Pier Road
It is not clear whether this was the actual name of a pub, or whether it was a nickname by which it was usually called. It was much patronised by soldiers stationed at Fort Regent, for whom this was the first pub they encountered on walking down to town at the start of a period of off-duty, or the last one they encountered as they returned home to barracks.

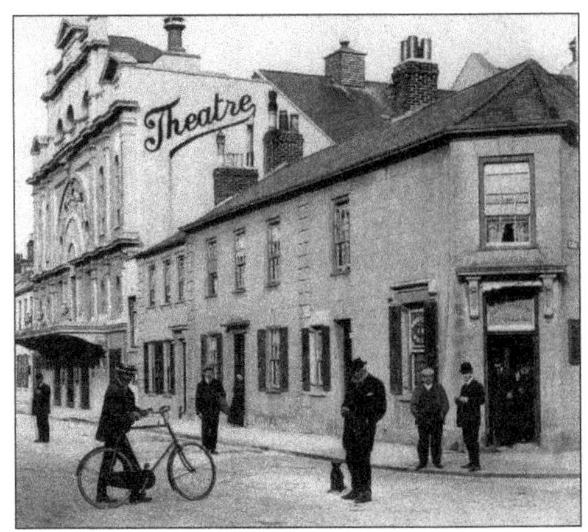

GLOSTER VAULTS,
Gloucester Street
Named, though not spelt, like the street, after the Duke of Gloucester, the third son of George III, who visited Jersey in 1817.

Gloster Vaults on the corner of Gloucester and Sand Streets and hard by the Opera House.

GRAND HOTEL; *MARINE HOTEL*
Grand Hotel (Jersey) Ltd bought the Marine Hotel (qv) from Thomas Le Geyt Curry in 1889. It was demolished and the new hotel built, designed by Thomas Colcutt (1840-1924), former president of the Royal Institute of British Architects. The foundation stone was laid on the same day that the statue celebrating the Diamond Jubilee of Queen Victoria's accession was unveiled at the Weighbridge, 3 September 1890.

Its doors were opened to the public in June 1891 and had extremely positive reviews in the local press. *British Press & Jersey Times* said that it was 'commodiously, not to say luxuriously furnished throughout' and that 'all visitors will have their every want carefully studied and met.' There were two billiard tables, to accommodate 'the British national game'. There were 170 bedrooms for guests.

Claude Debussy visited Grand Hotel in the summer of 1904 at a time that his personal life was mired in scandal. He stayed with his lover, Emma Bardac, the wife of a rich banker. It is believed that he wrote *La Mer* at the hotel. There were many distinguished visitors, including Prime Ministers of Canada and of France, the American Ambassador in London, the Rockefeller family, Lillie Langtry and Captain Prince Louis of Battenburg RN.

During the German Occupation, the hotel was requisitioned as the HQ of Fortress Engineer Staff 14. On 9 May 1945 German soldiers paraded in the yard at the rear of the Grand Hotel for the last time, where they dumped their arms and accoutrements, many of which were deliberately smashed before being thrown on the scrap heap. Crowds had gathered to watch the dejected looking German troops and naval ratings trekking to their country billets from the Grand Hotel. The hotel was left in a terrible state at Liberation time and the owners consequently applied to the Rehabilitation Scheme in order to get some compensation to put the building right once more.

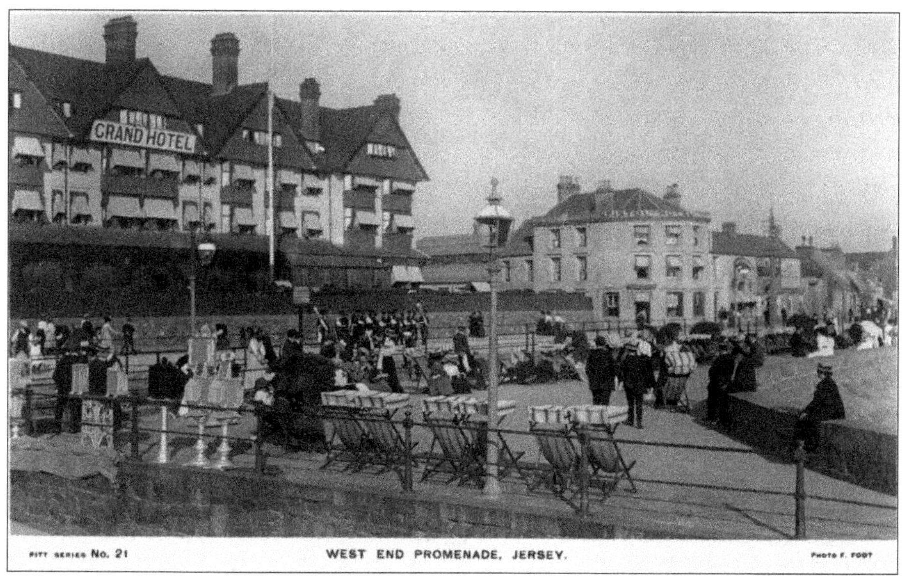

The Grand Hotel overlooking the Esplanade.
Note too the former Bristol Hotel in the middle distance

The hotel hosted the visit of Princess Elizabeth and Duke of Edinburgh on 22 June 1949. The red carpet unrolled for the occasion was to become a familiar sight during the following years, for the directors of the hotel decided that henceforth all lunches and banquets given by the States for Royalty would be provided at cost price. The Island would never have to pay an excessive amount.

In 1950 Mr L Sangan bought the controlling interest in the company that had commenced the hotel in 1890. This was liquidated in 1950 and a new Jersey company was formed.

Another reception for Royalty was held on the evening of Liberation Day, 2008, where a dinner was held for the Queen and Duke of Edinburgh.

GRASSHOPPER HOTEL, Mulcaster Street, c 1873.
In 1894 this was owned by G H Mitchelmore. The Premises were later occupied by the Royal Jersey Agricultural and Horticultural Society. The 'Grasshopper' which hung outside this hotel, is now in the Museum. It was 3ft 9in long from the tip of its antenna to its nether limbs.
At one time known as the Bath Hotel.

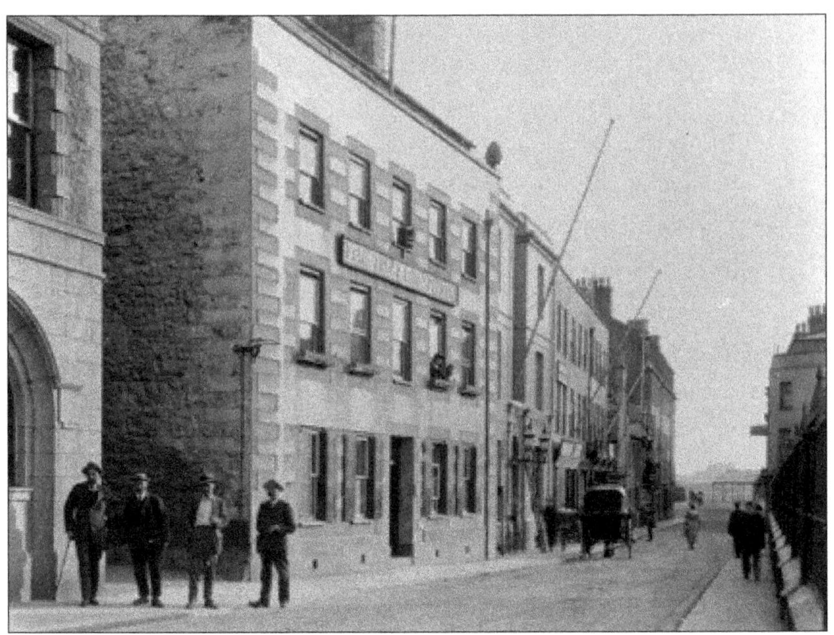

A group of cattle people standing outside the former Grasshopper Hotel which was purchased by the RJAHS for their Headquarters

HALKETT HOTEL, Morier Lane (now Halkett Place)
Opened 21 October 1886. Proprietor was Mr F J Le Maistre, occupier Mr J Berrow.

IMPERIAL HOTEL / **HOTEL DE FRANCE**
About 1862, a number of English and Jersey residents, realising the lack of a good hotel in Jersey, formed a company with the object of building a suitable hotel. Jurat Josué Le Bailli, president of the Chamber of Commerce and also of the Jersey Mercantile Union Bank, was its president.

The estate of the late Mr Ingouville was purchased and the old Maison Ingouville, 'La Fregonnière', was demolished. Work started on the conversion in August 1863. The contractor for the new building was an English company. Mr J Amy (master carpenter of Stopford Rd) was employed by the company to supervise the work. Sub-contractors were A Viel (Platrage) C J Benest and T Pirouet (part of the carpentry); Mr Benest was Constable of St Clement and later a Jurat.

There was a grand opening of the new 'Imperial Hotel' on 6 September, 1866: 'At 7pm a huge crowd of invited people were shown into a reception salon and soon afterwards walked in procession towards the banqueting room. The decoration of the magnificent room is in the best possible taste and the salon perfectly lit' (*Chronique de Jersey*). The guests included the Lieut-Governor, Bailiff, Jurats and Dean. There was room in the hotel to accommodate about 50 visitors.

Despite financial difficulties, the company functioned until 1878, when Jurat Le Bailly was sentenced to five years imprisonment – for fraud. The hotel was then sold to a different management

The hotel was bought by the Jesuit Order in 1880 and leased by them to French Jesuits, who had to disperse from their home country because of a tightening up of anti-religious laws. The building now became known as Maison Saint-Louis and was a seminary for young students studying theology, philosophy and science. The college was open from 1880 to 1940; in 1941 it was requisitioned as temporary accommodation for troops.

After the war the Jesuits thought of renewing their occupation of the property, but with vast social changes in France having taken place, which made their life considerably easier, they decided to sell and return to France.

The building was sold to Major J V Reynolds who, with his father decided to restore it as an hotel. As Philip Ahier writes (*Historical Hotels and Inns of Jersey*): 'They felt it wrong that such a magnificent structure commanding such a position overlooking St Helier should remain practically empty with the grounds overgrown and uncared for.'

The new hotel's name was the **Hotel de France**, in acknowledgment of its French Jesuit past.

The hotel opened on 15 May 1954, with 130 bedrooms and accommodation for 300 guests. Its first function was held at the end of the month. A large dining room was added in 1955 and the first conference was held in 1959, that of the National Skål Club. It was acquired by the Parker family in 1971, since when there has been major redevelopment of the buildings and grounds.

IMPERIAL HOTEL, LILLIE LANGTRY BAR, La Motte Street
Well known for its *Lillie Langtry Bar*

KING'S ARMS – See under Deal's Hotel

LA FOLIE
A harbour tavern, but located far from the area today used by commercial craft and visiting yachtsmen. When it was built some time in the first four decades

of the 18th Century it was positioned on one of the only two jetties available for mooring and protection from the elements, between the French and English harbours. The presence of its regulars - largely fishermen – gave it a unique character.

Its name may have had something to do with the perceived foolishness of building a house on the water's edge, or perhaps the whole harbour development in an area so far distant from the town centre and drying out completely twice a day, was thought to be a folly.

La Folie had the unusual claim to fame of a public house of being owned by the Harbours and Airport Committee. The original building was demolished and rebuilt sometime between 1723, which seems to be the reliable date for its origination, and 1850, when it was realigned to face the entrance of the Harbour.

It also enjoyed privileged status – in 1841 it was the only inn licensed to sell alcohol in the vicinity of the port. It was one of the Island's six Free Houses.

At the time of writing it stands closed and for a while was threatened with demolition as part of a controversial scheme to create luxury flats with private moorings, although that threat seems to have been removed (as of 2017). It suddenly closed on a Sunday evening and did not reopen. A new tenancy was sought – one did not materialise. It is a listed building. The building is still there, but is boarded up.

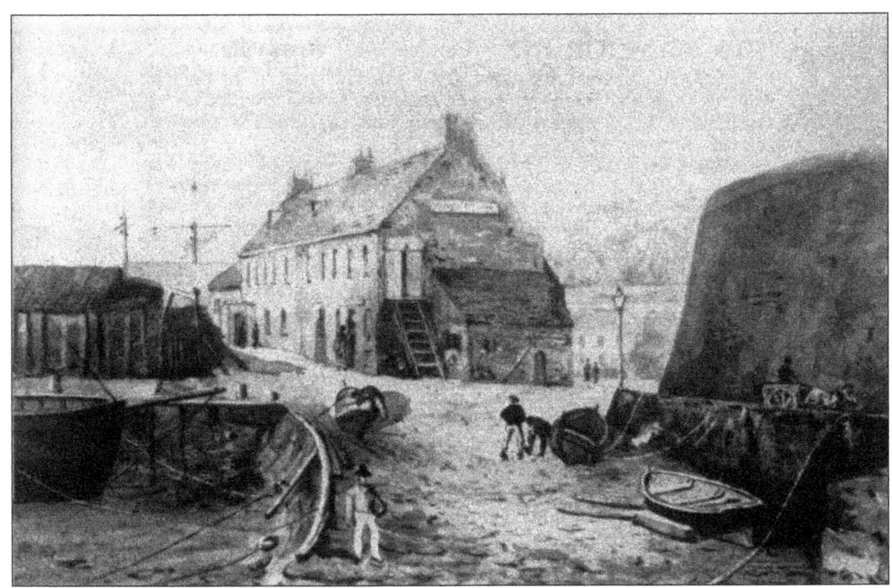

La Folie depicted in the early nineteenth century

In the days when growers would take their tractors and trailers, laden with potatoes, down to the docks, they were in the habit, while stuck in a stationary queue, of popping in 'for a quick one'. It had two drawbacks to becoming a listed building: (i) it cannot fit in any cooking facilities; (ii) the doors face the road rather than the harbour wall, so it was more difficult to enjoy an al fresco drink on a warm evening. A sign said: 'Visitors should beware of seasickness caused by the nautical chat of regulars.' It has been said that more fish have been caught in La Folie than ever been dragged from the seas around Jersey.

The licensee for many years was Bert Langford, who spent more than 40 years in the Island's licensed trade. It was a free house; a club atmosphere was encouraged and the pub was noted for a mammoth Christmas draw. The actor Rock Hudson was a visitor in 1953, during the filming of *Sea Devils.*

MINDEN HOTEL, Minden Place, on the site occupied in modern times by furniture or carpet warehouses. Terminus of a coach service to Leoville, St Ouen.

MITRE, *BLUE NOTE,* Broad Street
At one time the pub gave its name to the short thoroughfare connecting Queen Street to Broad Street, more properly known as La Ruette ès Haguais. It was for some years re-named as the **Blue Note** jazz bar.

OLD ENGLAND, Cheapside

OLD MARKET INN
Exact location unknown; the landlord there was Edward Ainsley who ran it from about 1856 and in 1865 moved to become landlord at the *Clarendon Hotel* in Market Street.

OLD SWAN, Corner of Wharf Street and Hope Street.
For some years this has been known as **THE OFFICE**

OXFORD, Union Street
At the corner of Union and New Streets, with a long frontage facing Union Street but with little depth. A second pub, a little further along Burrard Street, was formerly the *CAMBRIDGE* but was renamed the **BEER HOUSE.**

PARADE HOTEL currently called **CHIMES,** 24 The Parade

PEIRSON, *ROYAL SQUARE INN*

Probably one of the oldest extant inns in the town, built in 1749. It perpetuates the fact that the heroic Major Peirson – victor of the Battle of Jersey in 1781 – died nearby in the hour of victory. In that year it was the home of Dr Lerrier and its associations with the Battle; P J Ouless writes as follows:

> 'During the conflict a cannon ball, having passed through the hat of the Lieutenant Governor, Major Moses Corbet, shattered and carried off the lower jaw of Rullecourt, the French commander, on whim it inflicted a mortal wound. The two commanders – Corbet and Rullecourt – withdrew into the Courthouse, but Rullecourt's wound was hopeless. He never spoke again and expired the same night at 11 o'clock. He was carried into the adjoining house of M Lerrier (now the Peirson), a private gentleman, and some of the blood having fallen on the floor the stains have remained upon it to this day.'

Perhaps it was expected that Dr Lerrier's skill could have saved Rullecourt's life.

In September 1798 Sir William Taylor Money (1769-1832) then a young man, accompanied by two friends, visited Jersey, and his diary entry for 17 September was: 'Wigram and I breakfasted at Dr Lerrier's and surveyed the field of battle of 1781, where the gallant Peirson fell close to the Doctor's house, one side of which still retains the marks of the French artillery. The marks on the west side of the inn are still visible.'

It became an inn in the early 19th Century and was called The Royal Square Inn. At one time there were two painted notices on the walls: 'The Battle of Jersey 1781' and 'Here Peirson Fell'. Landlord of the Peirson Mr R Parris changed the 'Here Peirson Fell' plaque at the request of the Lieut-Governor, the Hon Sir Francis R Bingham (1924–1929) who had seen someone being photographed holding as glass and leaning against the wall. He was very much annoyed and considered it 'not a fitting act to a gallant soldier'.

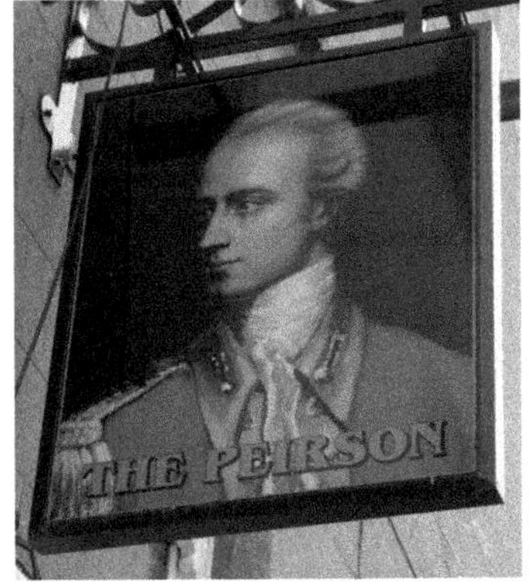

Thomas Parris, born in Honiton, came to Jersey in 1875 to manage the inn for the then licensee, Mr Brett. T Parris and Brett's widow bought the premises from Mr E J Gallichan in 1899. Mr Robert Parris (son of Thomas) was an engraver; his son, also Robert Parris, took over the Peirson in 1921.

Bass Charrington was the proprietor of the Peirson since 1971 and carried out alterations and improvements. It is now owned by the Liberation Group.

POMME D'OR

The site where the Pomme d'Or now stands was originally part of the foreshore. The sea wall ran along Bond Street and in front of it was a vast area of sand stretching out to Elizabeth Castle, with a few rocks strewn between. As the sand was only covered on equinoctial periods, in 1780 it was felt that the land should be reclaimed. The reclamation work took nearly 20 years but created the Esplanade, Weighbridge and Commercial Buildings. On this new reclaimed land, 1,000 plots were sold, mainly to St Helier residents.

The Pomme d'Or site was purchased by the Pellier family in 1802. Philip Pellier was a corn and flour merchant of high repute. He owned several mills and a large store in what is now the Weighbridge and Liberation Square area. In Wharf Street stood Pellier's Livery Stables and a house that they rented to a Mr Dates, who ran 'DATES' BOARDING HOUSE'.

The Pelliers gave up the stables in 1837, demolished them and constructed the Pomme d'Or Hotel, in their place. It was named after a well-known cider produced at 4 Wharf Street. The hotel was run on continental lines, under the supervision of Madame Boisnet, and soon won the patronage of the merchants along the Quay, the visiting captains and their officers. At that time it was situated between two other inns, the *NAVY HOTEL* and the *THREE TUNS*.

The hotel was mentioned in Auguste Luchet's *Souvenirs de Jersey*, written about 1844, in which he stated that it was 'under French management - an establishment replete with good things and noted for its gayety, where the house, the service, the attention, the wines and the brandies are all French.'

During the party political strife between the 'Roses' (liberals) and 'Lauriers' (conservative) in the early 19th Century, each party had a hostelry as their headquarters. The Rose faction met at the British Hotel in Broad Street, the Lauriers met at the Pomme d'Or.

In 1850 a complete renovation and redecoration began and by 1851 the Freemasons were holding their annual banquets in the hotel before the building of the Masonic Temple. The great French author, Victor Hugo, was one of the hotel's most celebrated guests in 1852 when he stayed there for a few days on his arrival in Jersey, before finding accommodation at 2 Marine Terrace. The renovation was completed by 1855 and the hotel now had 100 rooms, bathrooms, gardens and a dining room for 120. There were reading rooms, saloons, billiard rooms and shops.

The present Weighbridge frontage of the Pomme d'Or was originally a merchant's store, incorporated into the hotel as it grew in popularity during the second half of the 19th century.

The 31st anniversary celebration in 1861 of the Revolution in Poland was given at the hotel by Polish exiles living in Jersey and in 1881 a centenary banquet to commemorate the Battle of Jersey was held at the hotel.

The corn and flour store was demolished in 1882 and in 1886 the Weighbridge frontage was built. In 1895 Charles Pellier inherited the property following the death of his father, William. Charles joined the *BOULE D'OR* Hotel, situated on the corner of Conway Street and Wharf Street, to the Pomme d'Or.

Up to the start of the First World War, the hotel flourished. In particular, it attracted French visitors, although the fact that it was under French management occasioned an anti-French riot in 1900 on 21 May at a celebration of the Relief of Mafeking. The hotel deteriorated during the First World War. In 1920 the hotel was sold to a company known as the Pomme d'Or Hotel Ltd and an attempt was made to revive the hotel, which by now was derelict.

It was acquired on 5 February 1930 by George and Ada Seymour. The couple had visited Jersey on their honeymoon in 1919, fell in love with the Island and two years later, joined by George's parents, they formed what would become one of the Island's longest established family businesses.

At that time, the main entrance was in Wharf Street. The entrance was still flanked by the two inns, the Three Tuns and the Navy Hotel. These were purchased by the Seymours during the hotel's centenary year of 1937 and incorporated into the hotel. George and Ada had seven children, many of whom have worked in the Seymour Group.

The hotel's prime site overlooking the Harbour proved to be an ideal location for German Naval headquarters during the Occupation '*Hafenkommandant Jersey*'.

The hotel's finest hour was undoubtedly Liberation Day, 9 May 1945. After signing of the surrender of Jersey, at 14.00hrs, Generalmajor Wulf was sent ashore and told by Lt-Col. Robinson to meet him at 16.30 at the Pomme d'Or'. The initial landing party 'Omelette' followed Wulf ashore. This consisted of Lieut-Col. W P A Robinson, the commander of the Jersey Force, Captain Hugh Le Brocq and his batman, fellow Jerseyman Private Raymond Marquis, were also in the landing party. They landed at New North Quay to an overwhelming reception by Islanders. Col Robinson and his men had literally to fight their way through the crowds to the Pomme d'Or.

As the Advance Party neared the Hotel, Col. Robinson noticed that the swastika flag was still flying from the balcony. He asked for the Union Jack flag to be brought across from the Harbour Office, which had been draped from an upstairs window earlier in the day, by Surgeon-Lieut. McDonald and Sub-Lieut

Milne, and ordered one of his men to go to the hotel balcony, take the swastika down and get it out of sight. Huge crowds filled the Weighbridge area in front of the hotel, which had been selected as the Force's headquarters.

The Harbourmaster, Captain H G Richmond, had brought the Union Jack over to the Pomme d'Or and joined Colonel Robinson, who was on the hotel balcony with PC Bill Howe of the Jersey Paid Police. Very quickly they were joined by dozens of other uniformed liberators, so much so that the Pomme d'Or's owner, George Seymour, who had seen all four of his family's hotels taken over and largely trashed by the occupying forces, feared the balcony might collapse under their weight!

An impromptu ceremony took place at 15.45: Colonel Robinson mounted the balcony and addressed the crowd. After he had finished speaking the Union Jack was hoisted on the flagstaff by the Harbourmaster, Captain Richmond, as Colonel Robinson stood stiffly at the salute. The crowd then sang the National Anthem in a fervent manner and cheered and cheered again. This was the official seal of Liberation.

During the evening a large crowd gathered round the hotel and they sang and cheered while the British troops flung handfuls of cigarettes, sweets, biscuits

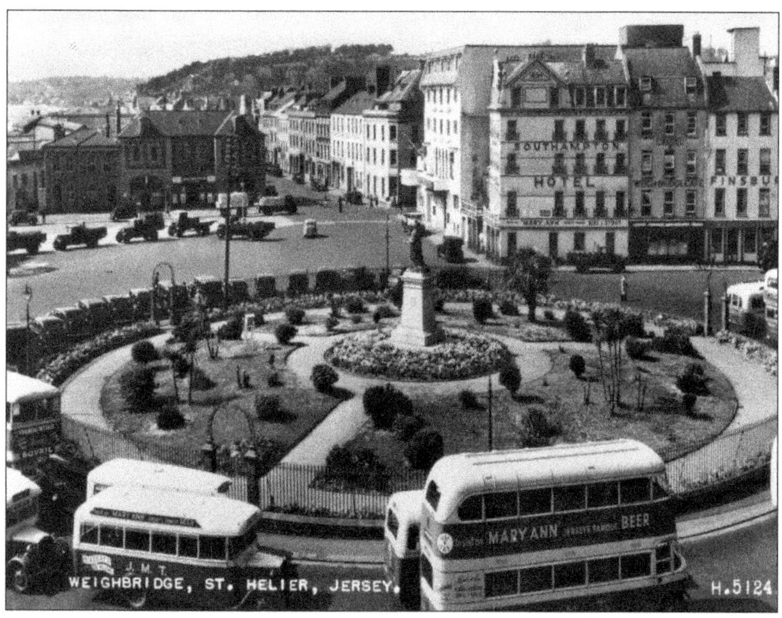

A postcard view across the Weighbridge in the 1950s featuring the former Southampton Hotel and, beyond it, the Pomme D'Or Hotel. Note too the double-decker bearing an advert which states 'Insist on Mary Ann Jersey's Famous Beer'.

and tea, sugar and milk cubes. Photographs of Hitler and the other members of his regime, which had hung in the hotel, were hurled to the crowd for them to deal with. The photos were torn to shreds and thrown back to the balcony amid cheers.

At the end of the Occupation, the Seymour company took over Le Huquet's coal store, which stood on the corner of Conway Street and the Weighbridge. Two thousand tons of rubble, resulting from the demolition of a German bunker had to be removed before the property could be remodelled in Conway Street.

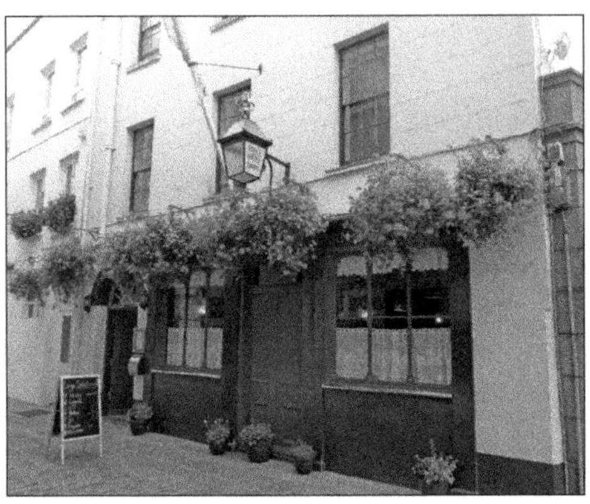

PRINCE OF WALES TAVERN, Hilgrove Street

Owned from the 1850s by Peter Drélaud and his family, who continued as licensees until the inn was bought by Randalls on 10 May 1994.

Mrs Peter Drélaud served in the tavern for 80 years, starting when she was aged 11. She was a very little woman and a stool was made for her so that she could see over the bar.

Interviewed by *The Morning Advertiser* in October 1948, she remembered the days when beer was 2d a pint and brandy and gin 1d a glass, on which the duty was only 2/6d per gallon, and all the public houses opened from 6am to 11pm.

THE PRINCE OF WALES TAVERN

Mr. Percy Drelaud   Licencee: Peter John Taylor

UNDER THE SAME FAMILY FOR OVER 110 YEARS
ONE OF ST. HELIER'S FEW REMAINING FREE HOUSES

FULLY LICENSED

HILGROVE STREET, ST. HELIER

Telephone 37378

PRINCE'S HOTEL, Havre des Pas

It was named after the publican, George Prince and his wife, Betsy, who settled in Jersey from England and ran this pub and hotel in the last quarter of the 19th Century. It had been a pub before their arrival, possibly called the *GREEN PIGEON*, or maybe the *CROWN AND PUNBOWL* (q.v). The façade with its canopied balconies remain in place in what is now a private dwelling.

RED LAMP, Peter Street / Ingouville Street
Built in 1846, by Goerge Ingouville, a wealthy builder who lived at La Fregonnière, a large house built on the slope above St Saviour's Road, which would in time be demolished and the *IMPERIAL HOTEL*, **HOTEL DE FRANCE** (q.v) built in its place. He constructed streets in the area, which he named after his three (illegitimate) children: Ann, Charles and Peter.

The pub survived almost until the end of the 20th Century, when it was re-named *SCRUFFY MURPHYS*, then closed, and is now the offices of a marketing and PR company.

RED LION, Halkett Place
Later called *FRIDAY'S* and now **THE HALKETT**
This once stood in isolation before the houses on either side were erected. It once had a slate step outside the front door. Originally two stories high, its walls were very thick. The cellar has huge granite stones forming its southern side, cemented together with horse hair and clay.

It was the starting place for St Aubin coaches in the 19th Century, The bus service from the Red Lion was in existence as far back as 1845, quoting Michael Ginns' and Eric Osborne's *Transport in Jersey*:

> 'The service, which left "The Red Lion" had, by 1858, had been in business for about 15 years, perhaps longer. A half-hourly service was in daily operation between 8.30am and 8.30pm between St Helier and St Aubin; the vehicles used were apparently double-deck horse buses of the type then commonly used in London. The end of this service came swiftly and surely in 1870, when the new railway to St Aubin was opened, and the company retired to lick its wounds and to operate a much less frequent service to St Brelade.'

In the *British Press Almanac* for 1871, there are details concerning a new bus service from 'St Helier, First Tower, Millbrook, St Lawrence Valley and Goose Green, leaving the Red Lion, Halkett Place, daily.' On Saturdays and Sundays there were different times for departure. At the bottom of the advertisement the fare for each journey was given as 2d. The stable yard attached to the hotel is still in existence at the back of the premises, surrounded by a high granite wall, over 40 feet high.

The sign of the Red Lion in 19th Century days consisted of a life-sized specimen, painted deep red. On Wednesday 30 October 1918, about midday, the lion came down with a mighty crash, owing to one of the brackets going awry: 'The shock caused the head and body to fall apart, the former rolling several yards before coming to a standstill in front of the shop adjoining.' The head was

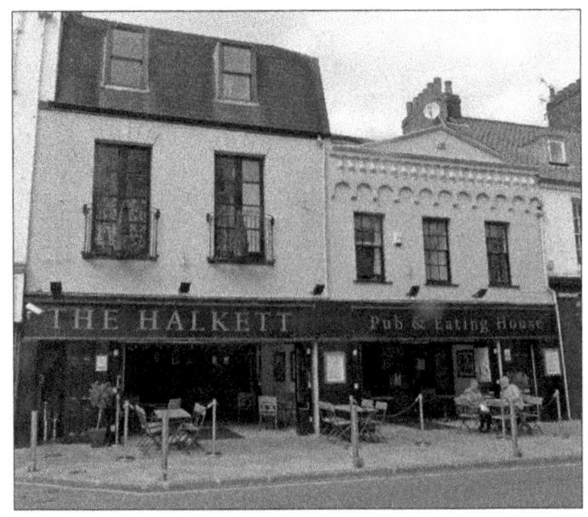

only slightly damaged, and was re-hung over the doorway. When Ann Street bought the hotel in 1949, it was removed and a new sign erected. The head of the damaged lion is still on the premises.

ROBIN HOOD HOTEL, Rouge Bouillon

This was a sort of prison during the bread riots of 17 May 1847. These arose as a result of the workers constructing La Haule Road, who were complaining at the high price of provisions, especially that of bread, in comparison to the very low wages they were receiving at the time, namely 2 shillings a day.

These workpeople gathered others from the shipbuilding yards at La Collette and those from the stores on Commercial Buildings and those working on the pier; they arrived in the Royal Square, shouting for cheap bread. The Riot Act was read outside the Royal Court House and the crowd dispersed from the centre of town. The Court put out an order through the Town Crier that no alcoholic drinks should be sold that day and that publican should close their doors. It was assumed that the riots were being caused by drunks.

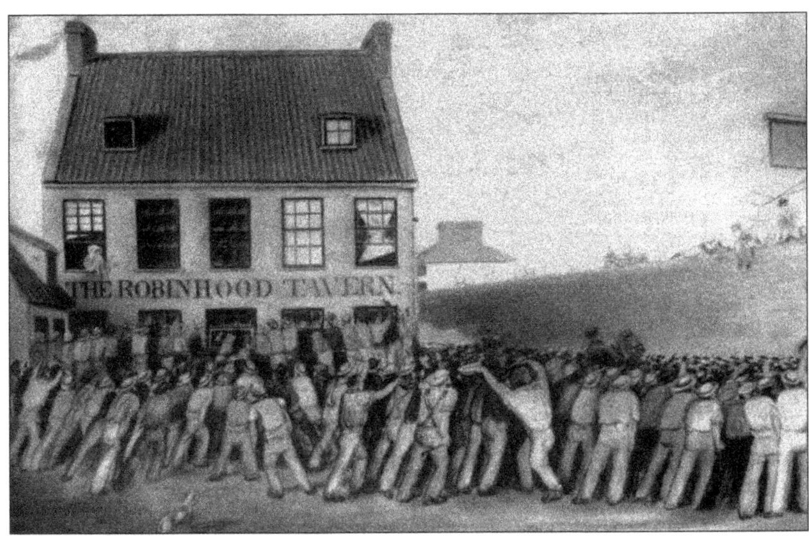

However, the mob, now armed with crowbars, pickaxes and hammers, proceeded to the Town Mill in Grands Vaux, which they attacked, grabbing bags of flour and loading them on to two waggons. At this stage, the Constable of St Helier (Peter Le Sueur), once again read the Riot Act outside the Robin Hood Tavern, as it was then known. One of the ringleaders of the rioters was arrested and lodged in the inn, but in the confusion that ensued he escaped by the back door, while the mob was trying to open the front.

The Military was summoned from Fort Regent and closed the road leading to the Robin Hood Tavern. The carts laden with wheat and flour were captured, re-harnessed to horses and taken back to the Mill under military escort. The police arrested more rioters and lodged them in the Tavern taking precautions they did not escape. The prisoners were later transferred to the prison in Gloucester Street and presented before the Royal Court. A military guard was left outside the Town Mill, the Robin Hood Inn and the general vicinity for a fortnight after the riots.

On Thursday 3 June 1847 fire broke out at the tavern, and before the first engine could reach it, the entire building was ablaze. It was eventually demolished, and replaced by the present building.

During the 1870s, the Robin Hood was the penny omnibus terminus. These were horse-drawn buses which travelled the town area.

The pub has had a series of owners since it was rebuilt, until 1969, when it was purchased by the Ann Street Brewery Company Ltd, in whose ownership it was retained. It has since become a 'partner pub' of the Liberation Brewery.

ROYAL GEORGE

There were two pubs in the mid-19th Century with this name. One was in Mulcaster Street, the other in Havre des Pas. Both would have been named after George III.

ROYAL HOTEL, David Place

Originally *Bree's Boarding House*, established 1858, although prior to that date, c 1848, 'E Bree's Boarding House' was in St Mark's Road.

When it opened it had 69 beds at 3 shillings a day and 26 beds at 3s.6d. a day; 69 guests at 8s. a day a day and 26 guests at 9s. a day. In 1875 it was called the *STOPFORD HOTEL* and subsequently changed its name to the *ROYAL (STOPFORD) HOTEL* (1891), *BREE'S ROYAL HOTEL* (1896) and finally the **Royal Hotel** in 1966.

An hotel brochure of 1894 stated:

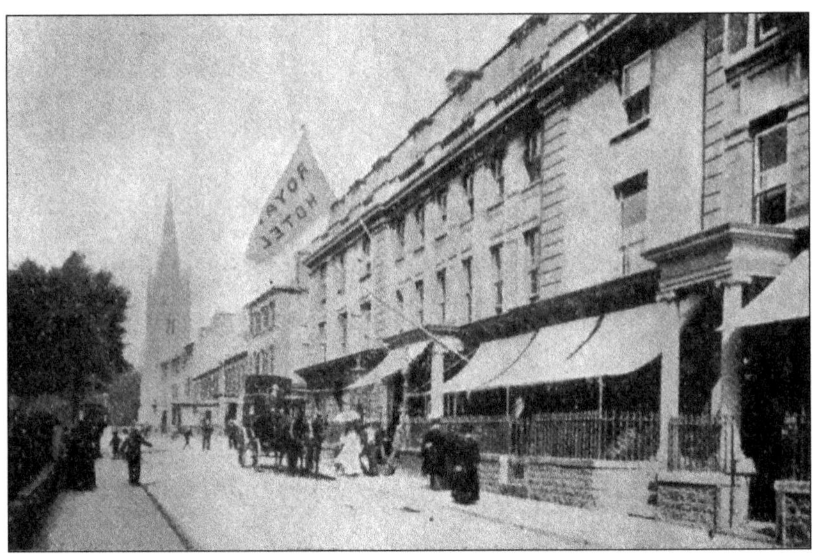

> 'The hotel is situated in the healthiest part of St Helier and is replete with every home comfort. The public rooms, which cover an area of 6,000 sq ft, and unsurpassed by any hotel in the Channel Islands comprise of spacious Entrance Hall and Lounge, noble Ding Room, Drawing, Reading, Smoking. Billiard and Commercial Rooms. There is a dark room for photographers.'

In the early days of the Occupation the hotel was used as billets for visiting officials and for officers newly arrived in the Island.

Major modernisation refurbishments took place in 1981 and in 1990 Dame Vera Lynn opened the Liberation Suite on the 45th anniversary of the Liberation of Jersey.

ROYAL YACHT HOTEL Formerly *ROYAL YACHT CLUB HOTEL*
This was opened during the 1820s or even before, possibly as the *LONDON HOTEL.* In 1833 an early guide book referred to it as The *LONDON AND YACHT HOTEL.* Ten years later it was known briefly as *HOTEL DE PARIS* before it became the *ROYAL YACHT CLUB HOTEL* in 1890. The hotel was situated in Mulcaster Street in what is now just a small corner of the modern four-star luxury hotel.

In the early days it was owned by a Mr Lowe although there was a succession of different owners throughout the 19th and 20th Centuries. Among the hotel's most distinguished visitors were, in 1848, the French King's fifth son, the Duc de Montpensier, and his two grandsons.

The hotel was used as a place for public meetings, such as one in 1837 in which 400 citizens met to petition the States for reform. A meeting to discuss a fitting commemoration of Queen Victoria's visit in 1847 resulted ultimately in the building of Victoria College. In 1855 it was owned by Mr G Chase; it was used as a meeting place intermittently for Masonic Lodge banquets at this time.

On 29 August 1872 saw a 'sumptuous' dinner given by the Harbours Committee to celebrate the Laying of the Foundation of the new La Collette Harbour; there were 11 toasts. The historian, Philip Ahier, records: 'While proposing a certain toast, Jurat de Quetteville called out to Mr Vickery, one of the deputies for St Helier at the time. 'Are you ready, are your glasses filled?' To which Mr Vickery replied, 'Yes, we are always working.' (A euphemism for elbow-lifting). The original La Collette Harbour Works were abandoned after £180,000 had been literally thrown into the sea. The Town Militia used the courtyard of the hotel for their summer training.

In 1874 Lillie Langtry held her wedding reception at the hotel, in what is a private dining room. About 1889-1890 it was purchased by Mr Geoffrey Parkinson, who improved and altered it.

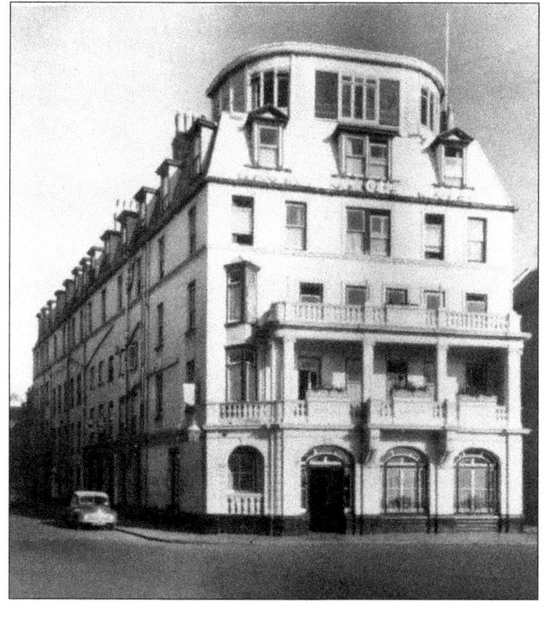

During the Occupation it was commandeered by the German Navy. In a recent excavation, items of uniform and weapon parts were discovered.

It was greatly extended in the early 21st Century, the hotel having by then become a somewhat run down pub. It was greatly extended and renovated, with a new entrance in the Weighbridge. It re-opened as an hotel in July 2007 in the wake of a £36m facelift. The huge redevelopment project took 18 months, working seven days a week.

One of the most popular features of the new hotel is 'The Drift' late night bar, which is very popular with a mainly young clientele with a liking for loud music.

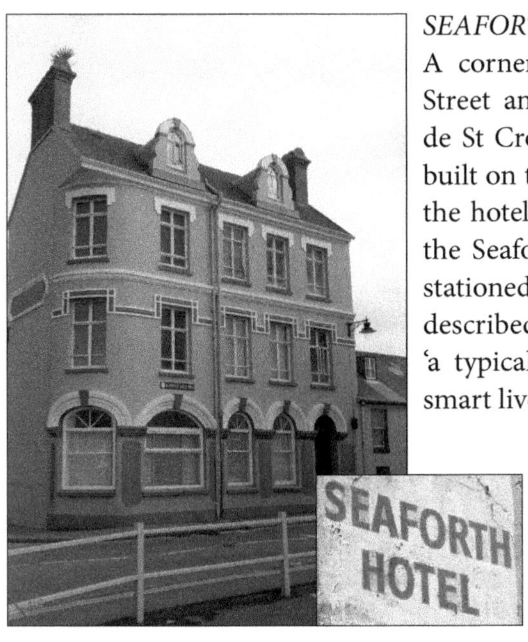

SEAFORTH HOTEL, Havre des Pas

A corner property at the turn of Green Street and Havre des Pas owned by Jean de St Croix was demolished and the hotel built on the site in about 1890. Presumably the hotel was named after the regiment of the Seaforth Highlanders when they were stationed at nearby Fort Regent. It was described in a monograph by Anita Fell as 'a typical Victorian public house with its smart livery of blue and yellow.'

The former Seaforth Hotel as it is today, having been coverted into apartments. A forgotten sign on a side wall betrays its former existence.

SEWARD'S CAFÉ, Royal Square

In 1843 a Mr Garland handed over the keys of his 'café' in Royal Square to the person who had bought the establishment from him, 23-year-old John Seward. Seward promptly put advertisements in the press and the Almanacs, such as: 'Sewards's Café, Royal Square. Strangers visiting the Island can be accommodated with board and lodging. Choice wines and spirits. Bass and Co's Pale Ale, Porter etc.'

Seward was not exactly a model landlord. Arguments with the landlord frequently ended with Seward hitting his opponent with the first blunt object to hand. He also disregarded gambling laws and opening times, but as Jurats and Centeniers tended to use the pub regularly, a blind eye was turned to these infractions. The newspaper, the *Jersey Herald*, however, campaigned against bad tavern keepers. Its owner and editor, Abraham Le Cras, was a reformer and its main writer was an independent clergyman who was a campaigner for the temperance movement. The newspaper had Seward's Café in its sights.

On 8 January 1845, at 10pm, Thomas Nicolle, a hatter based in King Street, tried to buy another drink. Seward refused to serve him; there was an altercation of some sort, which ended with Seward hitting Nicolle with a piece of wood and then chasing him across the square, while continuing to beat him. Nicolle swore revenge and returned at 1am with a pistol. To quote the research by Gavin Booth (1995):

'There was still a lot going on at that time. At the table nearest the window, a game of cards was in full swing. Chaos ensued when Nicolle discharged his pistol through the glass. When the police arrived, they found Miss Cook, a barmaid, in hysterics with a bullet wound in the arm; Simon Levi, a card sharp, dead with a bullet in his throat and Nicolle unconscious being beaten to the point of death by a livid Seward.

'When Nicolle awaited the trial that would see him transported for life, the *Herald* stepped up its targeting of Seward. The paper was unimpressed with the parish for renewing the Tavern's licence ten days after the event. Seward took these comments very personally and swore action.

'On 14 February 1846 Seward borrowed a hunting whip from a friend and made his plans. Le Cras, having been informed of this, sent a request for assistance to the Centeniers, but received no answer. At 1.30pm on the 16th, Seward ambushed Le Cras in Cattle Street and carried out what the *New Chronicle* called 'An American punishment'.

'Mr Le Cras managed to escape before serious injury was caused. But his mood was not improved by a comment by Vingtenier Mahy, who supplied the drink trade with stock. Mahy said: "So much the better of her has given it to him, that old b******! May he give it him again."

'Le Cras wanted action to be taken against Seward and Mahy, but was so certain he wouldn't get it, that he started a petition to abolish the current system and to incorporate the parish into a proper English city. As expected, no action was taken against Mahy, while Seward was asked to keep the peace.

'Things quietened down at the Café for a while, but continuing problems at the Café and several other inns led first to the temporary closure of all inns during 1847 and tougher licensing laws in 1849. By this time Seward had moved on to managing the Bath Hotel in Mulcaster Street, and later, the establishing of the Stag's Head at Snow Hill.'

SOLEIL LEVANT, Bath Street

Prosper Cocquet, a French publican, managed properties in Lower Bath Street and Hilgrove Street from the 1880s, but was not able to purchase them because of his French nationality, according to Jersey law. His daughters were able to purchase the properties because they had been born in Jersey.

Alexandre Liron purchased numbers 28 and 34 Bath Street from Victorine Cocquet, one of Prosper's daughters, in 1919 and later No 36 from his brother. Alexandre's family continued to own the properties known as the Soleil Levant, continuously from 1919 to 1971.

Alexandre was one of five sons born to Pierre and Augustine Liron, who were French immigrants and came to Jersey between 1881 and 1891. In the 1901 Census they are shown as agricultural workers in St Martin. By the 1911 census they were running the pub and lodging house in Lower Bath Street, where they had 10 boarders.

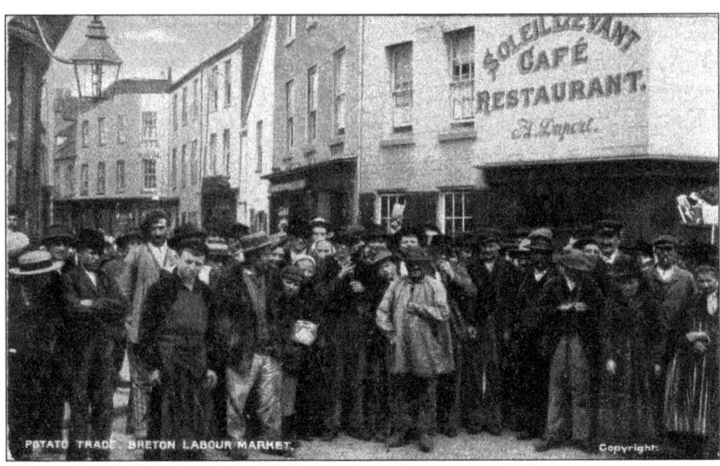

SOUTHAMPTON HOTEL, Weighbridge
Built 1864. Used to be a favourite starting point for charabanc tours pre-1914. It was also a favourite meeting place for potato growers and merchants. It was finally demolished in 2016 although the façade has been preserved (see illustration page 121).

STAR INN / HOTEL, 13 Hope Street and Wharf Street
Believed to have been founded in 1834 by Robert Gates and was then known as The Star Inn.

The original notice advertising the hotel, which appeared in the pages of *La Chronique de Jersey* on 22 February 1834, stated that Mr Gates

> 'has fitted up the above Inn with superior accommodation and respectfully solicits patronage and support. He has also executed an extensive Brewery and engaged a London Brewer of well-known ability and considerable experience to superintend this part of his Establishment and to ensure his customers a superior home-brewed beverage, wholesome, potent and cheap'.

From 1843 until 1940, when it was closed down, the hotel was listed almost continuously in the local directories. In the year of its closure it was machine-gunned by German aircraft during a raid on the Island immediately prior to the Occupation. During the Occupation it was used to billet German troops stationed around the Harbour area

The *STAR RESTAURANT*, which superseded the hotel, was a popular venue during the 12 years of its existence. It had a unique atmosphere, largely occasioned by the fact that many of the regular diners there were known to one another, so the restaurant resembled a club dining room. It closed its doors in 1961 and there were many who regretted its passing. The Star Grill room at Hotel L'Horizon perpetuates the name.

TEMPLE BAR, Stopford Road
Converted from a general store in the 19th Century, the proximity of the Masonic Temple gives a clue to its name.

UNION INN, Royal Square
Occupied a premier position in town, on the spot later occupied by the Public Library (now that part of the States buildings occupied by the Bailiff's Chambers and Judicial Greffe). The Union Inn is mentioned by Stead in 1809, although it was probably opened much earlier.

It was described by a French guidebook as the '*camp ordinaire*' of the Laurel party, whereas the British Hotel round the corner was the headquarters of the Rose party. The political sectarianism engendered by these two parties and the related consumption of alcohol at election times would deserve a chapter all to itself. The 'Union' is depicted in all engravings on that side of the square. It was pulled down in 1884 when the area was redeveloped as Jersey Public Library, which opened two years later in 1886.

The existence of another *UNION INN* in Minden Place is recorded in 1833; the innkeeper was Thomas Vardon.

UNITED CLUB, Royal Square
Although established in 1848, there is much anecdotal evidence that the building in which it is now housed, in the Royal Square, was being used as a meeting place much earlier than that, by seafarers based out of St Helier.

Wesley preached in the Long Room of the Club in the 1750s; it was known as Tozer's Saloon in the 1840s, and kept by Mrs Tozer in 1846.

The stone-vaulted lower floor, currently sub-let by the Club to the local Registrar's Office, once housed billiards tables and a second bar for members and guests, while the upper floors were for the use of members only. Susanne Dumaresq, Dame de la Haule, agreed to construct a more spacious Corn Market to replace the existing one on condition that she was allowed to build on the roof of that building for her own use.

VICTORIA, Minden Place
Now known as the **GREEN PARROT** Cocktail bar.
At one time there were four pubs with this name in St Helier. One, in Minden Place and the other three in Queen Street, Great Union Road and Esplanade.

VICTORIA CLUB, 8 Beresford Street
The 19th Century listed building was the work of the civil engineer Adolphus Curry, who also designed the Jersey Opera House and former Jersey College for Girls.

It was built in the 1890s as a private members' club and performed that role throughout its history. Its members never owned the property, and rising rental caused financial difficulties. Despite a cash injection to clear debts in 2010, the club closed shortly afterwards. It has since been re-opened by the Jersey Pottery company as **BANJO'S RESTAURANT**.

WELLINGTON HOTEL, St Saviour's Road
This establishment's previous names are *LA GRAPPE DE RAISINS, THE GRAPES, THE WATER LANE INN,* and the *IMPERIAL INN*. A most important hostelry in its heyday. Farmers and others coming from St Saviour or St Martin down St Saviour's Hill (*La Rue du Gouverneur*) bringing their goods to market in the Royal Square would have found it a convenient house to break their journey..

A bus service which commenced at the hotel was started in November 1788. This advertisement appeared in *La Gazette de Jersey* in its issue of 8 November:

> 'For the convenience of the inhabitants of St Aubin and of the neighbouring places, Mr Richard Monils proposes to inaugurate a bus service with a small covered conveyance in which passengers and their belongings will be transported from St Aubin to the Town and vice versa.
>
> It will commence on Saturday November 15 1788 and will continue every Saturday if there is patronage.
>
> This little vehicle will be more convenient than travelling in a bath chair, while the ladies and gentlemen who use it will not be exposed to the vagaries of the weather to which those who do the journey on horseback are subjected.
>
> In winter it will leave at the "Swan" in St Aubin at 9am, and from the "Bunch of Grapes", Water Lane, in the town at 3pm Fares: Adults 10 sous, children 6 sous.

> Each passenger is allowed 12lbs of luggage free of charge, above this amount, 40 sous per hundredweight. For each small package carried from one place to the other, 5 sous.'

This is the first recorded transport system in the Island.

By 1813 the name of the premises had been shortened to 'The Grapes', managed by Mrs Richard. In that year a number of Freemasons gathered and founded the 'Duke of Normandy Lodge'. In the early 19th Century, there were no houses above Tunnell Street, so The Grapes must have stood in isolation as a country inn.

The steep road opposite the inn was called *La Rue à l'Eau,* because before the advent of any system of drainage, rain water ran down the lane at a furious pace. When the Anglicisation of street names occurred, the name easily became Water Lane, and thus the inn became known as the Water Lane Inn.

Some years after the Imperial Hotel was built, the then owner of the Water Lane Inn (Mr E Vigot) decided to re-name it the Imperial Inn. When Water Lane was itself re-named Wellington Road, the hotel followed suit, and became the **Wellington Hotel**.

Ann Street Brewery purchased the property in 1930. The inn was completely modernised and the interior re-designed in 1974-75 and some improvements made to the exterior. Licensee in mid-1970s was Mrs A R Esnouf.

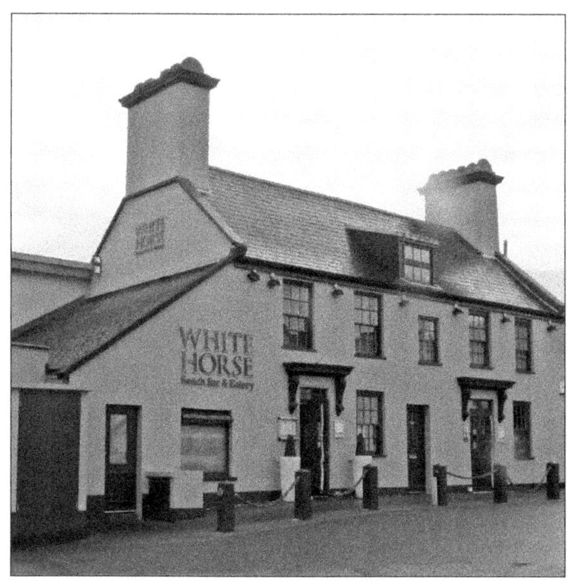

WHITE HORSE, *LE DICQ INN*, Dicq Slipway, St Saviour

Originally called Le Dicq Inn, but gained its present name because of a prominent advertisement on its frontage for White Horse Whisky.

The inn played a great part in the partisan struggles between the Charlots and the Magots – the two political parties of the late 18th Century. The Charlots supported Charles Lemprière, Bailiff of Jersey, 1714-1806, leader of the Royal Court party, the Magots were the opponents.

In those days it was traditional for candidates to bribe voters with food and drink, despite criticism in the newspapers and pamphlets of the day. For example, an election for St Saviour Centenier between Gideon Ahier (a Charlot) and John Godfray (a Magot, was described in the *Gazette de Jersey*:

> 'A plate of codfish was to be served for supper and in order to enhance the feast, someone in the Charlot party brought toasted pullets wrapped up in pocket handkerchiefs which could afterwards be used as serviettes. The fervid perspiration of the eaters kept them warm, it could even be said they had come straight from the turnspit.'

A week later, 1 January 1791, an article in the *Gazette* suggested that much dirty work had been in evidence at this 'extraordinary feasting'. The codfish had been wrapped in sour milk, the pullets had been drenched in vinegar and served in filthy handkerchiefs, stale and newly brewed cider had been mixed together, all these tricks could not have been beneficial to the guests and far from winning votes 'should have made the patriots reject the Charlot candidate with the greatest contempt.'

The paragraph concluded by urging all the patriots in the parish to vote in Godfrey as Centenier – 'Your most sincere friend'.

But electors were nauseated by the sabotage of the Magots. The St Saviour Constable, Jean Dumaresq, who had been a keen supporter of John Godfray, changed sides. The results of the election were Gideon Ahier, 101 votes; John Godfray, 93 votes.

Built on the borders of the parishes of St Helier and St Saviour, there are two slipways adjacent to it, one for each parish. An extension to Le Dicq slipway was built to prevent floods after the area was swamped in a great storm in 1811.

WILTSHIRE HOTEL, South Pier
Proprietor Mr Willingham, mid-19th Century. He also ran a twice-daily passenger coach service to Gorey via Hougue Bie.

YORK HOTEL, 2 Vine Street
Once a very popular commercial hotel – still in existence after 1900. Owned at one point by J Damer.

More 19th Century pubs in St Helier of which little is known other than their location

ARMY & NAVY HOTEL, Cross Street; Mentioned in 1820s
BATTLE OF WATERLOO INN, Bond Street

BERESFORD ARMS, Halkett Place, named after the last Governor of Jersey, Lord Beresford (1821-1854).

BELMONT ARMS, Belmont Road; Proprietor Mr Wyatt in 1861

BRITANNIA INN, Hill Street

BRITISH AND FOREIGN HOTEL Mr Labey mentioned as landlord in 1820s

CALVADOS HOTEL, Near Snow Hill. Destroyed by fire during the 1880s.
FOUR ALES: Mrs Esmond, 1820s

FREEMASONS, Peter Street

GREAT UNION, Great Unon Street

GREEN DRAGON, near the harbour in 1980s

HARP AND CROWN, Mrs Dwyer, 1820s

IPSWICH ARMS, Conway Street, 1854

MARKET INN, Halkett Street; Mentioned in 1820s; proprietor Mr Brabing. Walter Martyn listed as 'master innkeeper' in 1861.

MINOR'S HOTEL, Esplanade, c. 1875

NAPIER HOUSE HOTEL, Listed at 25-27 La Motte Street in the 1890s, the site was later occupied by the **Imperial** Hotel

NAVY ARMS, Mulcaster Street; 1840s
NAVY AND FRIENDS TAVERN, 8 Waterloo street. In 1820s kept by John Stroud. The building was still in existence in 1930s as a clothing shop.

OLD LONDON HOTEL, 1837; Hussey. On the site of what then became the Star Grill House.

PARADE COFFEE HOUSE, The Parade, 1820s

PLUME OF FEATHERS, York Street

PRINCE ALBERT, Conway Street

QUEEN'S HEAD, Aquila Road

ROSE AND CROWN, Sand Street

ROSE OF ENGLAND, Peter Street

ROYAL GEORGE HOTEL, Mulcaster Street

ROYAL STANDARD INN, Halkett Street, 1820s

TELEGRAPH INN, 7 Hilary Street

THREE TUNS, Wharf Street; now assimilated into the Pomme d'Or building

TURK'S HEAD, 12 La Motte Street, 1820s; the same building was being used a a bicycle shop in 1930

VAL PLAISANT, Val Plaisant

VINE INN, Vine Street, 1820s

WHITE LION HOTEL, Castle Street Proprietor in 1869 was Mr B Sherring

(ii) A TRIP OUT OF TOWN

'Of the villages of Jersey there is not a great deal to be said. Suffice it, that the island is divided into twelve parishes, each one possessing its church and a cluster of houses, and in almost all instances two hotels or taverns, which in almost every case are closely adjoining the church. Indeed, a good deal of parish business is carried on in these said taverns on Sunday morning after service'

A Hobble through the Channel Islands by Edward Gastineau (1858)

OUTSIDE of town, the improved state of roads and regular services by horse-bus and then by train opened up the Island to tourists and travellers in a way that would have been impossible in previous ages. The first horse bus started service on 15 November 1788, travelling every Saturday between St Helier and St Aubin.

The St Helier terminus was 'The Bunch of Grapes' – now the Wellington, at the foot of Wellington Road. At St Aubin it stopped at the Swan Tavern; the fare was ten sous. This service was followed in subsequent years by a number of different omnibus services operated by driver operators, livery stable keepers, publicans or by some combination of these callings.

In 1842 P Noel's the *Regula* travelled every two hours from 5 Upper Don Street to St Aubin, where it stooped at Mr Cowdray's Inn at the Market Place.

In 1871 there was a service from the Red Lion, Halkett Place, to Millbrook, then on to Goose Green via St Lawrence Valley. At a 2d fare, this was competitive with the cost of travelling on the new railway, but it only lasted two years.

Mr Willingham of the Wiltshire Hotel, South Pier, ran his 'Red Rover' service from his hotel to Gorey via Hougue Bie, twice daily.

St Mary & St Lawrence from Mrs Meech's Inn, Sand Street, return trips fare was 1s 1d or 10d single.

In 1888 there started a service from the Minden Hotel to Leoville, St Ouen, via St Lawrence and St Mary on Sundays, Tuesdays and Thursdays.

In 1889 there was an omnibus service for much of the day from the Aurora, Cattle Street, to St Aubin.

The Exeter Inn – 22 Queen Street – was also a favourite starting place for the country buses.

The coming of the railways completely changed the pattern of public transport. The inaugural train service to St Aubin was on 20 October 1870, stopping at The Railway Hotel, St Aubin, at which there were various evening attractions.

The Jersey Eastern Railway enabled passengers to attend events at Pontac Gardens, or the attractions of Grouville Common, such as horse racing and rifle shooting.

GROUVILLE

We know the names of two 19th Century pubs in Grouville, the *PRINCE OF WALES HOTEL* and the *ARMY AND NAVY HOTEL* - but their location is now unknown.

The *Registre des Taverniers de la Paroisse de Grouville,* in 1887, lists the following:

George Wickers	Princes Tower	La Rue
Charles Le Vesconte	La Roque Inn	La Rocque
Francois Le Vesconte	Grouville Central Hotel	La Rue
George German	Candour Tavern	Marais
Henry Algar	Fauvic Inn	La Rocque
Francois Moisson	Union Inn	La Rocque
Mrs Amelia Gray	Royal Golf Club Hotel	Marais

CENTRAL HOTEL, La Rue à Don

Already existed at the turn of 19th and 20th Centuries. Situated at the corner of La Rue à Don and La Rue des Côtils, it was a favourite meeting place for parish officials – at that time, the Parish Hall was just across the road, in premises that later became an electricity sub-station.

PRINCE'S TOWER HOTEL, Hougue Bie

An early tourist would certainly have stopped off at this hotel. Prince's Tower had been constructed by the late Admiral Philippe d'Auvergne, and was in every way what a 19th Century gentleman might have imagined a mediaeval tower to look like.

D'Auvergne died in 1816 and by 1822 the Prince's Tower was no longer used as a private residence but was developing as a pleasure ground. Facilities improved in the 1830s; the entrance lodge extended to create a new building known as Prince's Tower Hotel, a two-storey hotel that provided accommodation and banqueting facilities. In 1845 an old rustic lodge was rebuilt and housed a bar. By the middle of the 19th Century it had acquired a reputation for revelry.

The hotel became a popular venue for eating, drinking and dancing and by the late 19th Century it had become derelict. It was purchased by the Société Jersiaise in 1919 and subsequently demolished before they started the excavations of the mound that would reveal La Hougue Bie chamber tomb.

ST BRELADE

HIGHLANDS HOTEL

Built in the 1890s, but is reputed to be the successor of a previous hostelry located nearby, which was the haunt of smugglers. In 1966 the hotel was taken over by the Movement for World Evangelisation and modernised and extended by them. It is an unlicensed hotel, which is a surprising thing to find in Jersey.

ST BRELADE'S BAY HOTEL

There was an hotel near St Brelade's Parish Church which is mentioned by Stead (1809): 'An inn near the church where it may be necessary to recruit after the journey and where excellent accommodation may invite the tourist to spend the night.'

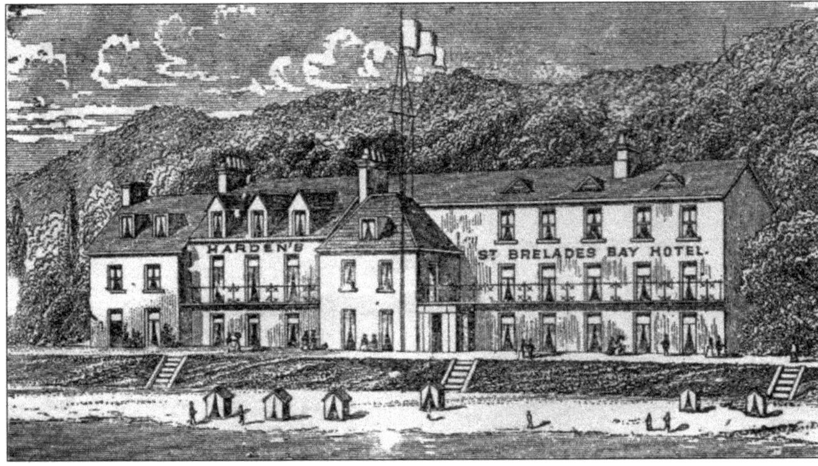

The house that would form the nucleus of the future hotel is shown in prints of the 1850s – a solitary building standing amid the dunes. It was bought by Randalls Brewery before 1875; the tenant hotelier, Mr Le Capelain, offered full board at 6s 6d a day, lobster lunches at 1s 6d and dinners for 2s 6d. In 1919 it was bought by the Colley family and the building was extended in 1930. In 1960 the management was taken over by his stepson, Digby Brecknell.

The hotel was requisitioned by the Germans from the very first day of the Occupation: it was the billets for the officers and men of the Luftwaffe reconnaissance squadron based at the Airport. By November 1941 it had become '*Soldatenheim II*'. It accommodated all ranks, with officers on one side of the main corridor and NCOs and ORs on the other.

As in all the other *Soldatenheime*, it was staffed by local civilians. Irish waiters were headed by 'Charlie the Czech', who had worked as head waiter at the Ritz Hotel in Colomberie before the war.

The Occupiers left behind six murals painted in the cocktail bar.

(ST AUBIN)

CURWOOD'S HOTEL

On the site of the Trafalgar or perhaps a bit further up the hill.

FARLEY'S HOTEL

'The visitor will always find a good dinner, comfortable bed and an attentive host. At this inn, the dancing assemblies are held during the summer months, which are always numerous and fashionably attended.'

HOTEL DE ST AUBIN

Also referred to as *Cowdray's Hotel*, referred to in 1863, and described as being on the corner of the main road, later occupied by a confectioner, Mr Gavey.

OLD COURT HOUSE INN

It is not clear for how long this well-known building has been running as a hotel; one can only say that this uncertainty suggests an earlier rather than a later date for this.

The building dates back to 1450; the original 'courthouse' at the rear of the building was restored in 1611. The front portion of the property, Osborne House, was a wealthy merchant's home with enormous cellars, which from the 17th Century stored privateers' plunder alongside legitimate cargo.

There are references in Chevalier's Journal to the cellars at St Aubin where the spoil from captured vessels was stored and sorted. An Admiralty judge had to decide whether the boat itself and its cargo were or were not lawful prizes. If so, they were sold, sometimes at auction. The house, which has cellars, was the venue for these operations. The house has four storeys and must have been the tallest house in the Island at the time for the newel staircase runs right up to the top floor. On the first floor is a very large room, believed to have been the Admiralty Prize Court Room, with 'PS 1611' incised on the lintel.

The hotel became world-famous as a result of the *Bergerac* television series, in which the hotel, under the guise of being the fictional 'Royal Barge' featured as being Detective-Sergeant Jim Bergerac's local. At an earlier date, both comedian Tommy Cooper and the singer, Yana appeared there.

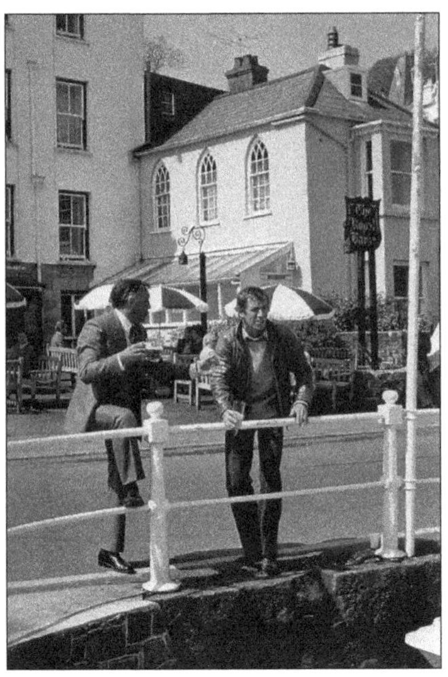

SOMERVILLE HOTEL

This former private house was running as an hotel in 1894, managed by a Mr W H Chapman, although it may well have opened earlier. The original house on the site, Somerville, had been the home of a former St Brelade Constable, G P Benest, during 1844 to 1860. This had burnt down and Mr Chapman rebuilt it, enlarged it and turned it into an hotel. A Swiss architect was employed to design the new building along the lines of a Swiss chalet.

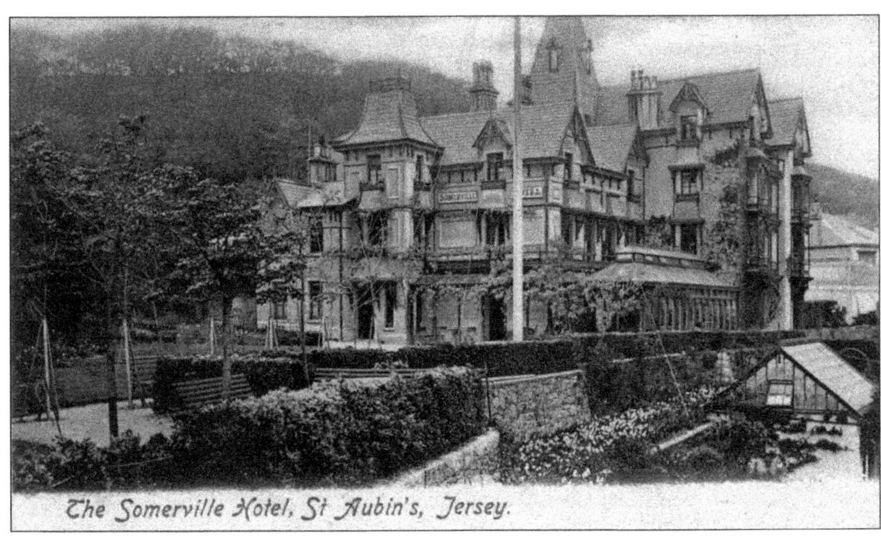

There were various changes of owners in the ensuing years. It was left in a dire state in 1945 by the Occupation troops and considerable reconstruction took place in 1946 before it re-opened as a 4-star hotel.

TERMINUS HOTEL

The Jersey Railway opened an hotel at the St Aubin terminus in May 1871. A bar was accessible direct from the platform; above it was a wide balcony with a saloon and coffee room upstairs. It was announced that a band would play there three times a week. To begin with, the place was well patronised and certainly attracted a lot of extra traffic for the railway.

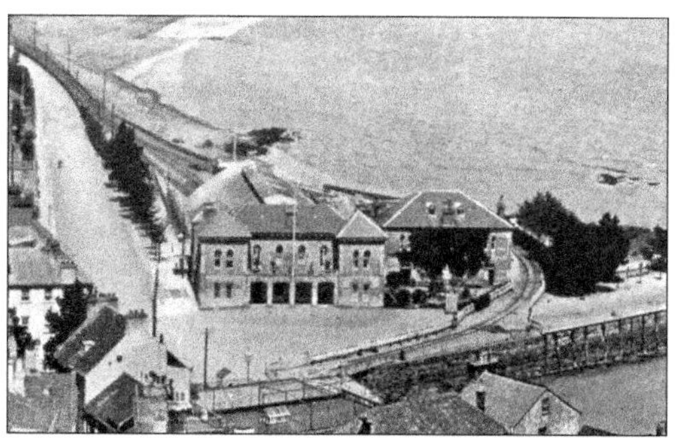

Detail of postcard showing the former Terminus Hotel, now St Brelade's Parish Hall. The extended line to Corbière can be seen as it sweeps around to the right when the terminus was no longer such.

During the winter, all the rolling stock of the Jersey Railway was stored in the St Aubin station, and on the night of 16 October 1936, a fire broke out. This destroyed much of the station building, 15 of the carriages, and damaged the Terminus Hotel. By the 1930s, the Jersey Railway was under pressure from the buses which could travel over a wider catchment area than trains could serve.

That was the final blow to the already struggling railway company, and it was decided to close the railway entirely. The Terminus Hotel later became the Parish Hall and offices, replacing the use of the Church Hall at St Brelade's Church for Parish Assemblies.

TRAFALGAR HOTEL, St Aubin

A painting of Nelson-type sailing ships, painted on the outside walls, was painted by Harold Hepburn in 1963. Although the hotel is named after the battle, the original building far pre-dates it, as is shown by the 1620 date stone appearing on the wall.

The original building was about one-third the size of the present pub. The present lounge bar is a combination of the old public bar and lounge bar; the public bar was entered from Mont Les Vaux, and the door was closed due its proximity to the traffic on the main road. The space is now occupied by a cupboard.

Karl Marx was a visitor and lodged there while on holiday in August 1879, accompanied by his daughter Eleanor ('Tussy'). Marx was 61 at the time and travelled to Jersey in the hope that the mild climate and sea air would improve his failing health. It was his second visit to the Island; he had previously visited Jersey 22 years earlier with his close friend and collaborator, Friedrich Engels, staying at lodgings in the Parade. He did not like the food at the Trafalgar, however: 'We are giving up St Aubin's because Tussy and I have a horror of a monotonous daily lamb and mutton diet, as a result of which I have become a reluctant vegetarian.' He much preferred the Hotel de l'Europe in Mulcaster Street, to which he moved.

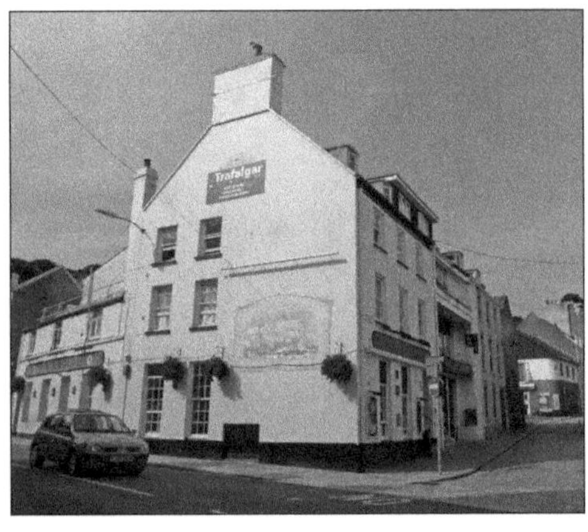

The Trafalgar Lodge of the Royal Antediluvian Order of Buffaloes was inaugurated at the Trafalgar Hotel in 1936. Its daughter lodge, the Duke of Normandie, was also initiated from the hotel.

Ann Street Brewery took over the pub in 1932. Mrs L Gould was the manageress in the mid-1970s.

ST CLEMENT

LA FONTAINE HOTEL, *PONTAC (LE RUE'S)*
St Clement Coast Road

Noted by Stead in 1809: 'for being certain of good treatment in all the comforts of plenty, cleanliness and civility. Near the Inn are several springs of fresh water, below high water mark, which occasion the place where they are found to be called Le Havre des Fontaines.'

Advertised later in the 19th Century as *Old Pontac Hotel*:

> 'Its private grounds offer unique attractions to visitors. The tastefully laid own Grounds (originally planned by Mr. Gibson of Battersea Park fame) afford every facility for lawn-tennis, garden golf, croquet, lawn-skittles, badminton, quoits, garden parties, picnics etc. The look-out of observatory tower commands an unequalled view. Tea and coffee served in the grounds. Everyone should see the famous maze, which is a facsimile of that of Hampton Court. Home comfort

> for tourists. Luncheons, dinners, teas and suppliers catered for with care and attention. Bathing tents. The hotel and grounds are not only under entirely new management, but have been renovated throughout and the hotel enlarged. The largest and finest ballroom in the Island. The floor is of equal quality material and built especially for dancing. Veranda, 140 ft in length. Large double folding doors leading on to the lawn. A C F Field, Proprietor.'

The hotel had an attractive garden, a bandstand, and regular firework displays. Its name was changed to Le Chalet Hotel at the beginning of the 20th Century and changed back to La Fontaine after the 2nd World War. There have been many different owners in that time.

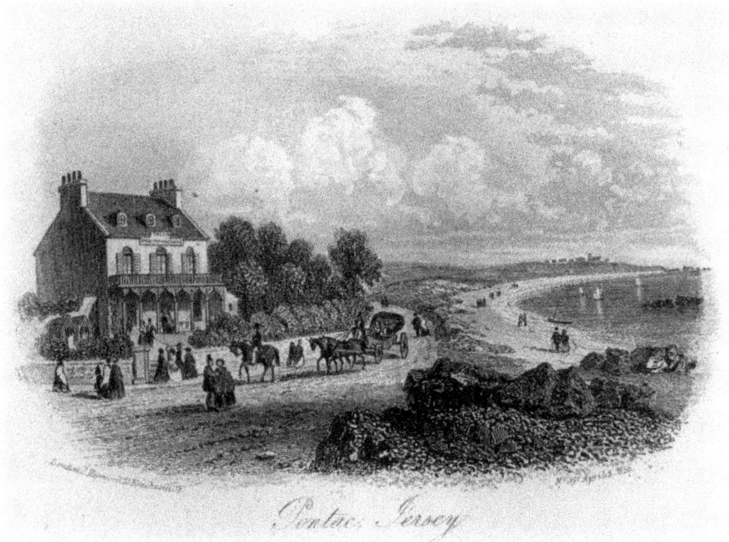

LE HOCQ HOTEL

The word 'Hocq' is the masculine form of La Hougue, meaning a mound of Neolithic construction – now long disappeared.

It is not known how old the pub is, but it is assumed that there has been a pub on the site for centuries. It may have been erected when the Tower and its short breakwater nearby were built; it was often the case that inns were opened to serve the workmen on isolated undertakings.

Le Hocq Tower, opposite the hotel, was built in 1779, or (a different source) 1783. So it was a pub for the small garrison – and off-duty soldiers are not saints – there is a report of a disturbance there in 1811. The Constable, John Le Neveu, complained to the Lieut-Governor, who wrote to the commander of the troops that he hoped he would order proceedings against the culprits.

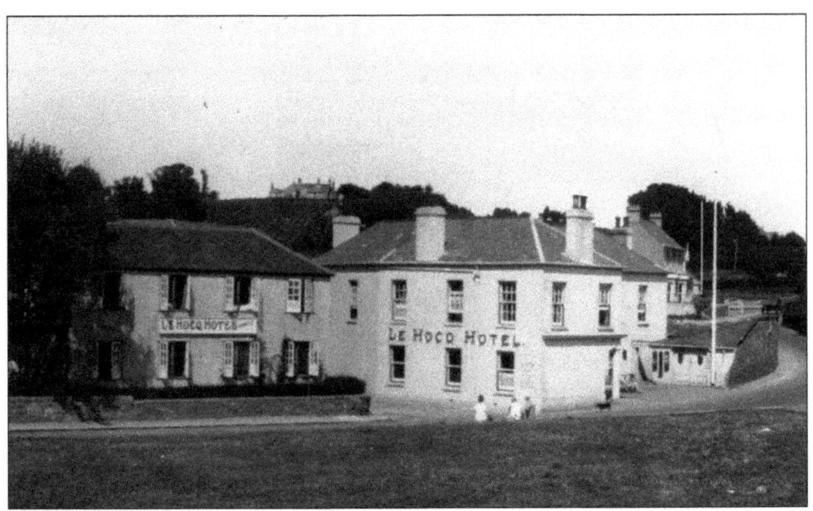

Quoting from the historian Philip Ahier:

'The highlight of the Parish of St Clement in former days [1920s] was the annual cattle show that took place at Le Hocq Marsh in 1 May every year.' [Site of the present Parish Hall]. 'As soon as the cows reached the cow tent, they were milked and the milk handed to Mrs Boleat [wife of the licensee] in exchange for rum, from which, with the addition of grated nutmeg, she made milk punch, which was drunk at the following meals, the times of which were most rigidly adhered to:

'About 10am there would be served "small" lunch, consisting of cold meats, ham, tongue, jellied veal with salads made with lettuce, tomatoes and beetroot. No potatoes were ever served with this meal.

At 3pm prompt, a four-course dinner was served. The menu for this meal never varied from year to year. It was conger eel soup, roast beef with new potatoes that had been freshly lifted from the fields nearby, and cabbage. Rhubarb and cheese concluded the repast. The milk punch and other alcoholic beverages helped to maintain the gaiety of the occasion.

'After the termination of the dinner, card games were the order of the day, during which time more beverages were consumed 'til at 9 pm, the farmers now feeling hungry, sandwiches were served.'

At one time the hotel possessed the only telephone in the area. It was generally understood that Mr and Mrs Boleat could be woken up if a night-time emergency occurred by the person wanting to use the phone throwing gravel at the bedroom window.

PRIORY

Very probably built on the site of an original priory, one of six mediaeval priories in the Island. The inn itself is 19th Century. It is now a private house.

ST JOHN

St John the Baptist's Feast Day (23 June) is Midsummer's Day and from time immemorial there have been festivities in the Parish of St John at that time – first at Bonne Nuit Bay, then at Frémont, and then, due to the embargo of the States in 1797, these were removed to the vicinity of St John's Hotel.

However, still in 1811 it was reported that 'on St John's Day and a few days thereafter a kind of fair, abolished by the States (for good reason) and yet still, at the same season, the neighbouring inhabitants and many from town resort to the public houses adjoining the church, to amuse themselves with dancing.'

Among the dances much in vogue was the jig, itself derived from French sources. This suggests that in 1811 there were at least two public houses near the church and that the dancing of pre-Reformation days had not entirely died out,

Two of these pubs are mentioned in Lieutenant Malorey's *Diary of a visit to Jersey in September 1798*:

> 'St John – a small village with a neat church. We supped at a little cabaret and required entertainment for man and horse. We were shown upon its walls large folio representations of the Procession of St Paul's and St Vincent's Victory… these were unsubstantial treats to hungry travellers, and as we could not procure '*quelque chose à manger*', we shifted our quarters to the sign of the '**PUNCH BOWL**' and we were speedily served with a pan full of eggs and bacon and a noggin of cider.'

Stead's *A Picture of the Island of Jersey* (1809) states: '.. In the public houses adjoining the church, [people] amuse themselves with dancing'.

Not so happy was an incident in 1821, when factional strife between the two political parties, Les Lauriers and Les Roses, was running high. The night before Philippe Durrell (a Rose supporter) was elected Jurat, a group of drunken pike and cudgel-carrying 'Laurelites' forced their way into a St John's pub (the name is not given) where the Rose supporters were drinking. They smashed windows, destroyed the stairs and wounded the innkeeper and his wife.'

In the *Strangers Guide to Jersey* (1833) under the Parish of St John appears the following: 'In this Parish and near the Church, the traveller may be accommodated with good entertainment for man and horse, there are two or three good inns, especially that kept by Mr Le Boutillier, adjoining the churchyard, whose politeness and assiduity for the comforts of his guests cannot be exceeded.'

Alphonse Luchet in his *Souvenirs de Jersey* (between 1843 and 1850): 'Adjoining the Church of St John there are two good houses where one may have a good feed and enjoy oneself, mainly on St John's Day' (the midsummer amusements were obviously still in existence.

ST JOHN'S HOTEL is mentioned in the *Jersey Times* of 1861, At Midsummer (St John's Day was 23 June) there were festivities – dating back from time immemorial in the parish. That year there was a tea and a *thé dansant.*

Ann Street Brewery acquired St John's Hotel in 1956 and it remained unaltered as 'the village pub' until 1971 when it had to be demolished. Although the building was undeniably inconvenient, and quite incapable of serving the needs of the local and passing trade any longer, it had plenty of character, and there were many parishioners who were sorry to see it go. It was replaced in the same year by the new St John's Hotel, on the site of its predecessor and offering as well a car park and a large light lounge.

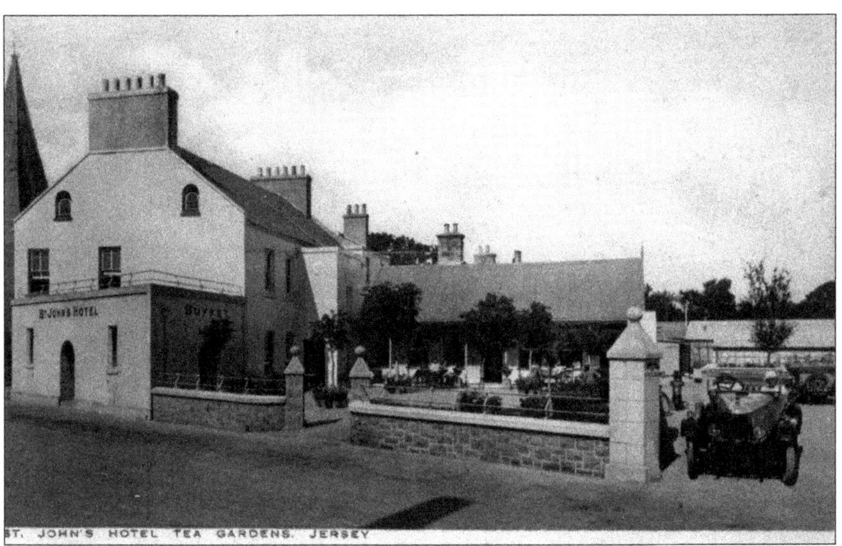
ST. JOHN'S HOTEL TEA GARDENS. JERSEY

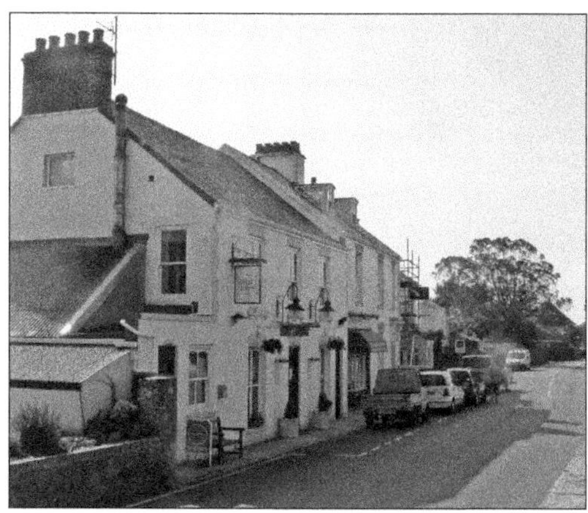

BRITISH UNION
now the **ST LAURENT**
The traditional parish pub.

CARREFOUR SELOUS HOTEL
The pub stood at the crossroads, named after the Selous family and was very much a centre for Breton workers; on a busy night during warm weather the wide space in front of the pub was filled by them. The area in front of the pub was also used by the Royal Jersey Agricultural and Horticultural Society for their 'Herd Book exams', which registered Jersey cattle.

It closed down at the end of the 20th Century and after conversion is now the Carrefour Health Club.

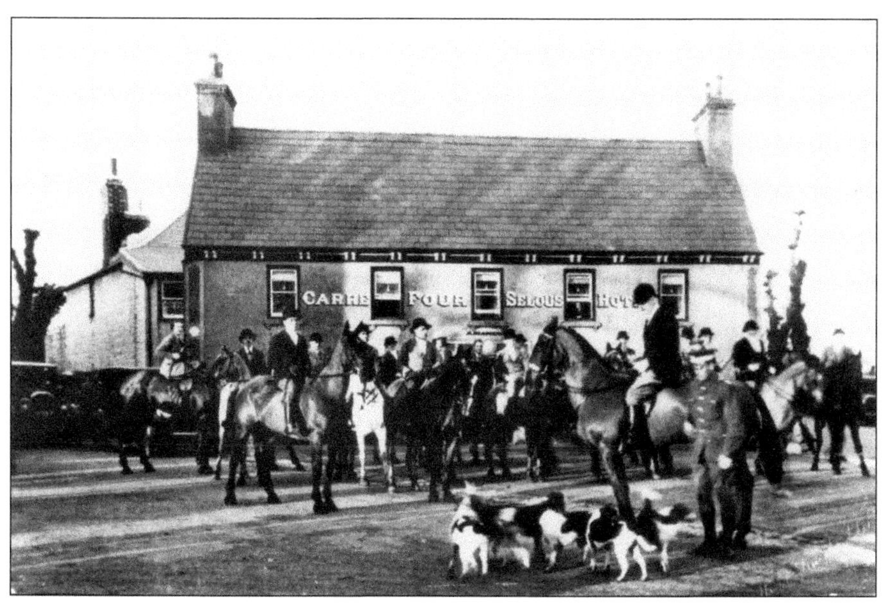

HALFWAY HOUSE, Millbrook

An inn for over 100 years. It was situated near the site where the Hire Shop now stands (2017).

Scene of a brawl in 1859, fuelled by alcohol, that resulted in the death of 38-year-old Henry Richard Cooper from Milverton, Somerset. He had been a witness to an altercation between two men, named Ellis and Whittle, following a boozy meal in the inn at which 'warm gin had been on offer'.

A witness was a Centenier, Thomas Dorey, who reported that others had taken sides in the altercation, including Henry Church, the landlord of the Bunch of Grapes in Dumaresq Street. Dory did not try to separate them out of fear for his own safety – besides, it was not his parish. Church, on the other hand, did try to stop the scuffle from getting out of hand and Cooper took exception to this – the two men squared up to one another.

Witnesses agreed afterwards that Cooper was the main protagonist and Church only did so with reluctance. He fought four successful two-minute rounds with Cooper but was hurt in the fifth and refused to fight on. He then left and Cooper returned inside to carry on drinking. Later, he went to the toilet and was violently sick. By 11.30pm he was seriously ill and the landlord, Francis Brown, helped him on to a couch in the kitchen. He eventually went to sleep, but it was obvious the next morning that he was terribly ill. A doctor was sent for, but he died later in moring.

ST MARTIN

DOLPHIN, Gorey

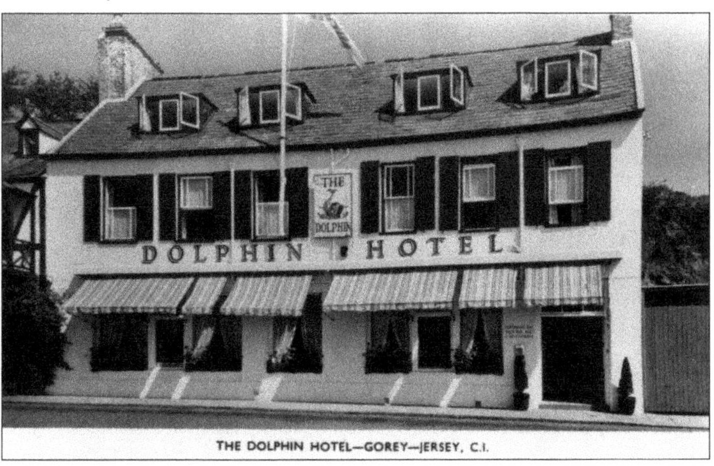

THE DOLPHIN HOTEL—GOREY—JERSEY, C.I.

MOORINGS HOTEL formerly the *British Hotel* or *British and Elfine Hotel*
In 1842, the *New Guide Book for Jersey and Guernsey* stated about Gorey:

> 'It is, in fact, nothing more than a large fishing village, every other house (or hovel) of which calls itself 'inn', 'tavern' or hotel, and of those numerous places of public entertainment – Payn's 'British Hotel' – is, we can vouch from frequent personal experience, superior, for both cheapness and quality of provisions, to any other inn in the place.'

In 1853 it was called the British Hotel and in time became the British and Elfine Hotel.

There is a story, mentioned by the Jersey historian G R Balleine in his *Biographical Dictionary of Jersey*, relating to a Lieutenant-Governor of Jersey, Sir Tomkyns Hilgrove Turner. He was, coincidentally, the son of a St Helier taverner, and made a very successful military career. Hilgrove Street is named after him. At the siege of Valenciennes (1793) he found his wife to be, Esther. Surprisingly for that time, her sister married his batman, Sergeant Cantell. The batman and his wife took over the British Hotel at a time when the oyster and shipbuilding industries had made Gorey prosperous.

Turner left Jersey in 1815 and was made Governor of Bermuda in 1825. He retired to Jersey in 1835 and was put in charge of Mont Orgueil, when he imposed a 6d charge on visitors wishing to see the castle. He did not collect the admission money for himself but left it to 'a veteran artillery-sergeant caretaker' who may or may not have been his brother-in-law, Sergeant Cantell, who had taken over the British Hotel 21 years before.

Mr P J Cantell is listed as the owner of the hotel in 1896.

The hotel was requisitioned by the Germans during the Occupation, and was renamed **The Moorings** by Group Captain J A P Harrison and his wife when they re-opened it in 1949.

It was completely modernised in 1969; it is currently in the ownership of the former Italian Consul, Mr Renzo Martin.

THE ROYAL

There was not much of a 'village' surrounding the parish church until the mid-20th Century – before then it was just an area of scattered houses. The Royal is not listed in the 1851 Census, although living nearby at St Martin's House were Samuel and Mary Le Four. Samuel's occupation was listed as ship owner and master and hotel keeper; by 1861 the couple had moved into the Royal; by 1871 he is described as a widower. The Royal is described in an 1874 almanac as 'hotel, grocer and baker. His daughter, Louisa, took over the pub on his death in 1883; in 1884 she married another experienced tavern keeper, Elie Falle.

The pub is mentioned in 1896: 'From the Royal a coach runs every Wednesday and Saturday to St Helier.' By 1901 the pub had passed to John de Feu and his wife, Marceline.

In St Martin, there were two pubs, the other being the CROWN, 'both by the side of the Cemetery'. Of the two inns, The Crown lost out, becoming the Crown Stores. The Royal has been modernised and extended by its present owners, Randalls.

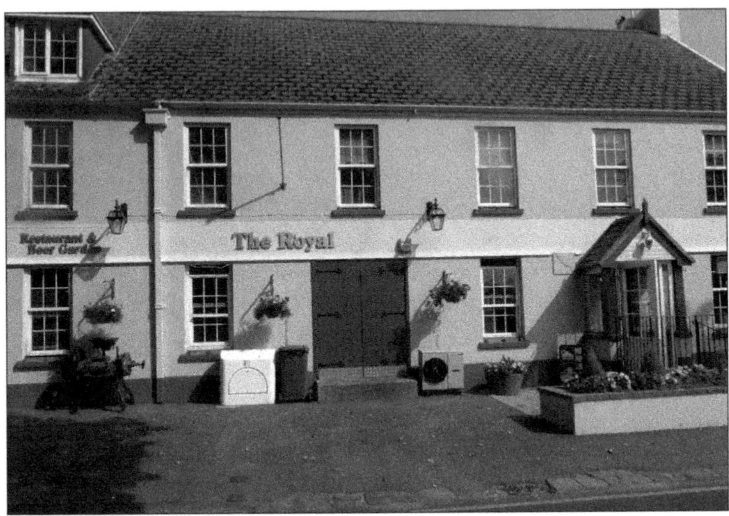

ST MARY

GREVE DE LECQ HOTEL

It is believed that the building was originally the officers' quarters for the barracks up the hill behind it. Both barracks and officers' quarters were built in Napoleonic times. It was already doubling up as an inn and occasional hotel in the 1830s to support the growing tourist trade. It was the first hotel at Grève de Lecq.

In the 1851 Census the hotel is listed as Grève de Lecq House, with a Mr John Toy from England as 'hotel keeper'. He ran it with his wife, Mary, and two servants – and had 11 children. In 1852 Albert Desmasur, the 13-year-old son of a visiting French artillery officer from Rennes, who was on a holiday visit to Jersey, died after injuries sustained from falling 30 feet from climbing rocks. He died the next morning. By 1861 a Mr T P G Poujol was the proprietor. He was still running it in 1881 at the age of 92, by which time he was a widower and being assisted by his grandson, Octave Duthiel.

The hotel attracted some prestigious guests, including a Viceroy of India and Prince Lucien Bonaparte, Napoleon's nephew, who stayed two nights while pursuing his interest in Jersey-Norman French.

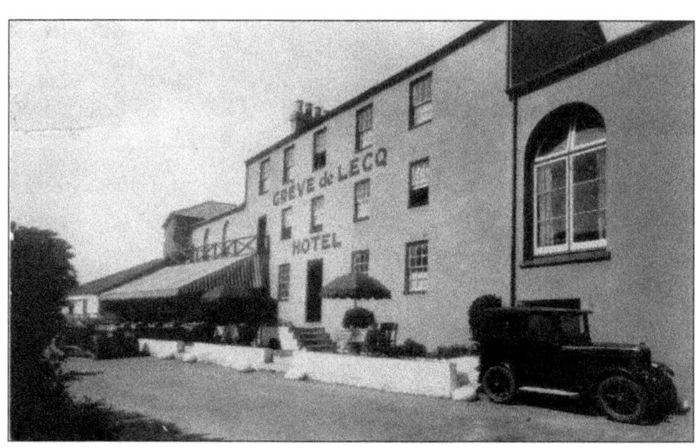

By 1871 Poujol had changed the name to the *Star and Garter Hotel* and was encouraging tourists to spend the night there before taking advantage of the services of a guide to explore the nearby caves. In 1872 a seven-course dinner was served to the members of the Grève de Lecq Harbour Committee, States Members and other influential Islanders, on the occasion of the laying of the foundation stone of the new harbour.

It is described in the 1888 *Jersey Times Almanac*: 'Delightfully situated near the sea, every accommodation for the tourist, stabling and pavilion for parties' and 'a great reputation as to its excellent cuisine and good liqueurs.'

The hotel was taken over in 1973 by Channel Hotels and Properties Ltd, but was later converted into Les Pierres de Lecq Apartments.

PRINCE OF WALES Hotel, Grève de Lecq

Built on sand dunes, a contract dated 1867 shows that a house had been built on the land by then, and sold to a Robert Randall.

It is mentioned in the 1881 Census as being run by a Samuel Parker, a Chelsea Pensioner and publican, although in 1901 it is listed as uninhabited.

During the Second World War, the hotel was used to billet men at 'Strongpoint Grève de Lecq'. A British airman, Sergeant Victor Dorman, was found by German forces north of the Paternosters, during an attempt to rescue airmen off the French coast. He was taken to Jersey, landing at Grève de Lecq before being dragged to the Prince of Wales Hotel where he was imprisoned. He was taken later to the German Military Hospital at the Merton Hotel.

ST MARY'S COUNTRY INN

It is believed that there has been an auberge on this site for centuries, although the current building is only a little over 200 years old. When it was rebuilt the builders would have used some of the original granite; the four bevelled stones on either side of the main entrance are evidence of a 17th Century building on the site. The new building became a meeting place for parish assemblies.

In the early 20th Century a telephone exchange was established in part of the building, supervised by a Boer War veteran, Mr Brideau, and his wife.

The pub was bought by Bass Charrington in 1987; until then it had been run by Bernard Le Gresley, whose family had owned the pub for generations and whose associations with the parish can be traced back to the16th Century. The pub was refurbished in 1989 and in 1991 the name was changed from St Mary's Hotel to St Mary's Country Inn.

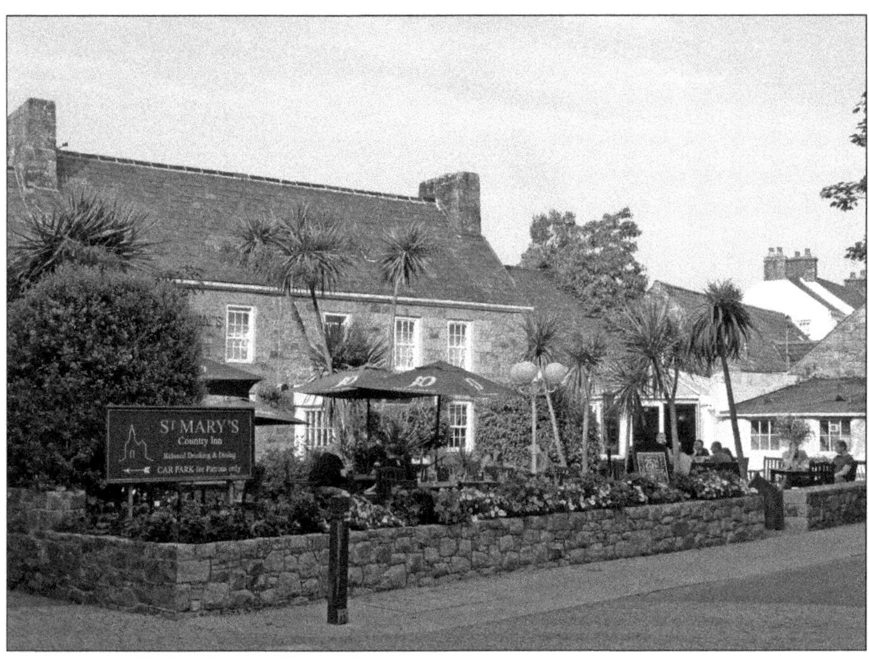

> 'When visiting Plémont, one will do well to desire the driver to stop at a small inn near the place – here the traveller may alight and here too he may find a room, a table and table cloth where he may spread his provisions; and where he may purchase abundance of delicious cream to add another luxury to his repast.'
>
> (*Strangers Guide*, 1833)

There were few if any public houses in St Ouen in the 19th Century, except, of course, the **Farmers Inn**. The granting of a Taverner's Licence was the prerogative of the Lord of the Manor and applications were not made to the Parish Assembly. The de Carteret family were always chary of granting licences. The only social meeting of an evening for the menfolk was the local shoemaker's shop – but there was not room for too many inside!

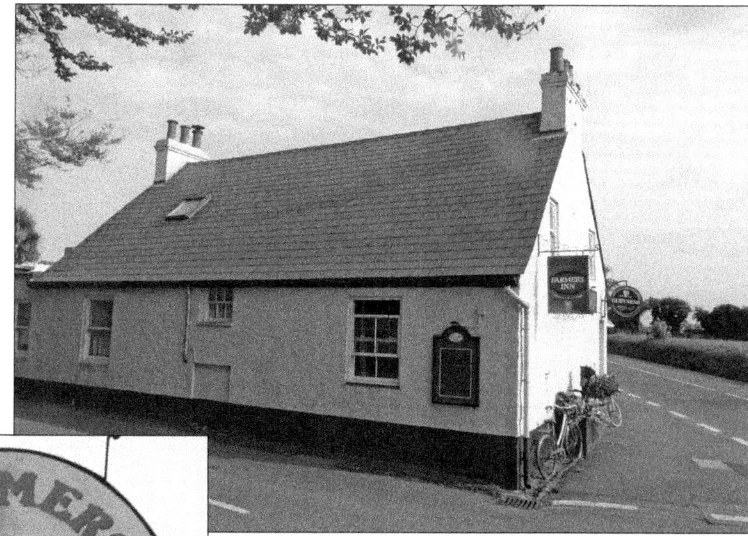

The Farmers Inn and its apt if somewhat faded pub sign

In St Peter, premises with the name '*Sign of the Three Oranges*', near St Peter's Church, was sold by auction 1 May 1820.

FORESTERS INN, Beaumont
The pub claims to be Jersey's longest serving inn, for the licence has been granted since 1717. It has been totally refurbished, complete with a thatched roof, and reinvented and reopened in 2017 as the **BEAUMONT INN**, 'Freehouse, Inn & Gastrolounge' as its sign has it.

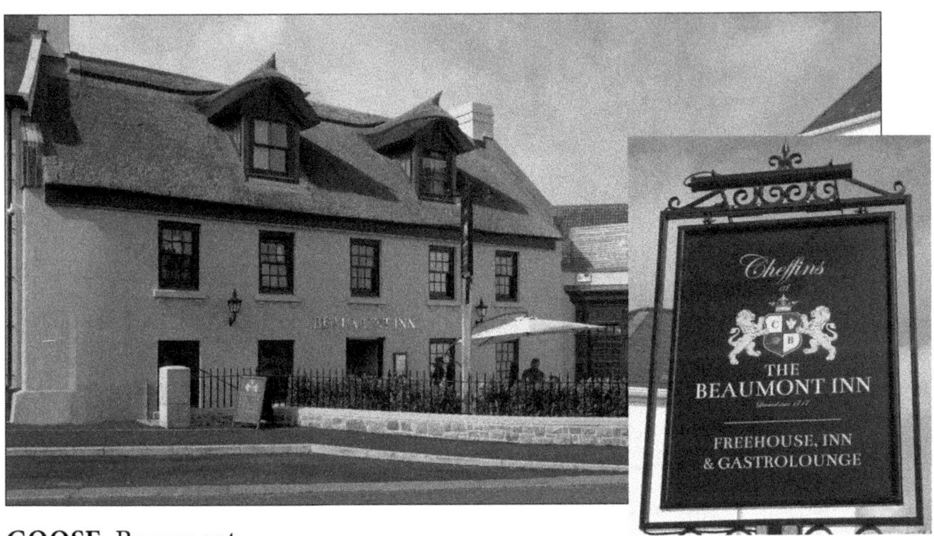

GOOSE, Beaumont
Originally the *BRITISH HOTEL, renamed the GOOSE ON THE GREEN, recently shortened to the Goose.*

THE STAR AND TIPSY TOAD formerly the *New Star*
Opened in the 1990s, but the predecessor, the *New Star*, was in existence for at least a century beforehand. This was renovated in 1992 by Steve Skinner, who also ran a microbrewery on the site

L'HOTEL DE ST PIERRE / ST PETER'S HOTEL
presently called the **SIR GEORGE CARTERET**
This was already in existence by 1824, owned by a Freemason (Jean Langlois) and used as a location for masonic meetings. By the early 20th Century it had become the *Alexandra Hotel*, named after the wife of King Edward VII, Queen Alexandra.

There was a vinery and rose garden at the hotel, presumably on the site of the current car park, and it was at one time a destination for charabanc tours

It was the HQ for Machine Gun Battalion 16 during the Occupation.

In modern times, it is better known as *St Peter's Bars*, then *St Peter Country Inn* and now the **Sir George Carteret**.

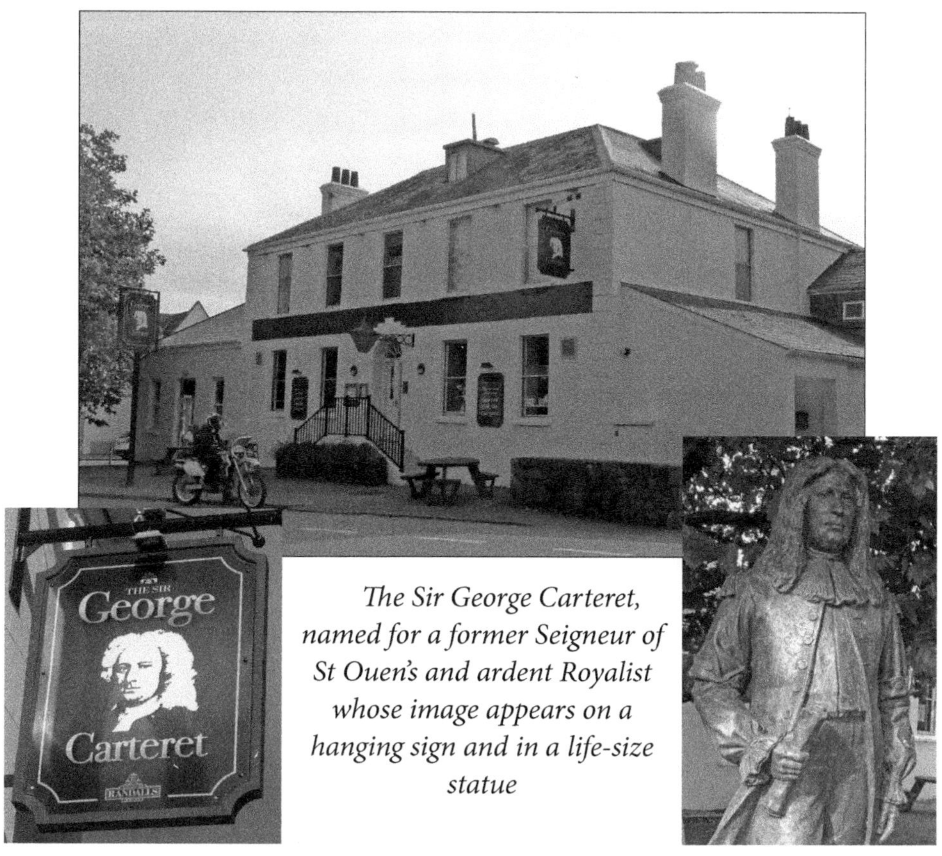

The Sir George Carteret, named for a former Seigneur of St Ouen's and ardent Royalist whose image appears on a hanging sign and in a life-size statue

TRINITY

BRITISH HOTEL now the **TRINITY ARMS**

In 1978 the Ann Street Brewery decided to replace the British Hotel with a new, purpose-built inn which would be more comfortable and hygienic than its predecessor.

Certain protests were voiced, including that of nearby resident, the late Alan Whicker, and a public meeting was called. The general consensus was in favour of a new pub, and so the project went ahead.

BRITTANIA, Bel Royal
The house belonged to the wife of Mr Hedley Le Quesne and was inherited by him on her death. It was at first leased to the Ann Street Brewery and then sold to it in 1969.

Two stories are recounted by the historian, Philip Ahier. The first is that in the early 20th Century a rider on horseback rode his horse through the door and right up to the bar. The second is that shortly after Liberation two children found 'a strange object' in a nearby brook. They picked it up and showed it to their father, who took it into the crowded bar. It was an unexploded bomb and the bar emptied quickly as it was brought inside. The Bomb Disposal Office was called for, and the bomb made safe without death or injury.

HARVEST BARN, Vallée des Vaux - St Helier
Before conversion into a pub in 1961, this centuries-old building was a mill, Le Moulin Nicolle, of probably 15th Century origin. During one period of its long existence it was a malt mill. It became a farm in the 19th Century and had become derelict by the 1950s. In 1958 the buildings were bought and renovated by Mr Gordon Turner and finished in 1961, when it opened as a free house. It was during the 1970s and 1980s in particular a very popular pub-restaurant. It was sold and closed early in the 21st Century.

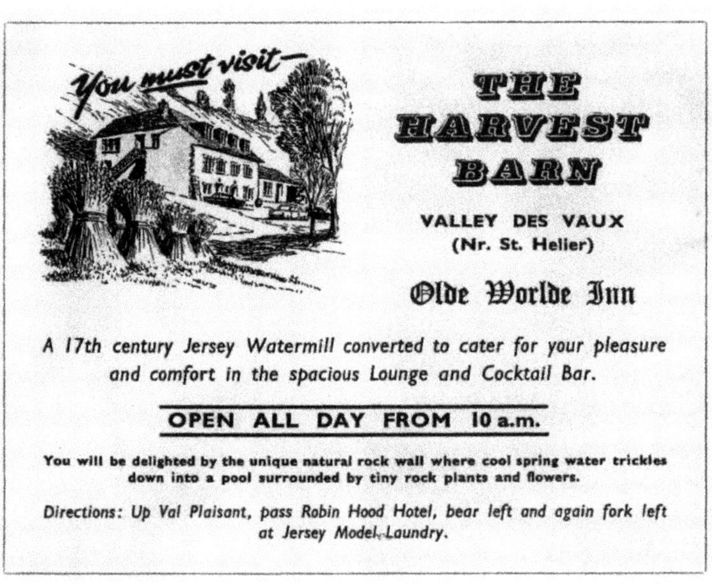

HOTEL DE LA PLAGE, Havre des Pas

Opened early in 1936 as a first class hotel. A newspaper 'advertorial' of the time stated:

> 'The hotel is, comparatively speaking, a new building and its design is modern without being freakish. Its clean, white exterior is a landmark and a definite asset to the appearance of Havre des Pas, while the interior is built with the sole object of comfort. Its assets include a Palm Court, and a Sun Lounge, and next door is 'Billy's Lido' where there is dancing both inside and in the open air; there is a first-class band and there is no charge for admission. It is one of the most popular rendezvous in the summer.'

It was in this hotel's restaurant that the con-man and safe-cracker, Eddie Chapman, was lunching with his lover and future fiancée, Betty Farmer, in February 1939. He noticed some plain-clothes policemen coming to arrest him, but escaped them by making a spectacular exit through the dining-room windows and escaped along the prom outside. Later that same night, in search of ready money, he burgled the West Park Pavilion, which happened to be shut that night and cracked the safe. The landlady of his boarding house had reported her suspicions of her lodger to the police'. Later that night he was arrested at the boarding house and began serving a prison sentence in Jersey. Two years later, during the German Occupation, he started his career as a spy, offering his services to the Germans as a turncoat agent. In fact he was a double agent, working for the British.

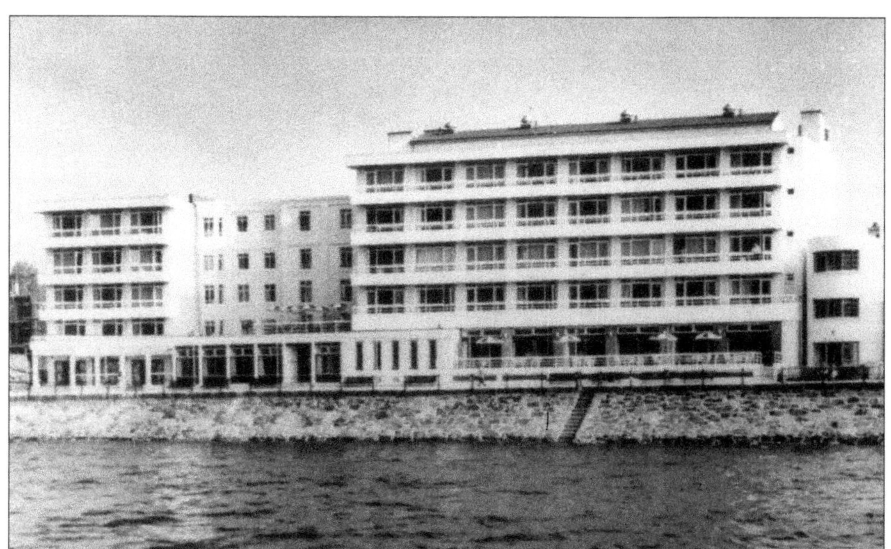

MILANO BARS, St Ouen

Situated off the northern section of Five Mile Road, Milano Bars was well known in the tourism boom years – the 1950s to 1980s – as a pub and a destination for 'Crazy Nite' coach tours. It was indeed synonymous with the bay's busiest period, offering a more casual atmosphere than establishments in town. The appearance of the flat-roofed Milano had not much in the way of visual charm and it was demolished in 1996, the site being returned to nature.

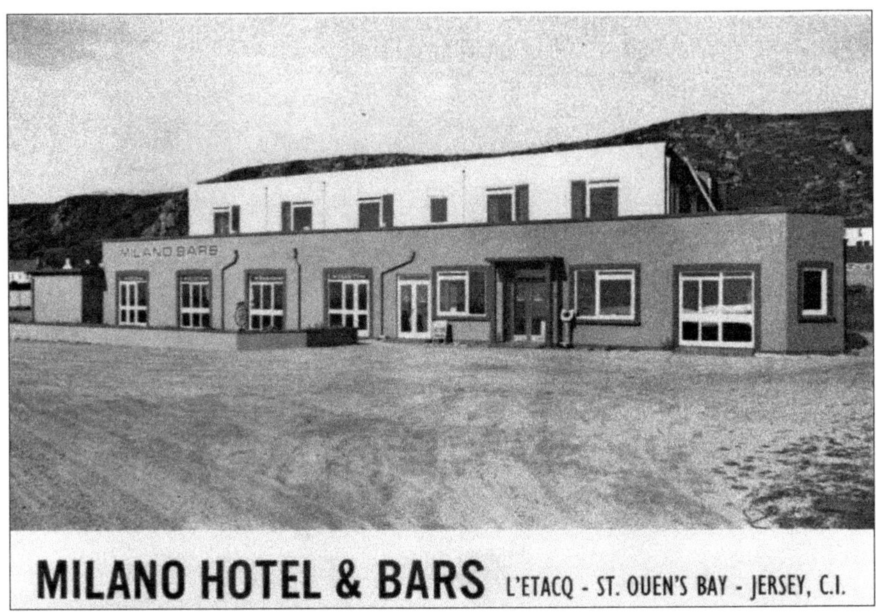

MOULIN DE LECQ, Grève De Lecq

Sometimes called Le Moulin de Vinchelez, this old watermill dates back to the 13th Century. In its earliest recorded form, Lecq is called La Wik, and may have stood for 'witch', indicating that remote part of Jersey was once a centre of sorcery – or at least of paganism.

In 1779 the mill was said to be '*en décadence*'.

The wheel was worked by the weight of water. It weighs 18 tons, has a diameter of 21 ft and is the largest water wheel in the Island. It was used for either grinding corn or as a fulling mill until 1929 when it was converted into a private home.

After 1945 a Mr C T Clarke ran a tea room from the premises. It was converted into a licensed inn by a Mr and Mrs R Ronald in 1954, and has been run as a public house ever since.

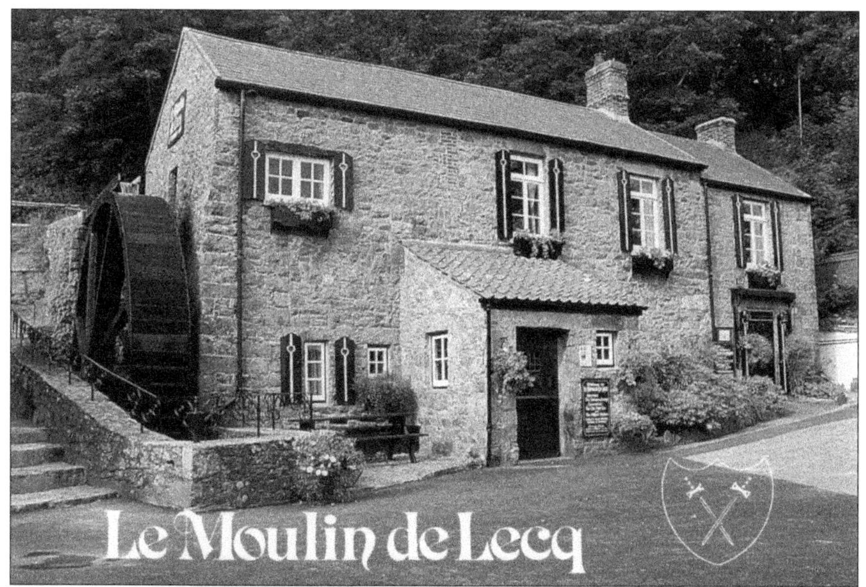

OLD PORTELET INN, St Brelade

Not an 'Old Inn' at all, but a picturesque former farmhouse bearing a stone which records the date 1606, but converted into a large pub to cater for the twentieth century tourist trade. It was much visited by evening 'mystery' coach tours which took in a variety of 'old inns' such as the Windmill Inn and Moulin de Lecq.

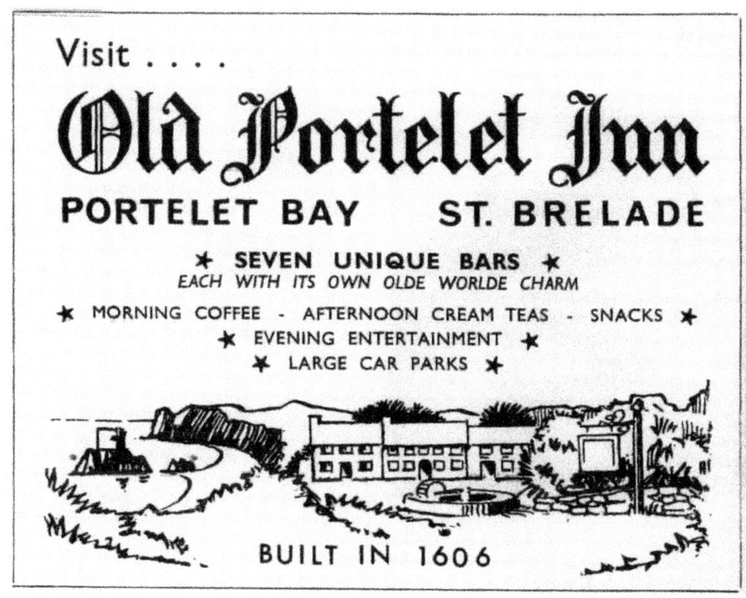

Old Portelet Inn

Price List

SPIRITS

GIN	1/8
WHISKY (Prop.) ...	2/2
DIMPLE HAIG etc.	2/9
LAMB NAVY RUM	1/9
DAIQUIRI	1/10
BACARDI	2/6
BRANDY ★★★ ...	2/6
BRANDY V.S.O.P. ...	4/0
VODKA	2/-
NIGGER HEAD ...	1/8

APERITIFS

GIN & VERMOUTH	2/6
GIN & DUBONNET	2/6
GIN & CORDIALS	1/10
PINK GIN	1/8
CINZANO	1/9
MARTINI	1/9
DUBONNET ...	1/9
ST. RAPHAEL ...	1/9
PERNOD	2/6
CARPANO	2/3
RICARD	2/6
GINGER WINE ...	2/-
CAMPARI	2/3

SHERRIES

CARLITO	2/-
WALNUT BROWN	2/-
ROYAL AMONTILADO	2/-
TIO PEPE	2/3
BRISTOL MILK ...	2/3
CELEBRATION CREAM	2/3
PORT	2/-

LIQUEURS

ALL LIQUEURS ...	2/-
EXCEPT	
AURUM	2/6
CHARTREUSE YELLOW ...	2/6
CHARTREUSE GREEN	2/6
GRAND MARNIER	2/6
DRAMBUIE ...	2/6
TIA MARIA ...	2/6

BEERS

WHITBREAD ...	1/4
DOUBLE DIAMOND	1/6
GUINNESS	1/4
PALE ALE from ...	1/2
BROWN ALE from	1/2
CARLSBERG PILSNER	2/3
CARLSBERG DE LUXE	2/6
HEINEKEN etc. ...	1/9
MACKESON ...	1/7
WORTHINGTON ...	1/4

DRAUGHT BEERS

WATNEY'S RED BARREL (Pint)	2/-
MARY ANN (Pint)	1/8
RANDALL'S BEST (Pint)	1/8

SPARKLING DRINKS

PIMMS No. 1, 2, 3, 4	4/-
JOHN COLLINS ...	3/-
TOM COLLINS ...	3/-
BUBBLY (per glass)	2/6
CIDER	1/6

MINERALS

FRUIT JUICES ...	1/3
COCA COLA ...	1/-
LEMONADE ...	1/-
SQUASHES	1/-
BABY MINERALS	9d

CHAMPAGNE COCKTAIL 4/6

TRY A HOUSE SPECIAL!!!

Price list from the 1960s

THE OLD SMUGGLERS' INN

This was reputed to be a centre of smuggling activities in Jersey. The building, originally built as cottages for fishermen, is said to date from the 14th Century. By the 1930s it had become known as the *Finisterre Hotel*, run by Jack Doig who was happy to relate that he was a descendant of a buccaneer, also called Jack Doig, who is reputed to have buried treasure on Cocos Island, off Costa Rica. The treasure has never been recovered, but not for want of trying. After the Occupation it was renamed the Old Smugglers Inn.

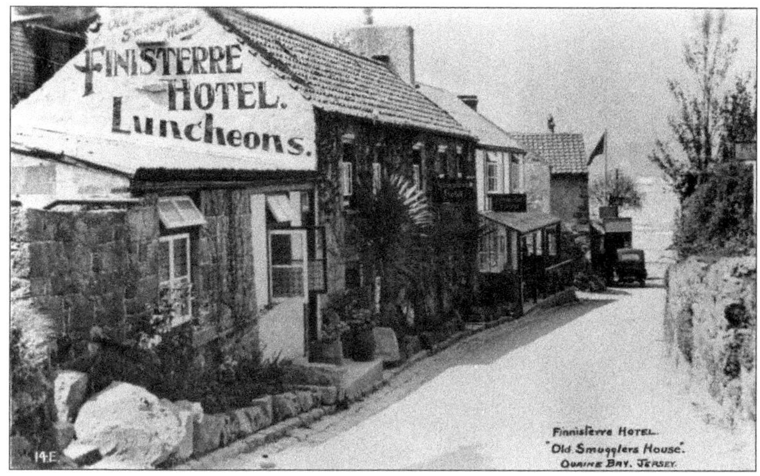

The Finisterre Hotel at Ouaisné, known today as the Smugglers Inn

PALACE HOTEL, Bagatelle

This was, before the Occupation, one of Jersey's foremost hotels. It had 150 rooms and enjoyed a panorama over the entire bay.

It began the war as a Wehrmacht Communications Centre and later became an officers' training school. Much of the planning for the German commando raid on Granville on 8-9 March 1945 was carried out here, but on the eve of the assault, a small fire broke out in a ground floor room used as a cordite store.

Because of the secrecy surrounding the forthcoming raid, it was imperative to protect the plans that lay scattered throughout the hotel so the Germans preferred to stand by and so the fire was allowed to increase its hold.

Instead of calling in the civilian fire brigade, the Kommandant decided to have his own men place demolition charges on all three floors to blow out a section of the hotel to stop the fire spreading along the building. Explosives were placed in position – but then the hotel suddenly exploded. Many buildings in St Saviour were damaged in the blast and nine soldiers were mortally wounded.

Although the firemen were now called in to stop the fire, it was dangerous work, as there were repeated detonations as small arms ammunition exploded. The shell of the building later had to be demolished because of the dangerous condition. There is a theory that the fire developed after an explosion perpetrated by Paul Muhlbach, an anti-Nazi soldier who was the son of the pre-Nazi era Social Democrat Mayor of Koblenz. The site is now occupied by Palace Close.

THE PRIORY

Devil's Hole, St Mary

It is believed that the name of 'the Priory' was derived from a priory that existed on the site in the Middle Ages, or that the farmhouse was built with stones from a nearby derelict priory after the Reformation, possibly on the site of the nearby property, La Falaise.

This old farmhouse was opened as a café by the Arthur family of St Mary before the First World War and later converted into a bar. Its location capitalised on the nearby tourist attraction of Devil's Hole, which had attracted tourists since Victorian times. It was purchased by C Le Masurier Ltd in 1954.

WEST PARK PAVILION

Familiarly known as 'the Pav', the building's history dates back to the late 19th Century. Its genesis was a corrugated iron building on the same site to stage a circus. Afterwards, 'the Tin Hut' closed but was re-opened in following years to stage a variety of concerts, pantomimes and dances. During the First World War it was used as a flour store. The Tin Hut was demolished and rebuilt as the West Park Pavilion in early 1930. It was re-opened on 1 July 1931 by the St Helier Constable, J T Ferguson; the first chairman of the company made the remark during his speech that the building was the only one of its kind this side of the globe. It became a popular venue for Island concerts and dances until the Occupation, when it was used to house Russian prisoners.

Its most glittering occasion was in 1956 when the Queen and the Duke of Edinburgh were guests of honour at a States luncheon held there. The building was decked out with flowers and after lunch the Royal couple appeared on the balcony to wave to the cheering crowds.

During the 1950s and 1960s it was a popular centre for ballroom dancing during the summer months and, as time went on, for discotheques.

A change of ownership in 1972 and refurbishment in a modern manner brought about a name change to *THE INN ON THE PARK*. It continued to host many famous stars of theatre and television. A local magazine article written in the 1980s stated: 'The Inn on the Park surely deserves to remain one of the Island's famous landmarks and the new owners, Anglo-Channel Leisure Investments Ltd, certainly intend to ensure that it does.

By 2001 it had been closed down and demolished. 'Oh no, not the Pav as well,' exclaimed the *JEP* columnist, Gordon Young, in his popular Saturday column, reflecting the affection many Islanders felt for it and reminding them of youthful pleasures and indiscretions. In its place now stands another block of flats.

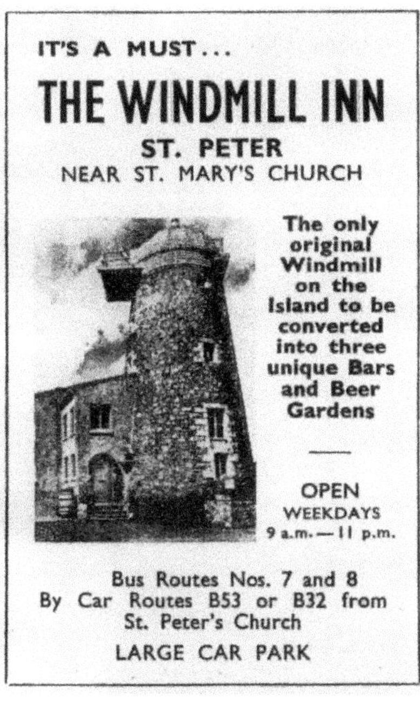

WINDMILL INN

Formerly a windmill, as its name and appearance might suggest, and known as 'St Peter's New Mill', It was built in 1837 and ceased functioning as a windmill in 1911, when its sails were dismantled and an oil engine replaced their motive power. It was converted into an inn in the 1960s and purchased by Ann Street in 1973. It was later converted into a showroom for the Catherine Best jewellery company with restaurant-café attached and this has recently re-opened.

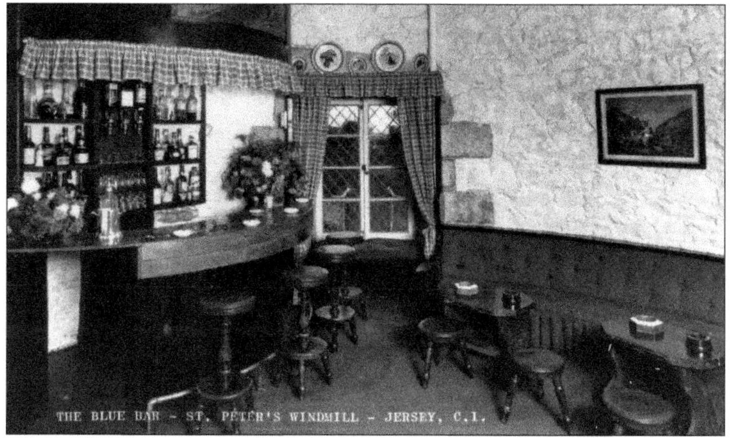

~ 10 ~

The Wine Importers

A guide book to Jersey published in 1811, titled *A Summer Stroll*, stated:

'The town of St Helier abounds with many handsome shops, which in their exterior exactly resemble those of England – they are all well-stocked and all produce of the East and West Indies are there, as well as wines and spirits are very considerably cheaper than in any part of Great Britain, but these excepted, almost everything else bears much higher price in time of war; but the restoration of peace could affect a reduction in provisions.'

The cheapness of alcohol in Jersey always attracted comment from visitors, from the beginning of the 19th Century to the latter part of the 20th Century. It is instructive to view the prices of wines – and the selection available – in the earlier part of the 19th Century:

In his book *A Pedestrian Tour through the Islands of Guernsey and Jersey* (1821), the author, William Gerard Walmesley, wrote:

'We were directed to a confectioner by the name of Bolton in the [Royal] Square for a variety of wines, which might be purchased in any quantity, even a bottle. Claret as low as 7s.6d per dozen and port wine 22s-6d.

'We ordered some port and Lisbon wine, and a substantial fruit pie to be sent to our lodgings. We settled our bill of expenses for our stay here of 13 days, which amounted to £5.11.6d, and including wine etc averaged about £3 10s per day for each of us.

'We dined on a French leg of mutton, which was delicious, and drank the health of our friends in England in a bottle of very good Frontignac. There are a variety of wines to be had here, consisting of Port, Sherry, Lisbon, Madeira, Tenerife, Mountain Sweet and dry, Frontignac, Claret, Champagne, Burgundy, Vin de Grave, Roussillon, St George, Picardin, Hermitage, Sicilian, Marsala, which are all low priced, except Champagne. The last sells for 6s a bottle. The best, of course, are to be found at the Wine Merchant's store, but the common sort are to be retailed in almost every shop. Cordials and liquors may be purchased at 2s per bottle, except Martinique, and some few others which are 5s 6d.

'English bank notes bear a premium of 1s 6d and an English shilling passes currently for 1s 1d.'

Thirteen years later, another English writer passed on the good news about Jersey prices to his readers. This comes from Henry Inglis' book, *An Account of the Island of Jersey* (1834):

'In the low price of wines and spirits, Jersey will compete with any place in the world.... Jersey has the command of all wines duty free and consequently the vintages of France, Spain and Portugal are all proportionately low-priced.

Port, 2yrs to 8yrs old	22s.6d to 25s per dozen
Inferior port	15s
Sherries	the same price as port
Barcello	14s
Marsala	12s to 14s
Vidonia	20s
Mountain	20s
Trent	22s.6d
East India Madeira	24s
Vin Ordinaire	6s to 10s
Light clarets	from 20s to 30s
First growths of best clarets	45s to 50s
Cote Rotie	45s to 48s
St George	12s
Burgundy, Chambertin	60s
Macon	25s
Vin de Grave, Barsac and Sauterne	from 15s to 25s
Champagne	50s to 60s
Rhenish	17s.6d
Hocks	40s to 50s

All of these prices are stated in Jersey currency, consequently 1s 8d must be deducted from every £1.

Cognac (such is rarely to be met with in England) costs 7s per gallon

Hollands (gin)	from 3s to 6s per gall, to 1s per bottle
Jamaica rum	1s to 1s 4d

Spirits of inferior quality (but not inferior to what is usually retailed in England) may be had at greatly lower prices.

One may therefore enjoy a glass of rum and water, sugar included, for one penny, and I am not sure that a few drops of lemon juice might not be squeezed into the bargain.

A man may comfort himself with a pint of old port for 11s, or drain his bottle of St George – rather a racy wine – for the same money, or old Marsala (better than it is found in England) for one shilling.'

A bill paid in 1835 shows the then current prices of beverages:

6 btts of sherry	12s.6d
Brandy	1s.6d per bottle
Rum	1s
6 doz porter	4s
6 doz ale	5s.6d.

An advertisement in 1837 from *The Caesarean* announces that Gillingham and Co at 2 Caledonia Place, Pier, was an 'importer of every description of English ale and porter', including Guinness Dublin Extra Stout.

For the benefit of readers who have never had the fun of explaining to a foreigner how to subtract £2.17s.9d from £5.2s.6d, 12 pennies (12d) = 1 shilling or, in today's money, five pence.

So, e.g. 1s.6d (the price of a bottle of brandy in Jersey in 1835) = 7.5 pence; 20 shillings (20s) = £1.

IT would be impossible to list every wine importer that has set up in business in Jersey. But a few of the more famous names of recent decades are detailed below. The longest established wine importer in Jersey was the company C LE MASURIER LTD.

The founder of the company in 1835 was Charles Le Masurier, a wine merchant. At that time, once wine merchants had bottled their imported stock and corked them, they immersed the neck of the stopped bottle in sealing wax and every merchant had his own seal. In the case of Le Masurier, his merchant's seal was an L superimposed on an M – the logo that remained familiar in the Island until relatively recently.

We do not know too much about the Le Masurier family: they were merchants; they were, confusingly, all named Charles; they lived in town.

In 1835, it is believed that one of a number of small businesses – that later were to coalesce into the Le Masurier company – was founded. It may have been

Nicholas Allain, wine importer and beer merchant of 36 Bath Street. Another strand in what would become C Le Masurier Ltd was Charles Le Monnier, wholesale and retail tobacco and snuff manufacturer and wine and spirit importer of 37 Broad Street (factory at 29 Commercial Street); Le Monnier and Sons, grocers, beer merchants and wine importers described in that delightfully old-fashioned phrase: 'Italian warehousemen'.... one or other of the businesses was established in 1835 – but which one of them it was is now lost in the mists of time. By the end of the 19th Century they were all absorbed in the Le Masurier trading name, as was also the Jersey Liqueur and Cordial Manufacturing Company and Kine's Springfield Brewery.

By 1875, 'F Clarke Wine Merchant' was trading from 3 & 4 Pitt Street; as C Le Masurier was trading from 3 Pitt Street, it seems probable that Le Masurier and Clarke were first of all neighbours and then round about the same sort of time Fred Clarke took over the adjoining business and continued to trade under the Le Masurier name.

Le Masurier's also wholesaled soap, tea, coffee, held the appointment of Honorary Agent to the Royal Yacht Squadron, made and supplied Jersey cider locally and exported to 'Gentlemen's Clubs' in London and higher class merchants and private customers in 'the Metropolis and the Provinces.'

The limited liability company was formed in 1911, but at this time Fred Webber Clarke had become chairman of the Le Masurier family business, although there was still a Le Masurier family connection with the company at least until the 1920s. From 1911 the history of Le Masurier company is the history of the Clarke family – if the Le Masuriers were all confusingly called Charles, the Clarkes were, equally confusingly, mostly all called Fred – except for the patriarch, Joseph Webber Clarke.

Joseph came to Jersey in approximately 1866 with his family, including his son, Frederick, then aged about 11. The family came from East Devon, possibly from the Honiton or Seaton area. Joseph was a butcher and fattened cattle in Le Coie, the water meadow area that would one day be the site of the Le Coie Hotel in Janvrin Road and that has now been redeveloped as housing on the town's busy ring road.

It was his son, Fred, born in Halburton in Devon, who was the first of the many 'Fred Clarkes'. He became the merchant and wine importer who bought out the Le Masurier family and took over the company, as well as building at least two major town houses to live in. By 1911, when the business was transformed into a limited liability company, there was a C Le Masurier wine shop at 7 Charing Cross.

Fred Webber Clarke enjoyed a long and profitable business career in Jersey. Apart from leading the Le Masurier Company he built houses, including West Park House in 1928. He died in 1934 at the age of 81, to be succeeded by his grandson, also called Fred Webber Clarke (junior) as head of the company.

Fred Webber Clarke's son, Fred Richard Clarke (born 1882), was educated at Victoria College and grew up in the wine business., as well as running a motor company, Omnials Ltd, which ran a motor bus service from Library Place to St Aubin. This particular business activity was not a great success: it ceased after a few months because the tyres didn't stay on the wheels. He was another astute businessman, who lived to the ripe old age of 99; his son, inevitably also called Fred Webber Clarke, became Constable of St Helier. He took over as chairman in 1934 and in the same year the company built the 'New L'Etacq Pavilion' – better known by its later name of The Milano. Also in that year the company leased the redundant buildings of St Peter's Barracks and ran it as the St Peterville Holiday Village until the buildings reverted to the War Office at the time of the Munich Crisis of 1938. The site is now buried underneath the Airport area.

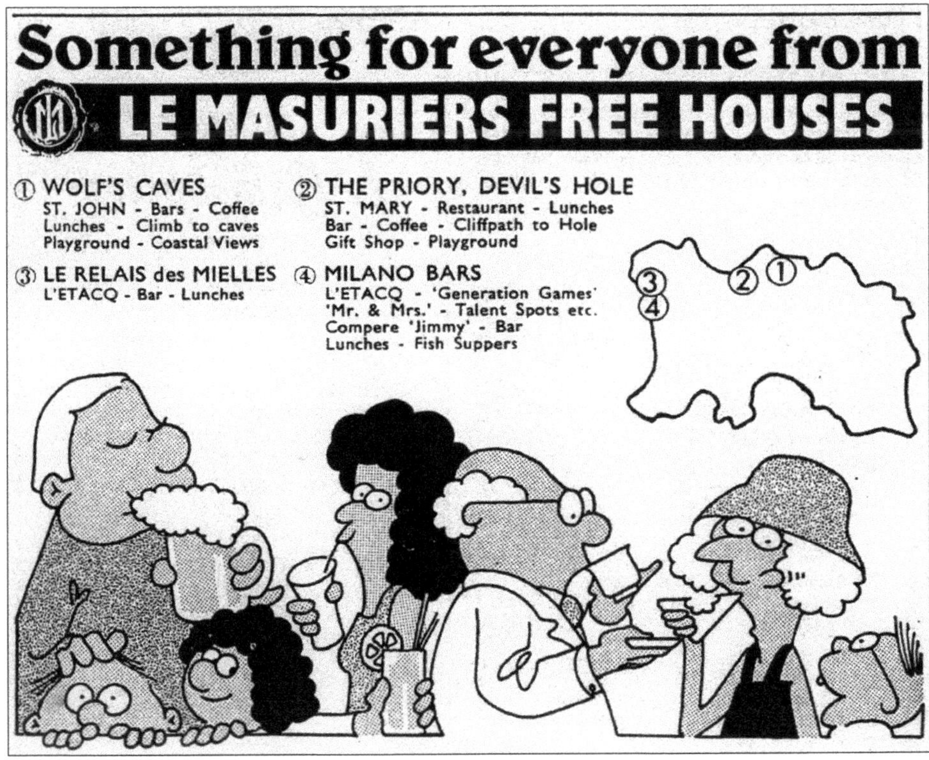

Advert from 1982

Many other Le Masurier properties were requisitioned during the Occupation; three of them were destroyed and several others vandalised. By then Le Masuriers had also acquired Wolf's Caves, the Sorel Pavilion, L'Etacq Hotel, La Moye Golf Hotel, the Prince of Wales and the Alexandra (Sir George de Carteret); in 1940 the wholesale wine merchants Charles Le Quesne was also acquired.

During the Occupation the latest BBC news was typed on bottle wrapping paper – a dangerous joint venture shared with the local fire brigade.

Liberation came and with it a resumption of the tourism industry. Fred Webber Clarke foresaw the tourist boom and proceeded to acquire suitable town centre properties for the popular Wine Lodge chain of shops. In 1956 he was elected Constable of St Helier, but died only two years later.

His son, Fred Philip Webber Clarke, took over the company and continued to consolidate and expand it.

However, on 4 April 1971 a disastrous fire all but completely destroyed their head office and bottling lines in Bath Street and James Street. Almost the whole complex of the extensive premises from Bath Street to James Street was lost. Records, equipment and hundreds of thousands of pounds worth of maturing wines were lost – The damage to buildings, stock and plant was estimated at hundreds

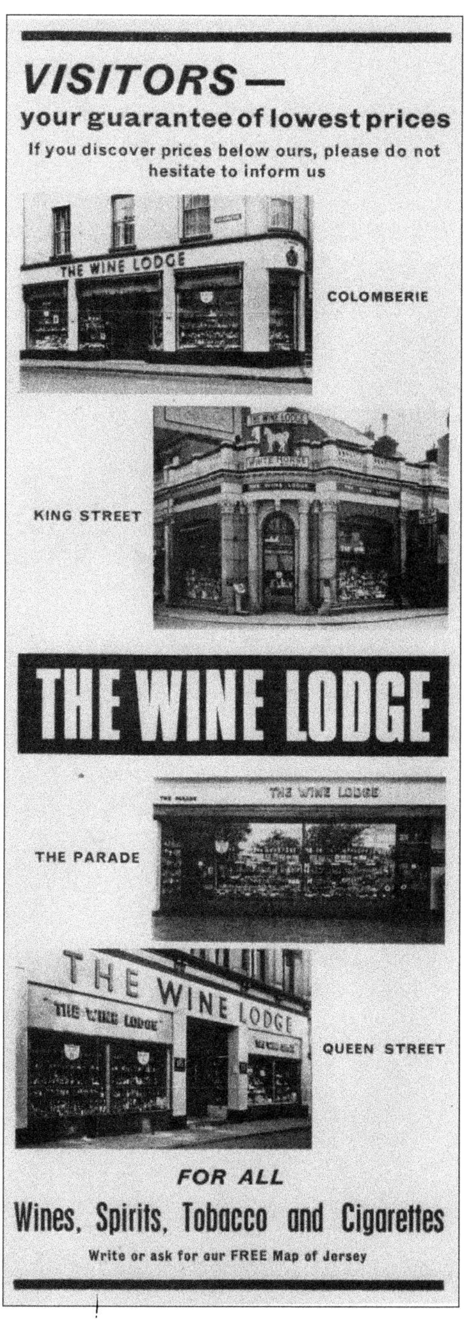

Advert for the several branches of Le Masurier's Wine Lodges which ran at the the heyday of tourism

and thousands of pounds. It was the most disastrous fire in town since that of the premises of Le Gallais and Sons in Bath Street 15 years before.

Fred Clarke listed the damage caused by the fire:

> 'The mineral water and wine bottling and cleaning plants. The retail store, the Wine Bar and the more modern Wine Lodge. The distributing and dispatch bays, the offices and boardroom, much of the equipment and stocks and also the suite occupied by the Jersey Hotel and Guest House Association. Also gone were hundreds of spirits – whisky, gin, cognac, rum and liqueurs, beers, mineral waters, soft drinks, bottles and crates. The scene was reported to be like a battle ground, with bottles exploding from time to time.'

In 1973 a new modern labour-saving warehouse and office block were opened in Stopford Road and Oxford Road, a site over which the first Clarke to settle in the Island had pastured and fattened cattle for his butchery business.

The year 1983 saw Fred Philip Webber Clarke become, in his turn, Constable of St Helier, and two years later the company opened its 20th public house – the Shipwright – in Peirson Road.

With the downturn of the tourism industry in the 1990s, the Le Masurier empire of Wine Lodges and pubs and countless little souvenir shops that also sold alcohol and cigarettes were gradually sold off. After the death of Fred Philip Webber Clarke in 2001 the company sold its drinks wholesale business to Randalls Vautier and leased its public houses, as well as selling off its licensed shops; the final one closed in 2006.

But the company of C Le Masurier has now become a prominent property company; like the Leopard in Just So Stories, it has not gone away, merely changed its spots. It always owned a considerable number of premises in Jersey; nowadays it also has property interests in the UK, Germany and Poland.

GEORGE ORANGE & CO LTD, 4 Wharf Street

George Orange (1811–1871) of St Brelade took over an existing wine merchant in 1849: the Metropolitan Wine Company, established in Garden Lane. In due course this was moved to 4 Wharf Street. He was succeeded by his son, Edwin Orange (1853–1917); Edwin's son, also Edwin, predeceased his father in 1910. A limited company was formed in 1924, with G F D Le Gallais (chairman), C H B Brockhurst (director) and Percy Vardon (managing director). Mr Le Gallais died in 1936 and Mr Brockhurst died in 1938. Mr Vardon became chairman and managing director, but died the following year. His widow, Gertrude Vardon became joint chairman and managing director and George Le Couteur, a director since 1938, became managing director. He took over as chairman in 1954. He died in 1970 and Martin Flageul, who had joined the company in 1962, took over as managing director in 1975.

He recalled the wine trade in Jersey in the 1960s: 'The majority of wine was high-quality French, a lot of it was bottled locally; sherry and fortified wines were massive. Tourism was huge and many tourists would take a bottle of sherry and 200 cigarettes back home with them. We used to bottle the sherries; Walnut Brown, Canasta Cream, all the Pedro Domecq range, Harvey's Bristol Cream... all bottled and labelled by hand.

Much of the imported French wine was also imported by the hogshead and bottled in Jersey.'

The Latest Drink

A BEER AND YET A WINE

SALT'S JUBILEE ALE.

BARLEY WINE.

NIPS, 3d. HALF-PINTS, 4d.

A Wholesome Beverage.
Recommended by the Faculty.

On Sale at all the leading Hotels.

Sole Agents: G. ORANGE & CO.,
Telephone 96. WHARF STREET.

Advert for George Orange, dating from 1913

Le Riche's Group acquired Orange in the early 1980s, and Martin Flageul then left the company to set up Victor Hugo Wines, as the wine merchant arm of Ann Street Brewery.

From G Orange's 1963–1964 price list, the wines shown below are detailed as a comparison with prices then and now (2017):

1955 Krug Vintage Champagne	30s per bottle
1956 Chateau Yquem	18s
1960 Ch Palmer	16s
1957 Pouilly Fuissé	13s.6d
1957 Chambertin	27s
1959 Liebfraumilch Blue Nun	11s.9d
Pouilly Fumé	12s
Spanish Burgundy	4s.4d
1955 Graham's Vintage Port	14s.6d
Cutty Sark Whisky	20s
Gordon's Gin	16s.3d

J F VAUTIER LTD

Traded from 57 New Street, taking over the company Jesse and Picot, believed to have started imported wine in 1830. Mr J F Vautier and F Pearce took over the company in the late 1890s; Mr Pearce had been the steward at the Victoria Club. He died in 1902, leaving Mr Vautier as sole proprietor. He remained as his head until his death in 1939 and was succeeded by his nephew, Mr R J Beer, who had been with the company since 1907. He died in August 1945 and the business became a private limited company. The share capital was purchased in 1978 by Randalls Brewery and continued to be run by Randalls as a separate entity from the brewery.

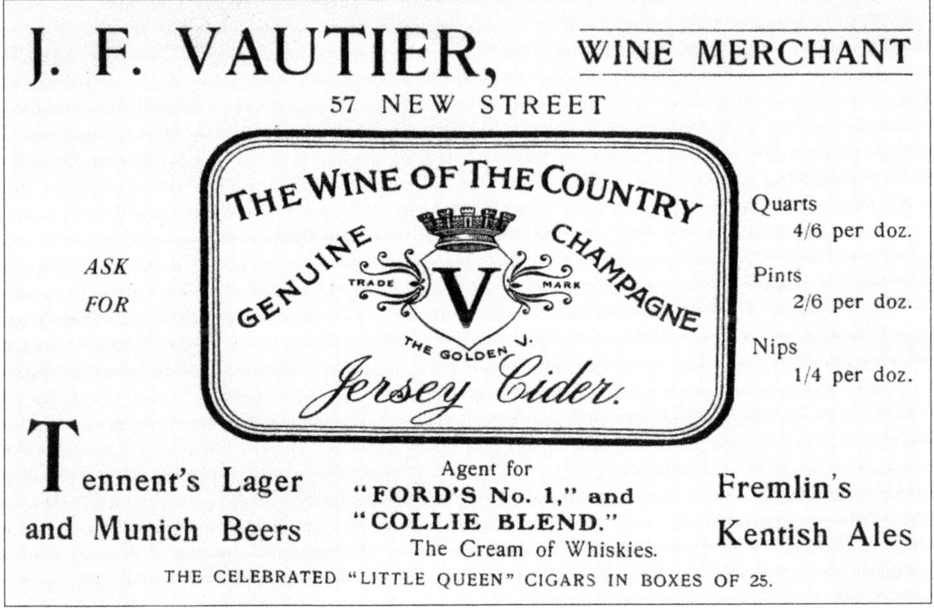

MERCHANT VINTNERS LTD

Founded in 1978, the partnership of Hamish Marett-Crosby and Eric Ruaro specialised in fine Italian wines, which were something of an unknown quantity in Jersey at the time. They worked closely with the AMIRA organisation of Italian hospitality professionals. In due course the company was sold to Randalls Vautier, which perpetuated the name as their wine merchant arm.

VICTOR HUGO WINES

Established in 1980, as the Ann Street group's wine and spirits arm with several retail outlets. The group had owned the Victor Hugo Hotel (now demolished and on the site of Victor Hugo Apartments) at Grève d'Azette.

'It seemed a good name for the new company,' said its first managing director, Martin Flageul. 'I checked out the biography of Victor Hugo, just in case he was a teetotaller, and of course he wasn't – he was known to drink a bottle of Burgundy in the morning before lunch. So that was how the name was chosen.'

Martin Flageul remained its managing director until 2012; he had previously been MD of G Orange & Co. He said that the greatest growth has been in the popularity of wine itself: not just a drink for a minority of people to be enjoyed as a treat, but as an everyday drink for the vast majority of people. The growth in popularity of rosé wines has been particularly marked.

The company is now part of the Liberation Group.

Other names of note:

Le Riches – part of the grocery company; Gorey Wine Company ; Bergerac Wine Cellar; Dunells; A C Gallie; Bath Street Wine Cellar; Vins Direct; Corkscrews

Agency businesses: Jaffé & Co.; J J Le Sueur; Leslie Rankin; A F Butcher

Wine education also came to the fore, with the establishment of a Jersey branch of the international body, the Guild of Sommeliers, and the Jersey Wine and Spirit Education Trust, which worked closely with the UK trust. Both these organisations did a useful and much appreciated job of improving the knowledge of wine and spirits of professionals in the wine trade and worked so successfully that Jersey got the best pass mark in the Certificate examination in Britain. But neither organisation survived the contraction of the tourism industry in the 1990s.

~ 11 ~

La Mare Vineyard and Winemaking in Jersey in modern times

Grape vines are no strangers to Jersey, for vines in sheltered terraces or against walls have been grown for centuries for eating grapes. Since the Occupation there have been three 'garden shed attempts' to grow grapes for wine but without success – La Mare Wine Estate in St Mary has been the first real commercial vineyard in Jersey.

The seeds of the idea for the vineyard at La Mare took root in late 1969. Robert ('Bob') and Ann Blayney bought La Mare, a derelict 18th Century farmhouse in St Mary with 28 vergées of land and set about its restoration.

Bob had begun his Wine Trade training as an 18-year-old cellar boy at wine shippers in the City of London. His family firm of wine merchants in the North-East of England, Blayney and Co, established in 1831, had built up excellent relations with leading families in the great wine centres of Europe and they taught him about 'wine' from the vine to the glass. Later, he became a Liveryman of the Vintners' Company and a Freeman of the City of London. He took over the family business at the age of 23 on the death of his father.

In 1968 Blayney & Co. merged with one of the big brewery companies and with his wife and toddler son, Andrew, he decided to join Ann's parents in Jersey where he became involved in the wine trade in St Helier.

He recollected: 'As a wine merchant I had long imagined having a vineyard of my own. Ann had been very sympathetic about this and, with the restoration of La Mare completed, agreed to help.'

Bob and Ann Blayney researched locally and discovered that there had been two trial plantings in Jersey on a very small scale since the Occupation, both being abandoned when the owners were unable to ripen the fruit of the chosen vine variety. Bob's experience in wine suggested that this was due to lack of

knowledge rather than climate difficulty.

Their research led them to plant, in 1972, a trial four-vergée vineyard with Müller Thurgau, a cross between Riesling and Sylvaner, which was thought to be the safe bet for Island conditions.

In 1974 they created a small, well equipped winery and laboratory in time for their first vintage that autumn. They were encouraged to plant a larger area of vines using Seyval, the French hybrid, as well as Scheurebe from Germany. The wonderful summer and autumn conditions in 1976 brought them an abundant harvest and the quality was good.

'Rather than race out and order a Bentley in our enthusiasm, we set out to enlist the best viticultural advice, and the famous Professor Helmut Becker from the German viticultural college at Geisenheim on the Rhine agreed to help us. He was attracted to Jersey and thought that the Reichensteiner and Huxelrebe vines on specially chosen rootstocks would suit us well. This big hearted and humorous Rhinelander virtually became our godfather; constantly helpful and from time to time allowing one of his key experts to come to Jersey to meet problems that had cropped up.'

He continued: 'Since our first trial planting we were becoming acutely aware that owning vineyards may seem a glamorous occupation but they devour money. It was said that to make a fortune from your vineyard you had better start with one first. We were failing on that test! Over the winter of 1975 we explored the possibility of opening La Mare Vineyards to visitors. As I had my 'day job' to keep me busy in town Ann took on the tourism side of La Mare Vineyards. That summer of 1976 we welcomed personally 22,000 visitors to La Mare and created another valuable tourist attraction for Jersey.'

They also made preserves, jams, jellies and mustards and opened a vineyard shop.

Over the winter months they shipped in loads of Seville oranges to make marmalade and Ann Blayney's team became known as 'Mrs Blayney's marmaladies'.

On Her Majesty the Queen's visit to Jersey in 1978 the States entertained her to luncheon at Hotel L'Horizon when all the Island great and good were invited.

'Our wine was being served which was a huge fillip to our confidence. To our astonishment Ann and I were invited too. We had the extraordinary pleasure of drinking the Loyal Toast to the Sovereign in her presence with our own wine.'

The vintages of 1980 and 1981 were tiny and made the Blayneys look for another product to sell to visitors – Jersey cider. (See pages 30-56)

Shortly afterwards, the success of La Mare Vineyards enabled Bob to swap his day job in St Helier for full time 'vigneron'.

In 1991 their soldier son, Andrew, who had been in the thick of the first Gulf War in Iraq, wished to leave the army and join his parents at La Mare. His enthusiasm for wine was inherited (he was fifth generation wine trade) and he was fired by the La Mare success. He suggested that during the cold winter months he should join a friend in Stellenbosch, South Africa, who was a wine maker, while his parents got on with the lengthy back-breaking job of pruning the vines. Each winter he became a 'flying winemaker' in Stellenbosch and eventually was complimented by being given his own entry in *Platter's Guide to South African Wines*. He brought home with him new wine making techniques and enthusiasms. Soon, La Mare was using new French oak casks for ageing wine and quality levels were impressive.

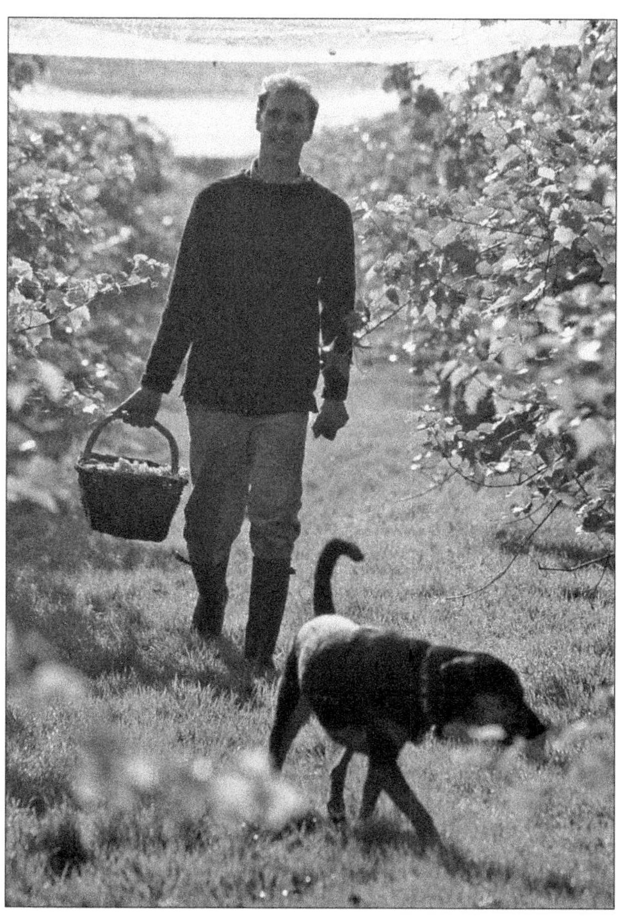

Andrew Blayney at La Mare Vineyards

He said: 'These were immensely exciting years. The quality of our wines was steadily increasing and in the fullness of time we also made a Jersey Apple Brandy, which won strong support. La Mare had become a successful venture and the family decided that Ann and I deserved our retirement.'

The sale to a wealthy English businessman, Trevor Owen, was arranged very amicably. Trevor was anxious that Andrew stay on and manage it but Andrew agreed that he would remain a part time director/manager and put in place a team to run it.

A general manager was chosen: Tim Crowley, an Irishman working in Jersey with a background in both farming and retail sales. The Blayneys had known him for some time and knew of his keen interest in La Mare. It was suggested to him that he might like to take over, initially under Andrew's leadership.

Apart from La Mare, there have been three other attempts to grow vineyards in Jersey.

One of these was the 'Clocher du Coin' wine produced by Bruno Rioda of St Ouen. He put his first 1,700 vines down in a 4-vergée field in 1973, and 1976 was his first harvest. He produced 1,000 bottles of wine, which he made using his own press on his farm in Jersey.

Unfortunately his 1976 vintage was also his last: 'I used to put netting over the vines to stop the birds eating the grapes. In 1977 a strong wind blew the netting off the vines and clouds of birds promptly settled over the vineyard and ate everything! I shot one or two, but the other birds were not at all upset by the untimely death of their friends and just went on eating. So I decided I wouldn't go on trying to make wine – the grapes were just too popular with the birds.!'

Another small vineyard in the 1990s was planted, grown on a steep hill near the Victoria pub in St Peter's Valley, using Seyval blanc, Regnier and Chardonnay varieties. The vineyard was then owned by David Dumosch Ltd, the agricultural merchants, which found it useful to employ their farm workers to harvest the grapes at a time of year when there was no work to do in the potato fields. The grapes were sent to Sussex to be made into wine. Wine was made during four successive vintages between 1994 and 1997 and sold as 'Le Perquage'. But the business model of sending the grapes away and then having them returned as bottled wine was impossible to sustain.

And yet another vineyard was planted and the wine named by Ralph Mauger 'Le Catillon' after his farm at Le Catillon, Grouville. He also sent his grapes away to England, and likewise found the difficulties of doing so greater than foreseen. At the turn of the millennium La Mare Estate was offered Le Catillon; the company bought it, but the vines were not top producers or of top quality and after a few years they were grubbed up.

The new owner of La Mare, Trevor Owen, confirmed Tim Crowley as manager and then as managing director. A previous wine maker at Brown Bros in Australia, Simon Day, whose family owned a vineyard in the UK, joined La Mare as a wine maker together with Andrew Blayney, who helped oversee the transition from the first regime to the next one.

An extensive re-planting programme has taken place at La Mare since that time, with only three rows currently left of the vines first planted by the Blayney family during their period of ownership. At the time of writing there are 18 vergées under vines. Simon Day returned to the UK in 2002 to take over his father's vineyard consultancy business but remains a consultant and visitor at La Mare. The winemaker is Daniel de Carteret, who trained in the New Zealand wine industry and took up his appointment at La Mare in 2006.

Speaking about La Mare wines at the time of writing in 2017, Tim Crowley said: 'The wine at La Mare is good, but we just don't have enough of it.'

In the past 17 years there has been much expansion at La Mare: new vines, new wines and new apple orchards planted both in St Mary and St Lawrence. A new winery was built in 2006, costing £2 million, purpose-built, temperature controlled and 'state of the art'. A new distillery has also been built, from which grape brandy is made and from which the first release is expected by 2020.

Tim said: 'Having a vineyard, together with a distillery to take care of surplus production, is quite a luxury and I believe it is unique in British vineyards.'

The estate sells to its own retail businesses – in town, at the Estate itself and at the Airport. The majority of the wine remains Seyval blanc, plus a small amount of Pinot Noir, and the other 'new' red wine varieties of Regent, Rondeau, Orion and Phoenix.

He added: 'The emphasis of our business is products based in our environment, made locally from what we can. What can the land produce? Vines, apples, cream from Jersey cows, raspberries and strawberries for fruit liqueurs. The criterion is that there has got to be a connection to Jersey.'

~ 12 ~

Spirits

'The baleful consumption of spirituous liquors has also prodigiously increased at the expense of the agriculture, the health and the morals of the people. The farmer no longer finds, as in good polity he ought to, the means of disposing of his surplus for the home consumption of the country'

Rev Edward Durrell, in introduction to new edition (1835) of Philippe Falle's book, *An Account of the Island of Jersey*

Both to the east, in Normandy, and to the south, in Brittany, farmhouse 'artisanal' distillation has been part of the local culture for generations. To what extent this was the case in Jersey it is difficult to say. The production of any sort of hooch would have been frowned upon by the prominent Methodist culture in local rural life, but that would not have inhibited those who wished to do so. At one time, spirits were also very cheap to buy.

It is known that some farms did install stills for producing an *eau de vie* in years of apple glut. In October 1837, the periodical *Caesarea* informed its readers that 'Mr G Whitfield was allowed to establish a distillery for the rectifying of spirits, subject to the same conditions as are other distilleries in the Island.' It seems, therefore, that a certain amount of distillation did take place in the course of the 19th Century.

Imports from Spain and Portugal in the early part of the Century included wine, brandy, fruit and salt. Wine and brandy were also imported from Sicily: one set of customs statistics details a total of 100,000 galls of brandy over the course of a year. From France, chief imports were wine, brandy and livestock, which form the principle articles of import: 70,000 gallons of wine, 50,000 gallons brandy and about 2,500 head of oxen.

Commentators of the time remark on the great quantity of spirits drunk – St Helier, like any English town, had its own 'Gin Lane'. Gin was generally referred to as 'Geneva brandy' and there were a variety of spellings such as '*dodevi*' and '*vedue*'. There was considerable trade with Holland and much 'geneva' imported, along with cheese, hops and tiles. The quantity depended on the price of brandy, consumers going for the cheaper option. The volume imported averaged about 45,000 gallons annually.

The continual imposition of ever higher excise duty over the years helped to remove the temptation of drunkenness from drinking cheap spirits – the influence of education and temperance also helped. In the end, those mostly affected were a different sort of person: not the labouring classes so much as the immigrant in retirement or with private income, with not much to do at home other than to drive into town to stock up with supplies of gin and other spirits.

If some farmers continued to make hooch for private consumption, they did so privately and very inconspicuously. The production of hooch increased during the Occupation, when imported spirits were difficult or impossible to buy. It has been alleged that one of the centres of production was the former premises of Boudin's bicycle shop in Bath Street. Customs took a very dim view of those who wanted to make their spirits at home, but at the turn of the 20th and 21st Centuries, things were about to change.

IT was Andrew Blayney of La Mare Vineyards who suggested that they consider distilling cider to make apple brandy. Bob Blayney recollected: 'Our advocate quickly told us that such activity on Jersey was against the law. Yet the chief of Jersey Customs was intrigued by the idea and began to investigate. He discovered that under certain circumstances it was possible and gave Andrew his blessing to drive off to Calvados country to find a traditional old copper "pot still" of the type that made the finest Calvados. At Lisieux he was introduced to a cider maker who had not used his still since the evening when the Allied troops freed his village following D-Day in 1944. He admitted that drinking freshly distilled apple spirit straight from this still that evening had knocked out every man in the village.'

La Mare once again called for help from an old family friend, this time from a well-known Cognac brandy family and 'who just happened to have an interest in Calvados as well'. A young graduate of a distilling college was lured to Jersey to join the La Mare team. Correctly conditioned maturing casks, empty of course, were quietly brought from France and in 1994 La Mare Distillery, under Andrew's control, was in business. It gained strong support and eventually it was on sale in the Heathrow shop of one of London's great wine merchants.

Under the successor leadership of Tim Crowley, La Mare continued with and expanded the project.

The Blayneys used the produce of their own apple orchard and buying in from neighbours; perhaps around ten tons of apples a year; La Mare is now (2017) taking about 150 tons and aims to expand that to close to 250 tons over the next five years. The trees to produce that volume of apples are already planted in the ground. In one site in St Lawrence there are 5,000 trees and there are very many apple suppliers throughout the Island.

Tim Crowley said: 'For our cider, we like to use our own apples only, but the brandy production is a great community project. We take apples from about 80 suppliers, ranging from a carrier bag full to about 20 tons maximum. Anything in between is accepted – and we pay a much higher rate compared to the UK. We don't want apples to rot on the ground, so we encourage everybody to bring them along. Every bottle of brandy has dozens of suppliers inside the bottle!

With the passage of time, there had been a vastly increased availability to La Mare of supplies of cider apples – they hope to double their supplies of apples from their own orchard within five years of the time of writing in 2017. This has helped them to build up stocks of apple brandy to mature and to allow for greater regularity of supply in the future, as well as to allow for sufficient stocks to be kept back to sell at an older, more matured age. For Christmas 2018 they plan to release their first XO 10 year old apple brandy.

Harvesting apples for their cider and brandy now takes up the lion's share of their time during the harvest season, said managing director Tim Crowley.

Their brandy is distributed both in the UK, through wholesalers selling to farm shops and fine grocery stores, but mainly within Jersey, at their own retail outlets in town, at the La Mare Estate itself and at the their duty-free Airport outlet, as well as to the local hotel and hospitality trade.

Another very popular product has been the La Mare Apple brandy cream liqueur, using Jersey cream, which rivals any of the industrially made cream liqueurs available on the market.

FOR years, Richard and Sarah Matlock at La Robeline had wanted to make a Jersey Apple Brandy from their cider. In due course they were able to acquire a 1950 'Parisienne' mobile still. Richard found the old, originally horse-drawn travelling still in the Pays d'Auge area of Normandy. He brought it to Jersey and restored it – and they have named it 'Sylvie'.

They are now producing their own *Eau de Vie dé Jèrri* and '*L'Esprit dé Jèrri*', colloquially known as '*La Pomm'thie*', a very smooth apple brandy, aged in oak barrels for a minimum of three years.

The early months of 2013 saw their first distillation of 'Spirit of Liberation' – *Eau de Bière*, made from Liberation Brewery's international award winning Liberation Ale. The brewery joined up with La Robeline Cider Company to use their French artisan continuous still. The 7.5% beer (slightly higher per cent than Liberation Ale at 4%) has produced a 60% spirit. This will then be cut to produce the Spirit of Liberation Eau de Bière at 40%.

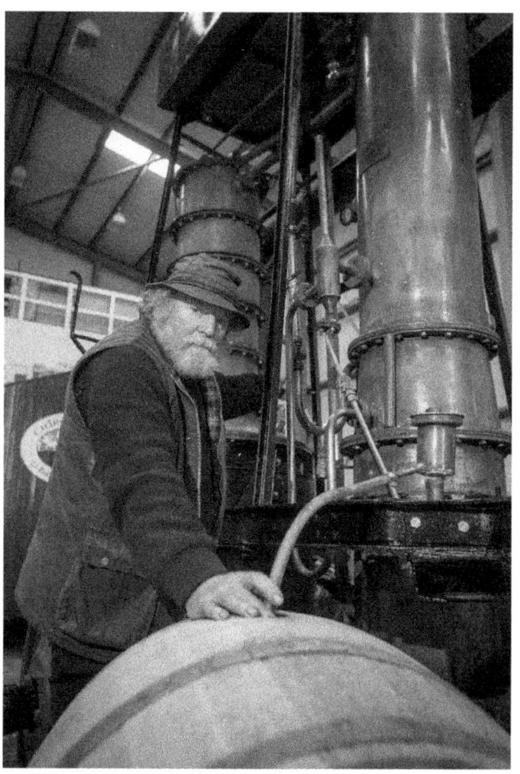

Richard Matlock at work distilling brandy
(Photo courtesy Gary Grimshaw)

Liberation group managing director Mark Crowther said: 'It is an experiment and we are still in the process of deciding on price, quantity and how we are going to brand the product. It is a work in progress! A great Genuine Jersey project to be involved in. 'The next stage will be to experiment with mixing our eau de bière in different cocktails.'

La Robeline also intend to launch an apple apèritif, like the French '*Pommeau*' (a mix of cider and spirit aged in oak barrels) and to expand the range to include cider vinegar.

IN recent times, (2013) La Mare has extended its range of spirits to produce a gin and also a 'Jersey Royal vodka' – using what would otherwise be waste potatoes to make a base neutral spirit. It has been difficult to establish these as brands. 'The trouble with gin these days is that it is trendy and there are hundreds of micro-distilleries making boutique gins,' said Tim Crowley. 'It is unique to make an apple brandy and even more unique to make Jersey cream liqueur with fresh Jersey cream. Gin does not have that advantage.'

He continued: 'We have learned that the Jersey Royal is not a great potato for making vodka, because the starch conversion is low. Big, dry English or Irish potatoes would be far better, which make "bowls of flour"'. Limited supplies of both gin and vodka have been made that balances supply with demand.

However, the La Mare vodka followed, by a few years, the sudden prominence in Jersey headlines of the so-called 'Jersey vodka project'.

THE idea behind this project was to make vodka from waste Jersey Royals and create a new product that would help the agricultural industry.

The advantages were summed up by the potato grower leading the project on behalf of the Jersey Export Potato Marketing Board, Mick Cotillard:

> 'Instead of struggling outdoors in vile winter weather in early January to plant potatoes, or to force the crop to produce as early as possible by covering the Island's fields in plastic, farmers could take their time, let the potatoes grow as big as they want and harvest them at leisure, for potentially the same return, without the environmental impact of waste potatoes rotting in the soil.'

The project was supported by some Islanders, criticised by others; the majority of Islanders, who had never previously thought of Jersey being a vodka producing Island, were simply amused.

The benefits to Jersey of proceeding with the so-called 'vodka project' were spelt out to an audience of supermarket managers and buyers, growers and farmers at a presentation held by the vodka project team of the Jersey Potato Export Marketing Board at Fort Regent in November 2003.

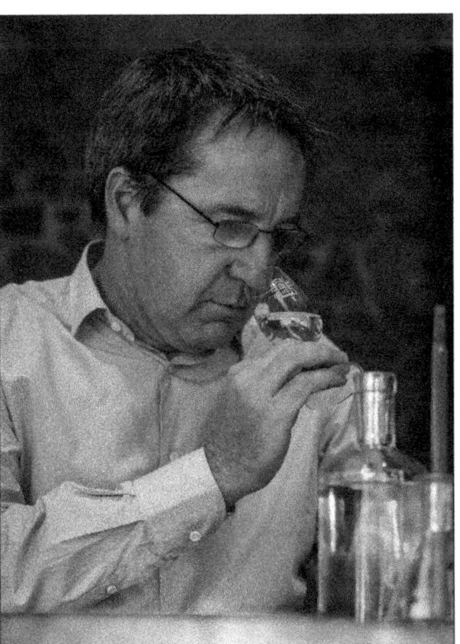

Tim Crowley tasting vodka
(Photo courtesy Gary Grimshaw)

Two Senators present, former Agriculture committee president Senator Dick Shenton and the then Agriculture president, Senator Jean Le Maistre, expressed their support. Senator Shenton said that it was the first time that the agricultural industry had come up with such a scheme to help itself, something that was 'excellent to hear'. Senator Le Maistre said that the project team deserved congratulations. 'People are clamouring for agricultural diversification,' he said, 'and this is one plan for that to happen'.

A potato grower, Ted Egré, said he had arrived as a sceptic but would now think again. Also present were States Members who were not so positive about the idea: St John Deputy Philip Rondel said he had not been persuaded by anything he had heard at the presentation, referring to the problems caused by alcohol, the traffic movements to and from the distillery 24 hours a day, seven days a week, and the impact on residents. And St Lawrence Deputy Maurice Dubras said he did not think that the many negative aspects of the scheme had been addressed in the presentation.

During the presentation, the project team said that benefits of the vodka scheme would include cash coming into the economy, a new tourism attraction in the form of a visitor centre, a new employer looking to fill around two dozen job vacancies and additional products in the form of bottled water as a spin-off from the very pure water supply needed for vodka production. More than £1m a year would be returned to growers. Public money spent on supporting the project (£105,000) was described by Mr Cotillard as 'a good and cost-efficient use'. Accountant Andrew Le Cheminant confirmed that the project was likely to return £0.38m to growers in the first year, rising to £1.38m within five years.

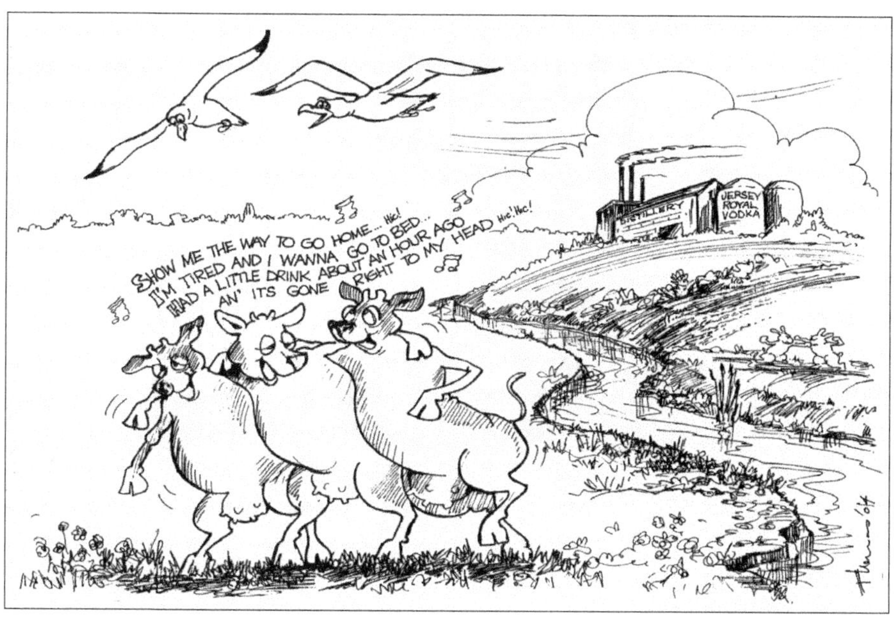

'Right that's a fiver you owe me ... I distinctly heard you say a distillery wouldn't harm the environment!' (Cartoon courtesy Al Thomas)

That meeting was probably the high point of the project. Whatever the merits of the scheme, a distillery needed to be placed somewhere, and no one could be found who wanted to live beside a large distillery. A proposal that it would be sited in a field near the gates to St John's Manor was not greatly appreciated by its owner or with other neighbours. Separately, members of the Jersey Farmers Union were having cold feet about the project, the proposed cost of which was rising astronomically. A general reaction was that they had expected a small-scale operation in a converted potato shed, not a multi-million pound distillery with visitors centre attached – that was by no means what they had envisaged or signed up for.

So the two separate issues of location and viability combined to defeat the project, and it was left to La Mare a few years latter to produce vodka on a much more modest scale, with the help of a grant from the Economic Development Department.

IN 2017, shortly before the book went to print, a new distillery was created, calling itself, reasonably enough, Britain's most southerly distillery' – since it is based at Le Hocq. The young distiller, Alex Curtis, makes 'Jersey Gin' and 'Rock vodka'.

The La Côte' Distillery is not only Britain's most southerly distillery, but perhaps also one of the smallest, since he uses his garden shed as a distillery. Inside the shed he keeps the mash tun, the copper still and the other equipment he needs to make his product.

He does not buy in a base alcoholic wash, he does everything from scratch, he explained, which explains the 'Genuine Jersey' designation for his products. That means buying in barley, using that as a base for the wash and then distilling that – three times – to make the spirit. So not poteen, by any stretch of the imagination, but a clean spirit with the scent of citrus, something to savour rather than drowning it with tonic, ice and a slice.

Micro-distilleries are very much a growth area in the UK economy, following the lead of the countless micro-breweries that have sprung up in recent years.

The predominant flavour for the gin is juniper and the vodka retains a trace off the barley from which it comes. There is very little barley grown in Jersey at the moment, but he hopes that might be changing. He creates the wash from barley and that creates the liquid that is distilled.

In the gin, he uses local herbs as the botanicals, such as juniper, coriander and rosemary, as well as more exotic botanicals. He varies the botanicals slightly with every batch he makes. But the most important ingredient is water – good quality Jersey water from the mains.

'It is more a bit of fun than it is anything else,' Alex said. 'Very much a start-up, a chance to experiment with botanicals and to produce interesting flavours, to enjoy myself – and, of course, to create a product that people might actually want to buy.'

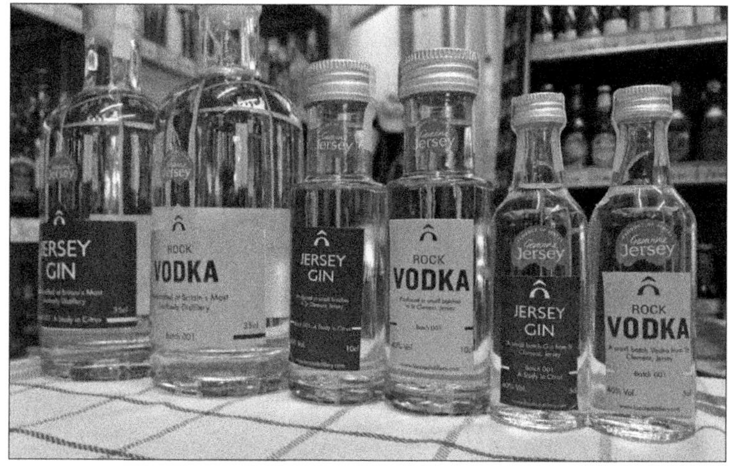

~ 13 ~

Water and non-alcoholic Drinks

> 'Could men be more satisfied with the common drink, water, I mean no people in the world are more liberally stored with water than we of this Island.
>
> 'Tis of my opinion, the greatest wonder of this Island that whereas 'tis but, as it seems, a great rock standing in the midst of the salt sea, it abounds beyond what is seen in any country under Heaven, with both fresh and excellent springs which gush out of the hard rock and bubble up everywhere, running in a thousand pretty brooks and stream among the Dales till they lose themselves in that great receptacle of water, the Ocean'
>
> Rev Philippe Falle, *Description of Jersey* (1694)

There are, as Philippe Falle says in his 1694 book, plenty of springs of good quality water in the Island.

Natural springs are said to come (in part) from France – and it was strenuously maintained at one time that these springs come from the Pyrenees region, flowing through an underground river system and through (it is nice to think) caverns measureless to man. What truth there is in these claims is not a controversy which this author is anxious to enter, but it is undeniable that Jersey is plentifully supplied with natural springs of excellent drinking water.

How this water was stored, treated and then supplied to the public, in past centuries, is another matter altogether. Hence is an early 19th Century comment: 'The pump water on this [east] side of the Island is all bad; a strong chalybeate spring is used for general purposes, which becomes turbid on its admixture with spirits.'

The David Place chemists, De Faye's (Royal warrant holders and suppliers of perfume to Lillie Langtry), decided to bottle water from their own bored well; the water came from the rock bed through a steel pipe – to all intents and purposes it was an artesian spring. De Faye's Natural Spring Table water (non-aerated) was sold at a price of 4s.2d. a dozen in the early years of the 20th Century. This was eventually given up because it was no longer economic. The spring from which it was taken is still in existence outside the shop, but the purifying, testing and bottling became too expensive. Keeping a French mineral water was less expensive than producing their own.

OF all the massive undertakings entailed in the construction of Fort Regent, perhaps the greatest one was the sinking of the well. Work commenced in December 1806 and was not completed until two years later, in October 1808. The pump and machinery for lifting the water through a height of more than 200 feet was manufactured by Henry Macauley, a noted marine engineer of the day. Although it was claimed that the pump could be worked by men or horses, it was also noted that: '24 men working for two hours, without fatiguing themselves, can with ease pump into the cisterns 800 gallons of water.'

IT is one of those 'believe it or not' facts that the Schweppes company producing aerated mineral water and soft drinks, was for a while owned by a Jersey partnership.

The production of mineral water was begun in the late 18th Century by the talented mechanic, jeweller and amateur scientist, Jacob Schweppe. Herr Schweppe had been born in Germany, but moved to Geneva as a young man and made a name for himself there before moving to London to pursue business opportunities with his inventions that helped create the aerated water industry. He and his daughter, Colette, worked profitably there and in 1798, as he prepared for retirement, he sold three-quarters of his company to three Jerseymen, Robert Brohier and Henry and Francis Lauzun.

Robert Brohier was a great-grandson of Matthieu Brohier, a merchant and a refugee from Provence after the Revocation of the Edict of Nantes in 1685. Both of his sons married into Jersey families and had trading links with Southampton in the 18th Century. One of Brohier's activities in the Island was the manufacture of soap. His nephew, Henry Brohier, a medical student, wrote a thesis for his medical degree at Paris University in 1821 on the subject of natural and artificial mineral waters, clearly inspired by his uncle's association with Schweppes. He married the sister of a Bailiff of Jersey.

Henry Lauzun was a captain in the Royal Staff Corps and as a surveying draughtsman for the Duke of Richmond – worked on his 1795 map. Francis Lauzun, probably the brother of Henry, married Robert Brohier's sister.

Henry was commended by the States for his work, under General Don, of constructing military roads – 'Captain Lauzun of the Royal Staff Corps who… has acquitted himself in a manner which reflects honour on his zeal and ability.'

The partnership of 1798 of the thee Jerseymen was dissolved by a deed dated 3 May 1824. The two Lauzuns departed from the business. Since 1801 Robert Brohier had had the largest share in the business. He had taken up residence in the company's Margaret Street premises in London and had assumed responsibility for the commercial management of the business. He was the last member of the firm to have known its founder personally. Another shareholder was Richard Annesley Sparkes. He sold the business in 1834, by which time he had acquired the interests of the Brohier family.

THE Jersey company, A E Smith and Co, produced and bottled a range of soft drinks, latterly from their premises on the Longueville Road. Production ceased in 2003 with the closure of its bottling plant. It was then owned by the C I Traders group.

A rival company – described as a Mineral Water Manufacturer – was established by John Ernest Le Dain in the 1930s. Mr Le Dain had had a drink problem so perhaps this was his road to reform. The works occupied a premises at 22 Hill Street and the company is listed in the *Jersey Almanac* between 1935 and 1957 when they eventually sold out to Smith's. Le Dain's produced a wide range of soft drinks and their bottle labels attest to the professionalism of the enterprise – one is depicted on the front cover of this book and another here.

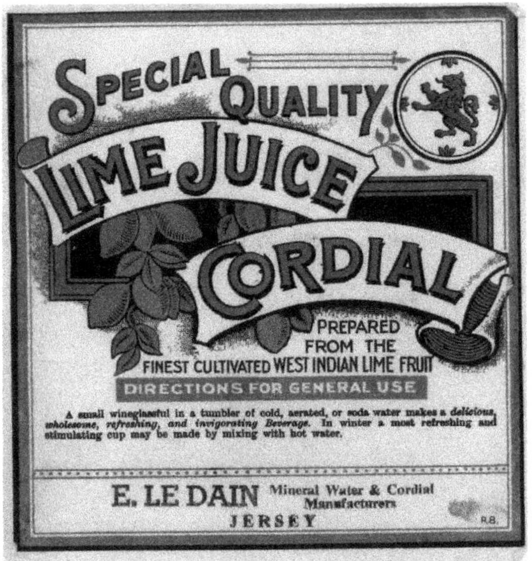

~ 14 ~

Modern Times

(i) SCENES FROM THE 20th CENTURY; PRE-WAR

In 1901, Adam Black wrote in his guide book, *Guide to Jersey* about the hotels in town and the horse omnibuses lining up at the head of the pier to await passengers disembarking from the Mailboat.

He quotes the prices charged by the major hotels of the time:

[1]Pomme d'Or, 7s.9d; [2]The Star, 6s.8d; [1]Royal Yacht, 8s.6d; [2]Weighbridge, 5s.8d.

On the Esplanade: [1*]Minor's Hotel, 8s.6d; [1*]The Grand Hotel, with baths, from 9s upwards, both fronting the sea.

By the side of the Town Church: The Grasshopper, 6s.

Opposite the entrance into the Jersey Parliament House: the [1]Halkett Hotel, 7s.

Head of Broad Street, in good situation: the [1]British Hotel, 7s.6d to 9s.;No 31 Broad St, the [2]Temperance Hotel, 6s.6d. In David Place; [1*]Bree's Hotel, 8s.6d and upwards. The Hotel Calvados near the station of the Eastern Railway.

(The figures indicate the class of the hotel, the asterisks those good of their class.) He also states that there was an abundance of furnished apartments and lodgings all over the town and Island. The most fashionable quarter in the town was the neighbourhood of St Mark's Church.

FOR the Battle of Flowers in 1912, Charlie Chaplin played in Jersey at the Opera House as a star performer of Fred Karno's Comedy Company production of *A Night in the English Music Hall.* Chaplin played 'an inebriated swell, trying to light a cigar from electric light. On 15 August, at the Battle of Flowers, he so disrupted the performance that he was reprimanded at the Town Hall.

THE Striped Monkey (*Le Singe Rayé*) was a racy place of entertainment, which opened in June 1928. It was located in Cross Street, above the building that later housed Orange & Co, wine merchants. In its opening, it was advertised as the 'weirdest, queerest, cutest and most attractive café in the Island. 'Music was supplied by the 'Jungle Jazzes Band. It was run by Senator George Troy and his partner, Percy Waymark Hoar.

Outside it was painted pink, and showed monkeys running up palm trees. Inside the decoration was a combination of South Sea Islands strands, tropical jungles and a grotto in which 'queer animals' were depicted. Admission was free and so many people booked for the first week that there was no room for dancing, because extra chairs and tables were placed on the dance floor.

In 1991, someone who had been an habitué there told the *Jersey Evening Post*: 'Young ladies hung out there. There was a lot more drinking than dancing and a lot of smooching and I was twice thrown out because I was only 16 and under age.' Another lady remembered passing it in 'careful decorum on the other side of the road. Victoria College House boys used it for surreptitious, nocturnal assignations.'

And another recollection: 'There was no need for doormen, because nobody thought of fighting in those days. No one remembered it closing down – it just faded away.'

A NEW licensing law was passed by the States in 1929. It provided for:

* Two categories of hotel licenses (first class and second class)
* Ordinary licenses
* Boarding House licenses
* Licenses for places of entertainment (2 categories)
* Restaurant Licenses
* Club Licenses
* Off-Licenses
* Merchant's Licence.

The fee for a first class hotel was £100; a 2nd class hotel was £50, ordinary and wholesale licenses were £50; a club license £25; off-licence £15, boarding house £20 and for a first-class place of entertainment £200. The costs were deemed too expensive by the *Jersey Critic*.

A fire occurred at Le Quesne Wine Stores in Burrard Street on 20 August 1930, and in November of the same year, a serious fire also occurred at Daly's pub (now The Lamplighter).

Five people were rescued from Daly's, including a baby, after a ladder was found by the head porter of the nearby Royal Yacht Hotel.

From: *The Islander*, 15 February 1939:

> 'Sherry Parties – the most fashionable way of entertaining friends today is by means of Sherry party. A Sherry party is held in a private house (or private room in a club, hotel or restaurant) between 6pm and 8pm.
>
> 'The advantage of a Sherry party over a luncheon or tea party is that the hour at which it takes place enables the host's or hostess' men friends to come along after the day's work.
>
> 'It is essential that the Sherry should be really good Sherry and it is customary, in addition to cigarettes, to provide light hors d'oeuvres, such as olives, sandwiches, cheese straws, potato chips etc. all of which go admirably with Sherry.
>
> 'A Sherry party is thus by far the most economical way of entertaining large or small groups of friends. Furthermore, there is no waste as Sherry remains good and sound in a decanter indefinitely and, if not used, can be consumed at leisure subsequently.'

(ii) SCENES FROM THE OCCUPATION

AS the threat of war approached in late 1938–1939, Air Raid Protection warder training and shelters were constructed on the site of the old Sandringham Hotel, Colomberie.

ON 17 June 1940, General Charles de Gaulle decided to escape from France, flying out from Bordeaux Airport with Major-General Edward Spears, Churchill's personal representative to the French premier, Paul Reynaud. The French government, in its temporary refuge in Bordeaux, had decided to seek an armistice with Hitler and de Gaulle feared arrest if he stayed in France. The aeroplane stopped to refuel at Jersey Airport, and Spears took the passenger to the Airport canteen; de Gaulle asked for a cup of coffee. Spears later wrote:

> 'I handed it to him, whereupon, taking a sup, he said, in a voice that indicated that, without implying criticism, he must nevertheless proclaim the truth: that this was tea and he had asked for coffee. It was his first introduction to the tepid liquid which in England passes for either one or the other. His martyrdom had begun.'

De Gaulle was invited to lunch at the Alexandra Hotel in St Peter while refuelling took place. There he bought a case of whisky, apparently, though as he did not enjoy the taste of whisky it must have been Spears who bought it as a gift for Churchill. The cost of the 'House of Lords' Old Scotch Whisky would have cost General Spears £3.18s.6d, at the cost of 3s 6d a bottle. Shortly after their de Havilland Flamingo plane took off from Jersey for the last leg of their journey to England, they were pursued by a German plane which they were able to evade and land safely – de Gaulle was in London the same evening. The next day he made his first BBC broadcast appeal.

THE notorious German bombing raid on the Channel Islands took place on the evening of 28 June 1940. The Old Court House Hotel in St Aubin was hit, and so was the Pomme d'Or, where one bomb crashed through the roof. Mr Ferrand, the landlord of the Bunch of Grapes (Lamplighter pub) was killed.

The recollection of Anthony Faramus, then working at the Continental Hotel in St Saviour Road:

> 'By June 1940 'weeds had started to sprout up the lower face of the building and litter was strewn about. The bar was open and lively, with the staff enjoying the supply of alcohol at the bar. Without legal title, we were squatters by permission of the management in exile, having been granted open-sesame to lock, stock and barrel.'

In the negotiations between the civil government and the military regime of the Occupiers, minor matters were open to discussion and compromise. The first of these was a decision on the opening hours for public houses. For the first two weeks of the Occupation, closing time had been set at 9pm. Alexander Coutanche (the Bailiff) suggested a one-hour extension. This was agreed by the Commandant, Gussek, providing that only beer and wine were served; spirits were reckoned to be too provocative. He may have been right, though in the event he was to find out that the likeliest offenders were among his own troops.

Most of the Occupation forces kept themselves to themselves and used the German recreational facilities that were provided for them. There were *Soldatenheime* – the German equivalent of Naafi Officers' Club at Fort d'Auvergne Hotel; Other Ranks had their own facilities at the Mayfair, all ranks could use St Brelade's Bay Hotel for relaxation during their off-duty hours.

They were run by Red Cross Sisters, who were themselves strictly controlled in dress and behaviour – no lipstick or nail varnish was allowed and hair to be cut short. The only greeting allowed was *Heil Hitler*! Officers had separate rooms in the all ranks clubs and proper respect due to rank always adhered to. The clubs served food, but as the Occupation went on, this was likely to be sparse and disappointing.

The alternative to the *Soldatenheime* was to drink too much, in private, and drunkenness became a continuing problem, especially as troops' morale worsened during the course of the Occupation.

Quite early on after the Germans had occupied the Island, they took over the Ann Street Brewery, The sugar stock apparently was not taken into stock by the German brewer but was shared during the first and second year of the Occupation among the workforce in the brew-house.

He apparently said that under the German *Reinheitsgebot* (German Beer Purity Laws) sugar was not necessary for the production of beer; the only ingredients that could be used in the production of beer were water, barley and hops.

The *Reinheitsgebot* is no longer part of German law, it has been replaced by the Provisional German Beer Law, which allows constituent components prohibited in the *Reinheitsgebot*, such as yeast, wheat, malt and cane sugar, but which no longer allows un-malted barley.

German breweries are very proud of the *Reinheitsgebot*, and many of them (even brewers of wheat beer) claim to still abide by it.

In 1942, the States Department of Essential Commodities: informed the public, with reference to: 'Cider Manufacture and Sale (Jersey) Cider.

By this Order it is prohibited to manufacture, sell or offer for sale any cider except under licence of the Department.

ON Hitler's insistence, no strongpoint was to surrender as a result of a shortage of food or water – the troops were expected to hold out to the last round of ammunition.

Most positions were equipped with drinking water supplies contained in the ubiquitous Trinkwasser tank and each bunker had a large stock of locally produced aerated water (usually, but erroneously, referred to as 'Vichy Water').

In St Ouen's Bay, most defence positions were additionally provided with boreholes which contained a hand-pump and a cistern holding seven cubic meters of fresh water. One such bunker was also provided at Battle HQ at Le Coin Varin, St Peter.

THE Victor Hugo Hotel at Grève d'Azette, run by a M and Mme Blatié, was a German brothel during the Occupation. The young Joe Mière was an apprentice at Axis Supplies Engineering Works, Hilgrove Street in 1942, was sent by his employers to deliver light bulbs that had been ordered. It was a noteworthy experience for him and he enjoyed chatting to the French prostitutes – but he did not tell his girlfriend, who would have been shocked.

'ALTAR wine was very difficult to obtain, but supplies were found in France. The wine was no longer available in bottles so that small casks had to be purchased and brought to the Island. The most sensible place to store the wine proved to be the boys' vestry where all our cassocks and cotters hung up in rows on coat hooks. Equally sensibly, no drinking vessels of any sort were left to tempt foolish young boys. However, it was not an uncommon sight to see a neatly buttoned up cassock and clean cotter prostrate on the floor underneath the cask's little wooden tap while the wine dropped gently between the open lips.'

Leo Harris

(iii) SOME SCENES FROM POST-WAR JERSEY

In December 1952, the Bristol coaster the *Brockley* was wrecked on D on the Minquiers. A party of Jersey fishermen went aboard and found 14 cases of Bristol cream sherry. These were hidden on the Minquiers from Customs, and were brought back bit by bit to Jersey under the floor boards of Bob Viney's boat.

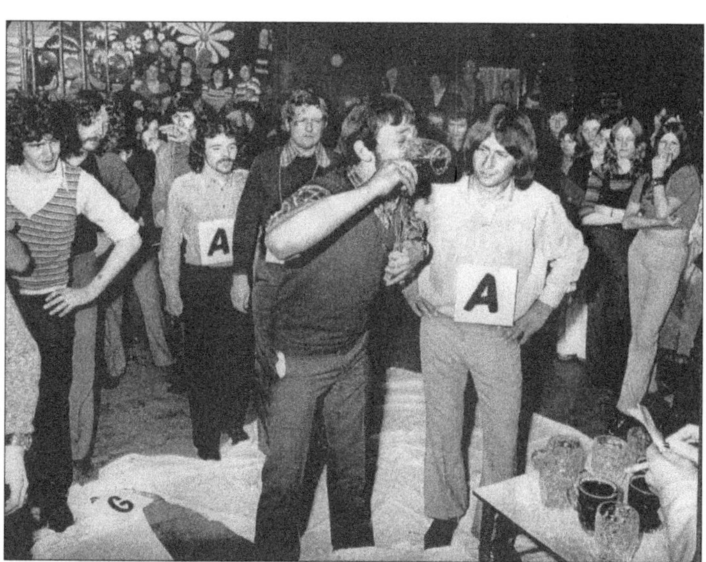

A beer drinking contest at the Plaza Ballroom on Leap Day Night 1972. Girlfriends had to wait patiently until gallons of the local brew, Mary Ann, were consumed before they could pop the question (© Jersey Evening Post)

Fred Le Feuvre, the publican of the Seymour Inn retired in 1979. He took with him some of the furnishings of the Inn, such as the dartboard, to a hut on the Minquiers owned by Gordon Com. It was the scene of subsequent jolly evenings with his friends, and became known as the most southerly private drinking den in the British Isles.

ART WALLSER, a Jerseyman who returned to Jersey having served for a short time in the Navy and then taught Art in the West Country, created his alter ego, Gene Le Bean, named after his son Eugene. The two or three frame comic strip first made its appearance courtesy of the *Jersey Evening Post* features editor, Peter Stuckey, and was preserved in a series of books. Gene was a crabber always portrayed smoking a large pipe spouting a volcanic amount of smoke and ash, (as did Art) and a huge pair of wellingtons always oozing water. He had cut holes in them to let the water run out. He also had a boat called Beryl (named after a dimly remembered hymn ('for those in Beryl on the sea').

He was permanently well oiled, and with his friends, Victoria Pier and Archie Rondel, he offered an alternative and mildly subversive comment on his times. Eugene can frequently be seen as the young curly haired boy by Gene's side.

LOCALLY brewed Lady Hamilton Pale Ale went on sale to the public for the first time at the 2011 Beer Festival. It was the creation of Nigel Romeril and was sold alongside a hundred other real ales at the three-day Jersey Beer and Cider Festival.

In June 2011 he was granted a licence to sell his beer from his family's farm. His Brewery is called the Pocket Brewery. Just as this book is going to print, another micro-brewery is setting up in business in St Ouen, calling itself the Stinky Bay Brewing Company. Partners are Digby Ibbotson and Matthew Topman.

THE Jersey Beer and Cider Festival, started in 1988, is organised by the Jersey branch for the Campaign for Real Ale (formed in 1976 by a group of Jersey Real Ale drinkers). Jon le Sueur, committee member, said in 2012 that 'Lots of people are switching to local beers from industrially-made brands, which of course benefits the economy and the craft-style brewing that Camra aims to promote.

> 'The Liberation Brewery has done an enormous amount of work to increase the scale and promoting of real ale in general. The work they have done has made people more attuned to drinking local ale and increasing the variety of real ales on sale.'

The 2016 Festival, which celebrated the Jersey branch's 40th anniversary, exhibited over 100 real ales and ciders in what was the Island's biggest marquee, with two extra marquees on either side of it; for the duration of the Festival it is the Island's largest licensed area.

Shortly before publication of this book, the organisers announced that as it was impossible to run the festival profitably, there would be no festival in the future – certainly not in the way to which the Island had become accustomed in the past 29 years.

~ 15 ~

Health and Sobriety

The evil effects of intemperance – the arguments for and against statutory interference in the freedom to drink moderately and ethical imperatives to refrain from over-indulgence in alcohol have remained constant over centuries.

The evils of drinking were graphically illustrated in a 'representation of tableaux vivants' held on 12 August 1856 at the Queen's Assembly Rooms, Belmont Road. The programme consisted of:

1 The Happy Meeting
2 The first introduction to the bottle
3 Drunkenness and its effects
4 Distress occasioned by the bottle
5 Beggary, but still clinging to the bottle
6 Cold and Want, causing death, the work of the bottle
7 Brutal violence, through the use of the bottle
8 Murder, with the instrument of misery, the bottle
9 The bottle has done its work
10 Gin, its effects personified
11 Signing the pledge
12 Water and its happy results

Half of the profits of the entertainment were devoted towards the support of St Andrew's Sunday School and the other half for the Temperance Society.

THE Salvation Army is still prominent in Island life, operating mainly from its Citadel in Minden Street. There used to be a second town corps in Newgate Street and others in Trinity, Gorey, St Aubin and St Ouen – at a time when there was not so much travelling between the parishes.

The present citadel had moved from place to place, but settled down in

Minden Street in 1920 in what was then the Prince of Wales Rooms. At one time it shared the Queens Assembly Rooms in Belmont Road with the Jersey Militia.

The Jersey Temperance Federation produced a booklet in 1927 comparing the consumption of alcohol in Jersey with that of Great Britain. The conclusions of the report were that Jersey people consumed 25,159 gallons of Spirit, or Alcohol, at proof strength and there was double the amount of licensed houses in Jersey than in an average English community of the same size.

THE article below appeared in the publication the *Jersey Leader* on 16 July 1937. With due allowance made for the difference between 1937 and 2017, the article is worth reading with today's conditions in mind:

THE DRINK TRAFFIC

Once in a while someone of more or less prominence gets up and takes a wallop at our old friend, John Barleycorn. It is then that we are treated to a display of statistics which in the aggregate are usually misleading. That there is more than the ordinary consumption of liquor in Jersey is undeniable but as to who does the consuming is another question. It is well known that the visitor traffic can account for a good proportion of the liquor sold, also that a not inconsiderable amount is carried back to England.

Possessing as we do a large number of well-to-do residents who normally would spend on luxuries such as these more than the average, helps to swell the total still more, and when a few thousand diggers on an annual spree are thrown in for good measure, we are well on the way to accounting for much of the excess consumption over normal local requirements.

Unfortunately, in dealing with what is euphemistically termed the Drink Traffic, too much is left to the imagination of people with strict temperance views, and not enough care is exercised in arriving at a strict and intelligent analysis of the situation. Statistics too often tend to mislead, at the best they mean little, unless accompanied by a complete exposition of conditions governing them. Such peculiar conditions do exist in Jersey, and if there is an excess of drunkenness, as claimed, which I am inclined to think is often more apparent than real, then the cause of this intemperance should be verified. As an advocate of free trade in drink, I am yet to be converted to the idea that restrictive legislation can make people more temperate.

There are other means, and these are usually overlooked by so-called temperance advocates, who, while honest enough in their opinions, are least fitted to entrust with the task of improving conditions in this respect. Drinking, like eating and other pleasures of life we indulge in, are things that require cultivation; those who have learned how to use and not abuse are in a far better position to provide the remedies than people who possess an extreme, if sincere, bias.

Plumb-line

A second extract from this publication follows. This was printed on 12 November 1937:

TEN MILLION PINTS OF BEER

SIR – I was amused to read your comments on the amount of beer drunk in Jersey.

I have looked up the figures and find that 521,532 bottles of spirits were drunk; 3,621,224 bottles of wine, in addition to the 9,386,096 bottles of beer you have mentioned.

There are two ways of looking at these figures, You can think, with envy, of the amount of money the wine merchants and publicans must be making, or one can spend a few pleasant minutes working out just how long that amount of beer would last you, allowing one pint for every 15 minutes, which is a comfortable pace one can keep up for many jolly hours.

I have done more: I have worked out how much each person drinks.

Taking the Island's population as 40,000 adults and 90,000 visitors, the consumption per head works out as follows:

1½ pints of beer a week

1 small glass of whisky each 10 days

1 glass of wine every month.

No one could get drunk, or keep drunk on that modest amount. In fact, I know many who drink as much and consider they are almost teetotal.

W MORRIS

***It would be interesting to try this exercise these days.

In 1952 a branch of Alcoholics Anonymous was established in Jersey. A report at the same time in the *Evening Post* stated:

> 'AA exists solely for the rehabilitation and care of dipsomaniacs. Every drunk cured by AA becomes a member of the movement and will willingly do all in his or her power to help other fellow sufferers.'

The founder member in Jersey was a woman in her 60s, who is likely to have first 'found sobriety' in London AA before moving to Jersey. With one other member in Jersey to begin with, over the next 60 years or so thousands of Jersey people – some regarded as hopeless cases – found sobriety. They came from all walks of life – the only requirement of membership, then and now, being a desire to stop drinking.

A prison group of AA was formed in 1971.

Bringing this up to date, once again we learn – this time, from reports of the Medical Officer of Health, that Jersey's consumption per capita is one of the highest in Europe. Every year around £11,000,000 is spent on alcohol in Jersey. The government enjoys the revenue from alcohol impôts duty. The alcohol industry provides employment opportunities. There is a downward trend, which started in the 1990s, but we consume more alcohol per capita than our UK and French neighbours.

Over a third of young Jersey adults binge drink – in Jersey, young women keep pace with their male peers!

Within the EU, alcohol has been identified as the third highest risk to health, ahead of obesity and behind only tobacco and high blood pressure.

Our current consumption figure of 14.2 litres per capita is roughly equivalent to about 180 bottles of wine, equates to half a bottle a night and an average of 27 units per week for everyone aged 16 and over. This means that on average, all Island adults are exceeding recommended sensible drinking limits. Of course, the reality is more varied than this as some don't drink at all and some drink more than the average.

Alcohol accounts for 42 deaths a year, around five percent of all deaths in Jersey.

Drinkers over 25 mostly drink wine, with beer being the second most popular choice. A small percentage of Islanders (around 3 per cent) have a very heavy drinking problem. Regular drinking amongst the middle-aged and elderly population can be a problem.

The Health Related Behaviour Questionnaire survey conducted in schools every four years reports that 40 per cent of 14–15years are drinking alcohol.

Alcohol is thought to be involved in the majority of violent street crimes and public order offences in Jersey.

Police data shows that around 4% of all road traffic collision involves drinkers who have failed a breath test and that the highest offending group are 21–40 year-olds, causing three out of nine traffic accidents in the last ten years.

Teenage girls over-indulge more than boys.

In general outlet density is positively associated with alcohol consumption and alcohol related problems. The cheaper it is, the more is consumed.

One cannot quarrel with these findings, but perhaps they do need to be treated with some caution, much as the 1937 correspondents of *The Leader* took then current temperance publicity with a pinch of salt.

The statistics may indeed be a cause for concern, but public education on the misuse of alcohol has never been so greatly understood as it is today.

The dangers of drinking and driving, of alcohol as a contributory factor in domestic violence, of binge drinking by young people, of the dangers to health and well-being by excessive consumption, and of under-age drinking – all these are better understood these days than at any time in the past. The public is not so foolish, on the whole, as to imagine that excessive drinking is good for you.

Unfortunately, too many official bodies tend to behave as if the public was, collectively, under-age, on the one hand treating it like a milch cow for collecting taxation income, on the other hand making it more and more difficult to buy and enjoy, inoffensively and legitimately, the pleasures of a moderate consumption of alcohol.

Anyone with memories long enough will remember the television and cinema advertising of cigarettes some half a century ago. Anyone watching an old black-and-white film knows that all too predictably, the characters, when they are not talking, are puffing at cigarettes. Most schoolboys of the mid-20th Century will remember how the majority of their schoolmasters were always puffing on their pipes.

There has been a revolution since then, led by the health campaigners drawing attention to the dangers of tobacco. In a sense they are quite right: tobacco is dangerous, although perhaps the balance between health education and the freedom to behave as one might want, within the confines of the law, does need some re-balancing. The change in smoking habits within fifty years suggest how possible it might be for a similar revolution to occur as far as the consumption of alcohol is concerned. A modern form of Prohibition seems, at times, all too likely. It is in a sense, part of the new Puritanism in our post-modern sad age.

As the *Jersey Evening Post* stated in an editorial on 2 March 2009 on the findings of the 2009 Medical Health Reports: 'Although alcohol can be a friend as a personal pleasure and a social lubricant, if used in excess it soon changes character and becomes the mortal enemy of individuals and society.' Or, as Shakespeare said in Othello: 'Good wine is a good familiar creature, if it be well used'.

The final word can go to St Paul. It may not be politically correct in today's terms, but political correctness was very low down in his world view: 'Be no longer a drinker of water, but use a little wine for your stomach's sake and your frequent infirmities.' (Epistle to Timothy 5, 23)

~ 16 ~

Epilogue

GOING TO THE PUB: Yesterday – today, tomorrow?

I know where Men can still be found,
Anger and clamorous accord,
And virtues growing from the ground,
And fellowship of beer and board,
And song, that is a sturdy cord,
And hope, that is a hardy shrub,
And goodness, that is God's last word –
Will someone take me to a pub?

G K Chesterton

It seems incredible that in every historical time, up until the earlier years of the last century, the 'public house' or its equivalent had one important aim: to provide comfort, warmth, leisure and conviviality for those who were unable to achieve that at home.

If a home had no heating and there was not enough money to buy regularly sufficient fuel or candles, or if you wanted to avoid the landlord, there certainly was another place more like what home should be, but wasn't – and that was the public house. There one might find warmth; there one might find company and sympathy; there was conviviality.

In today's vastly changed social circumstances, none of the above is so likely to apply. A pub might be 'a lifestyle choice', it might be an enjoyable night out, it might be a convenience; it might have a big screen to enjoy televised sports events in the company of fellow-minded enthusiasts – it is unlikely to be a necessity.

Factors such as the much publicised and very true dangers of drink driving and the equal danger of failing a police breathalyser test have caused many country pubs, in particular, to lose much of their business. Whatever one might think about the future advent – at the time of writing – of driver-less cars, at least one point in their favour is that their possible popularity in future years might see a renaissance in the fortunes of the country pub.

Many pubs, recognising that to attract customers there needs to be more than alcoholic drink available, have reinvented themselves as 'gastro-pubs' or at least now serve meals more full and adequate than the traditional bar snacks (or the not so traditional microwaved burnt offering).

Speaking to Chris Lake of the *JEP* when interviewed by him in 1994 about the changing world of pubs, the retail manager of Randalls Vautier, Robin Denton said:

> 'The past ten years have seen some of the most dramatic changes in drinking habits. If, in 1980, you could buy a toastie in a pub, it was a sophisticated place to be. Nowadays customers are far more discerning. They are, rightly, choosy in where they go and what they drink.
>
> 'It's a sign of the times, perhaps, similar to a customer's approach to shopping.... It wasn't that long ago that you could go to a supermarket to buy either a sliced or an un-sliced loaf. No longer. The choice of bread seems limitless. But that is what the customer wants and expects. That is one of the reasons why we made a conscious decision to give more choices of beer than ever before.'

Dick Spink, the tied manager with what was then Ann Street Brewery, remarked in the same interview that he believed town and country pubs were going their own separate ways and described how many of those in St Helier were changing from ale houses to French-style brasseries, while the country parish pubs were turning to real ales and offering eateries for all the family. The situation has become even more marked since that article was written, almost a quarter of a century ago.

In the early 1990s three 'theme pubs' opened, located a short distance away from one another: The Merchant Trader at the Weighbridge, focussing on the old three-cornered trade between Jersey, Canada and South America; the Corinthian in Mulcaster Street, focussing on sport and, just up the road, Chambers, of which *JEP* columnist Gordon Young wrote:

> 'I have never been gobsmacked by a pub in my life – never, that is, until I walked into Chambers. For a start it is enormous, certainly, I would imagine, the largest pub in Jersey. Secondly, the theme of the law courts has been so well-designed that the establishment is more like a series of places of refreshments than a single pub. These range from a comfortable gentleman's club to a magnificent ancient court of law, with, in between, a library and what must be the longest bar in the Island.'

Anyone in the on-license trade must ask: 'Where does the pub go from here?' Its future seems uncertain in a time when, after working at your place of employment, it is more likely you will return home to spend your few leisure hours with the solitary delights and introspective charms of being 'on-line' than in convivial company in a pub.

It must also be admitted that drinking in a pub, in the company of others, is a social activity, with responsible bar staff ensuring that their customers do not drink more than they can carry. In comparison to that, there must be plenty of front doors in Jersey that hide the private drunkenness and over-consumption that takes place within.

Publicans must try ever harder to maintain their customer base. In recent years there have been too many pubs closing down. They must exemplify the virtues of community, friendship, good food and drink and good cheer – and in that sense, be counter-cultural, since there are far too few public spaces in modern times where all these virtues together can otherwise be encountered.

In short, they need to emulate that pub described by J R R Tolkien in *The Lord of the Rings*:

> There is an inn, a merry old inn
> beneath an old grey hill,
> And there they brew a beer so brown
> That the Man in the Moon himself came down
> one night to drink his fill.'

APPENDIX A

DID YOUR ANCESTORS SELL ALCOHOL?

IN the *Jersiaise newspaper* of 28 January 1841, there is a list of all those who sold alcohol applying to renew their licences. This provides a complete list of all outlets in St Helier for the period. The list includes cafes and 'boutiques' (the equivalent of an off-licence today) and a billiard hall. This list was researched by Alexander Glendinning and published in the 1993 Société Jersiaise *Bulletin*. There were 144 re-applying and a handful were not approved; these are marked with an asterisk.

Jean Alexandre	5 Parade Place	Boutique
James Almond	Grande Rue	British Hotel
George Averty	Minden Place	Union Inn
G L Baker	Ann Street	Gas Light Inn
William Baker	9 Belmont Road	Piece and Love
Robert Beecroft	Moulin-de la Ville	Robin Hood
J Binet	39 Parade Place	Town and Country Inn
M Bisson (V Beazely)	Weighbridge	Queen Victoria
Marie Bisson	Hill Street	Robin Hood Inn
B Bivest	24 Royal Square	Café L'Harmonie
H J Blackmore	Church Lane	Globe Coffee House
Eugene Boisnet	7 Wharf Street	Pomme D'Or
Mary Briggs	Cheapside	Prince Albert
John Brown	20 Hill Street	Boutique
Nicolas Brown	Mulcaster Street	Star Tap
Samuel Buckland	Premiere Tour	Sportsman's Inn
John Bryant	6 Peter Street	Devonshire Inn
Elizabeth Clarke	19 Queen Street	Boutique
Daniel Coates	5 Pier Road	White Hart
William Coles	16 Burrard Street	Boutique
Ch Collins	Upper Don Street	Shakespeare Inn
Clement Coutanche	Mont-a-L'Abbe	(nothing listed)
Elie Coutanche	33 Sand Street	Town Battalion
Mary Anne Croom	34 Halkett Place	Boutique
Joseph Cummings	Aquilla Road	Victoria First
John Damer	2 Vine Street	York Hotel
Thomas Daw	5 Kensington Place	Trades' Union
Rt-Geo Dawson	Parade Place	Love and Unity
Thomas De Gruchy	Halkett Place	Old Jersey Inn
Pierre de la Cour	Dicq	Sailor's Return
James Demain	Aquila Road	Beehive
Elie Deslandes	Esplanade	Castle Inn
E De Ste Croix	C du Nord	Success to trade
Daniel Deslandes	Mont Cochon	Travellers' Inn
Ph Dorey	Premiere Tour	First Tower Inn
Phil Esnouf	Premiere Tour	Union and Friends' Inn
Philippe Fauvel	35 Queen Street	Boutique
Francis Ford	Pier Road	Royal Hotel
C J Forrester	24 Queen Street	Admiral Jarvis

Thomas Francis	Waterloo Street	Divan
Edouard Gallichan	26 Royal Square	Pierson Inn
Ph. Gallichan	9 Hilgrove Lane	Victoria Inn
Thomas Gallichan	La Motte Street	Half Moon
Elie-G Gallie	5 Wharf Street	Weighbridge Inn
Josué Gavey	Haut de la Parade	Carters' Inn
Michael Gee	Old Street	Wooden Walls of Old England
Jean Gelender	22 Hill Street	Boutique
William Gibbs	Sand Street	Blue Bells
John Giles	18 Hue Street	Sawyers' Arms
Henry Gilman	Mulcaster Street	Navy Arms
Hugh Godfray	Cattle Street	Aurora Inn
Jean Godfray	Pied-des-Creux	Clarence Inn
Esther Gruchy	Mont Cochon	Boutique
Jean Gruchy	29 Dumaresq Street	Boutique
Thomas Hales	Weigh Bridge	Old London Hotel
John Hall	(nothing listed)	(nothing listed)
Elie Hamon	Rue	Sailor's Wellcome Home
Fanny-Cary Hannise	Simon Place	(nothing listed)
John Hardy	Troopers' Yard	Tap
Philip Hardy	1 Troopers' Yard	Tap
Robert Hicks	Mulcaster Street	Spread Eagle
Jean Huard	Great Union Road	Victoria Inn
Charles Kaines	Burrard House	Boutique
(*) John Kimber	22 Pier Road	Fox and Goose
C Labey	47 Sand Street	Rose and Crown Inn
Harriet Lambert	20 Union Street	Hampshire Inn
Rd. Landbatherland	Havre des Pas	Green Pigeon
Esther Langlois	Burrard Street	Ring the Bells
P Le Boutillier	16 Bath Street	Wellcome Inn
J Le Cornu	3 Caledonia Place	Calendia Hotel
(*) Ph Le Cras	Moulin de la Ville	Army and Navy
Pierre Le Croix	Hilgrove Lane	Entreeaux Artisans
Geo.-H Le Feuvre	7 Francis Street	Brown Bear
Jean Le Feuvre	45 Hill Street	Boutique
Phle. Nic Le Feuvre	66 Colomberie	Brothers Inn
Philippe Le Gresley	4 Sand Street	Swift Inn
Abraham Le Gros	Parade Place	Golden Anchor
J Le Levre	40 Seale Street	Rose and Crown Inn
Jeanne Le Maistre	Cattle Street	Caesarea Inn
Anne Le Masurier	Queen Street	Boutique
Jeanne Le Riche	Havre-de-Pas	(nothing listed)
Thomas Le Riche, jun	Mont-au-Pretre	Mont-au-Pretre Inn
J-George Le Sueur	7 Mulcaster Street	Boutique
Wm. Letto	Gloucester Street	Carpenters' Arms
Elie Le Veslet	3 Royal Square	Union Inn
Francis Levens	Burrard Street	Boutique
Pierre L'Hotelier	30 Grande Rue	Rising Sun
Nic-Jean Le Vesconte	5 Pier Road	Boutique

William Lloyd	George Street	Castle Bridge Inn
Peter-James Machon	Havre-des-Pas	Victoria Inn
James Madden	Kings Street	Boutique
Th M'Allen	Gloucester Street	Ship Builders' Inn
A Manzell	4 Mulcaster Street	Café des Italiens
Richard Maryon	6 Waterloo Street	Druid's Head
William Maryon	Charles Street	(nothing listed)
Joseph Matthews	Bond Street	Plymouth Inn
Michael M'Avoy	6 Conway Street	Belfast Arms
Francois Menier	Patriotic Place	Steamer
John Mesquita de Sousa Perrira	20 Beresford Street	Billiard
George Monck	Beresford Street	Beresford Arms
J Mourant (V Renouf)	11 New Street	Golden Grape
Jean Mourant	25 King Street	Victoria Inn
Josué Mourant	Morier Lane	Navy and Friends
Marie Mowatt (V Godfray)	York Street	Hero
Dennis Murphy	49 Sand Street	Weary Traveller
Edouard Noel	Haut de la Parade	Boutique
Philippe Noel	Beresford Street	Steam Boat
Victor Osmont	Conway Street	Mariners' Arms
Joseph Paul	1 Great Union Road	Boutique
James Paull	19 Charles Street	Red Lion
Alfred Picot	21 Royal Square	Royal Square Hotel
Marie Picot	John Street	George III
Anne Pinel (V Le Feuvre)	Pier Road	Boutique
Philippe Pinel	Haut de le Parade	Boutique
Richard Pinney	17 Union Street	Three Nations
Stephen Pique	26 Bond Street	Waterloo Inn
James Pugsley	Caledonia Place	Devon and Cornwall Inn
Robert Randall	48 Ann Street	Malsters' Arms
Francis Renouf	Havre-des-Pas	Royal George
Philippe Renouf, fils Clement	22 Conway Street	Royal Square Inn
Peter Sinclair	Weigh Bridge	British Tar
Jane Romeril	Queen Street	King's Arms
Manuel Sebire	Hilgrove Lane	(nothing listed)
Jeanne Sinel	Pier Road	Lord Nelson
(*) Hugh Smallacombe	Dorset Street	Seven Stars
John Smallacombe	Parade	Royal Sovereign
Charles Squire	Queen Street	Exeter Inn
Jean Stark	Market Place	Royal George
James Stoneman	Parade	Exeter Inn
George-Francis Sullivan	Chaussee	La Folie
James Stokes	Market Place	Market Inn
J Strout	10 Waterloo Street	Navy and Friends
Lewis R Summers	Mulcaster Street	Albion Inn
Patrick Sweeney	10 Wharf Street	Butchers' Arms
Ths. J Touzel	Colomberie	Shipwrights' Arms
Francis Vardon	Don Road	Brickmakers' Arms

George Vardon	2 Minden Place	Victoria Hotel
Mary Walter	Hilgrove Lane	Sailor's Return
(*) R Wellman	Providence Street	Crown and Anchor
Ch Whale	14 Halkett Street	Coach and Horses
Richard White	Havre-des-Pas	Boutique
Wm Williams		
Truss Wilson	Weigh Bridge	Weigh Bridge Inn

There are also 24 new applications. These are not necessarily for new premises; some are new managers:

	Mulcaster Street	Devonshire Inn
Jean Ahier	Colomberie	Boutique
Mss Elizabeth Bellman	Pier Road	Commercial Inn
Frédéric Bisson	Sand Street	Hero Inn
John Dyer	Pier Road	Devonshire and Dorset Inn
Henry Ellison	Old Street	Golden Cross
Mss Jeanne Fauvel	5 Waterloo Street	Friends' Inn
Mss Jeanne Gallichan	Mont-a-L'Abbe	Union Inn
Richard Gray	Victoria Place	Cornwall Inn
W Hull	Sand Street	Dorset and West Country Inn
Lach Hibbs	Market Place	Kent Coffee House
Jean Le Riche	3 New Street	Boutique
Jean Mauger	18 Sand Street	Boutique
Elias Norfolk	35 Sand Street	Bunch of Grapes
Jean Quérée	Albert Street	Boutique
William Squire	34 Hill Street	Boutique
Samuel Stone	New Street	Prince Albert
Geo. Syvret	Royal Square	York Inn
Daniel Vonberg	Bath Street	Boutique
Rt Wickett	Première Tour	Devon and Cornwall Inn

APPENDIX B

List of hotels, taverns, breweries and wine merchants from 19th Century Almanacs

The Stranger's Guide to the Island of Jersey: Commercial Directory, 1833

INNS & HOTELS

Albion, Thompson. Mulcaster St
Britannia, Brée, 32 Hill St
British Hotel , Almond, Broad St
Caledonia, Le Cornu, Pier
Commercial, Gregory, Pier Rd
Commercial Hotel, Mrs Paton, Don St
Deal's Hotel, Pier Rd
Le Sueur's, Mauger, Hill Street
London and Royal Yacht Club, Miller, Pier
Market Inn, Brabin, Halkett St
Nelson's, Nelson, 13 Bond St
Old London Hotel, Mrs Collins, North Pier
Union Inn, Le Veslet, Royal Sq
York Hotel, Mrs Le Gros, Royal Sq

TAVERNS AND PUBLIC HOUSES

Admiral, Davy, Sligo St
Army and Friends, Godfray, York St
Basket of Flowers, Dory, Parade Place
Battle of Waterloo, Pique, Bond St
Beehive, Brown, Vauxhall,
Beresford Inn. Renouf, Beresford St
Blue Pigeon, Falle, 6 Queen St
Britannia, Le Bailly, Cheapside
Britannia, Sarre, Castle Bridge
British and Foreign, Labey. Hillgrove Lane
Brother's Inn. Le Feuvre, 34 Colomberie
Caesarea Inn, Hocquard, Cattle St
Carpenter's Arms, Letto, Seale St
Carter and Friends, Noel, 10 Conway St
Carter's Inn, de la Cour, 8 Nelson Place
Clarence, Godfray, Claremont Rd
Cock and Bottle, Gallichan. Royal Sq
Crown and Anchor, Touzel, Gloucester St
Crown and Thistle, Finnie, Pier Rd
Dolphin, Martin, Pier Rd
D Williams, Homey, King St
Engineer's Arms, Howe, Pier Rd
Fifteen Balls, Alexander, John St
Four Alls, Esmond, Hilgrove Lane
Fox and Goose, Kimber, 7 Hill St
Friends, De Gruchy, Beresford St
Friends and Liberty, Falle, 9 Hope St
Friends' Inn, Hubert, 38 New St
Gas Lighter, Romeril, Bath St
George III, Powel, John St
Gloucester, Langlois, Conway St
Golden Anchor, Le Gros, Parade
Grapes, Renour, 33 Sand St
Half-Moon, Steen, Chapel Lane
Harp and Crown, Dickson, Pier Rd
Harp and Crown, Dwyer, Hilgrove Lane
Horse and Groom, Tucker, Ann St
King's Head, Beazley, Nelson Place
Jersey Inn, Bichard, Cheapside,
Kent Coffee House, Godfray, Market Place
King's Arms, Touzel, Queen St
Lord Nelson, La Folley, Cheapside
Masons and Friends, Fallaize, Roseville St
Mason's Arms, Horn, New St
Military Arms, Nuttall, Pier Rd
Navy and Friends, Stroud, Waterloo St
Navy and Friends, Gallichan, 11 Beresford St
Nelson and Jarvis, Hocquard, 26 Queen St
Nelson's Arms, Pingdester, Beresford St
Old Farmer's Inn, De La Haye, 23 Parade
Pensioner's Arms, Corcoran, ParadePlume of Feathers, Luce, York St Plymouth Inn, Short, Bond St
Queen Adelaide, Richard, Minden Place
Rising Sun, L'Hotellier, 20 Broad St
Robin Hood, McAteer, Mulcaster St
Royal George, Lucas, Mulcaster St
Royal George, Machon, Cheapside
Royal George, Renouf, Waterloo St
Royal Square Inn, Royal Square
Sailor's Arms, Hamon, Conway St
Sailor's Inn, Gould, Sand St
Steam Packet, Peek, Pier Rd
Swift Inn, Langlois, Market Place
Tailor's Arms, Touzel, 29 Colomberie
Temperance Coffee House, Le Hardy,Ha;kett St
Three Crowns, Squire, Hill St
Three Tuns, Scrivin, Wharf St

Town Battalion, Coutanhce, Parade
Tradesman's Inn, Sjarland, Burrard St
Traveller's Inn, Morris, 27 Hue Sr
True Briton, Smith, Union St
Union, Down, Sligo St
Union, Vardon, Cattle St
Vine Inn, New St
Waterloo, McKenzie, Conway St
Waterman's Arms, Frankard. Conway St
Weary Traveller, Bostock, Sand St
Welcome Home, Le Boutillier, Bath St
Weighbridge Inn, Gallie, Nelson Place
Wellington Inn, Cabot, York St
Weymouth Inn, Hussey, Pier
White Hart, Dunscombe, Morier Lane

WINE AND SPIRIT MERCHANTS

Cuming, W, Pier
Durell, P, 61 New Street
Fauvel, C, Colomberie
Gabourel, J. 33 Colomberie
Hemery Bros, Hill Street
Millais, A. 35 Sand Street
Perchard, P, KIng Street
Stalker, 2, Winchester Place

The Royal Almanack, FR 1837

Brewers

Blandy & Co, Castle Bridge Brewery
Brorn & Co, Beresford St
De La Taste, Old James St
Matthews C, Parade Place
Quirk J B, Old James St
Turner T, 7 and 9, Gloucester St

Inns and Hotels

Albion, Hoblyn, Mulcaster St
Britannia, Brée, 32 Hill St
British, Almond, Broad St
Caledonia, Le Cornu, Pier
Commercial, Gregory, Pier Rd (Billiard Rooms)
Deal's, 6 Pier Rd
Diana, Stone, Pier Rd
London and Royal Club, Williams, Nelson Place
Market Inn, Brabin, Market Place
Navy and Friends, Stroud, Waterloo St
Farmer's Inn, De La Haye, Parade
Kent Coffee House, Levens, Market Place
Old London, Hussey, Pier
Royal Hotel, Pepin, Pier Road,
Union, Le Veslet, Royal Sq
Weigh Bridge Inn, Gallie, Nelson Place
York , Royal Square

The Jersey Express General Almanac and Directory, 1866

Hotels and boarding houses

Aurora Hotel, Philip Canning, 8 Cattle St
Banks' British Union Hotel, 57 Esplanade
Bentley's Hotel, 4 Mulcaster St
Bouley Bay Hotel, W Newbegin, Bouley Bay, Trinity
Bree's Boarding House, Stopford Rd, David Place
British Hotel, Mrs Cantell, Gorey
British Hotel, St John's, Charles Jennings
British Star Hotel, J De La Haye, L'Etacq, St Ouen
British Hotel, C A Green, Broad Street
Brook's Family Boarding House, 14 Esplanade
Channel Islands' Hotel, R Gribble, corner of Mulcaster Street
Clarendon Hotel, Mrs Ainsley, Market St
Great Eastern Hotel, St John's, Mrs Whittle
Hotel de l'Europe, Mme Délepine, 11 Don St
Hotel de la Pomme d'Or, Madame Boisnet, Wharf St
London Hotel, H Miners, Mylcaster St
Mon Sejour Boarding House, F Treleaven, 53 David Place
Navy Hotel, W Nerry, Wharf St

Royal Hotel, Mrs Stone, Pier Rd
Royal Yacht Club Hotel, Mrs G Chase, 1 Caledonian Place, Pier
Royal Victoria Hotel,N Philips. 4 Esplanade
Shaw's Hotel, 1 Edward Place, Parade
Southsampton Hotel Hoitel, T W Sinnatt, 1 Pier
Star Hotel,Mrs Travers, 13 Hill Sr
St Aubin's Hotel, James F Coudray,
St Aubin
Temperance Hotel, D Beazer, 10 Bond Street
Trafalgar Hotel, D Morse, St Aubin
Union Hotel, F Prosser, Royal Sq
Way's Hotel, 2 Bind StYork Hoitel, J Damer, Royal Sq

Innkeepers

Ahier Ph (Inn), 4 Cattle St
Ahier Ph, 16 Halkett St
Allix G, Merchant's Inn, South Pier
Appleyard J (New Hospital Inn), 3 Gloucester St
Aubin J, Victoria Inn, 9 Minden Place
Babot W, Weighbridge, Pier
Baker H T, 43 Colomberie
Bartlett W (Royal Oak Inn), 21 Parade
Bartlett C, corner of Commercial St and Conway St
Bartlett H, 7 Troopers Yard
Bennett E T (Royal Square Vaults)
Binet J G (Union Inn), 2 Minden Place
Brett G, Pierson Inn, Royal Sq
Brett J (Crown Tavern), troopers Yard
Briard W.A (Welcome Home), 55 Lower Bath St
Broomer, W (Old England Inn), 10 Cheapside
Brownsea W, 10 Stopford Rd
Brown Mrs 8 Stopford Rd
Buckland Mrs (Clock Tower) 79 King St
Buckland Mrs, 1 La Chasse
Carroll T, Yarborough House, Stopford Rd
Cayzer H, Dorset Inn, Dorset St
Chanter C D, 77 New Sreet,
Clarkson R, Birmingham Inn, 9 Waterloo St
Clarke L, Mail Packet Inn, 13 Caledonia Place
Cole G, Red Lion Inn, Halkett Place
Coutanche Mrs, 29 Seaton Place
Dawson, corner of Don St and Burrard St
Deslandes D, Travellers' Inn, Mont Cochon
Gallichan Mrs, St Saviour's Rd
Germin A, Café de Parish, 12 Halkett Street
Giles R, Star and Garter Inn, corner of Union and Hue St
Giles W, Charing Cross
Hay C, 1 Great Union Rd
Hall Mrs, 33 Dorset St
Hamon C, 11 Museum St
Hamon, Friends' Inn. St Aubin's Rd
Hansford J, 7,1 Dorset St

Brewers

Banks Z, New Springfield Brewery, 3 Trinity Rd
De La Taste J H, 1 Wesley St
Kine, T, Trinity Rd and 24 Charing Crpss
Marcus B, Gas Lane]
Qurk T B 1 Minden Place
Randall R,10 Clare St

APPENDIX C

EUNE DRANME JERRIAISE: A Jèrriais primer of drinking

This list was compiled by Geraint Jennings; his permission to use this material is acknowledged with thanks. An expanded version may be found on the Internet: http://members.societe-jersiaise.org/geraint/jerriais

Mary-Ann, la milleuthe biéthe en Jèrri. (Mary Ann, the best beer in Jersey)
Tchiques announces

(Some advertisements for Mary Ann, from way back when)

Tch'est que ches pouor vos Mess Phlipp?
Mais ne Mary-Ann diantre. Tu sais bein que ch'est la meilleuthe.
Deux d'gouts de whiskey ou de gin?
Nennin, j'aime mus une Mary-Ann.
J'pense bein que t'es couomme mé et que ch'est une Mary-Ann?
Vèrr, viyant qu'il n'y a rein de milleur en Jèrri.
Tch'est que tu veurs prendre man vi?
Une Mary-Ann pouor seur, car il n'y a rein de dithèt.

Almonas des Chroniques de Jersey, 1934

Tchi ch'est qu'une Mary-Ann?
Moussieu n'est pon Jèrriais, car y'saurait que ch'est la milleuthe biéthe.
Tch'est que tu veurs prendre man vi?
J'pense bein que t'es couomme mé et que ch'est une Mary-Ann?
Mary-Ann as-tu pensé à mé?
Ergarde dans lé pagat et tu trouveras une Mary-Ann.
T'en vint-tu béthe une fais?
Véthe, et une Mary-Ann m'f'ra grand plaisi.
Quand nous est failli une Mary-Ann fait hardi d'bein pour vos ravigoter un miot.
Mary-Ann, la milleuthe biéthe en Jèrri.
Pouortchi qué tu prends tréjous une Mary-Ann?
Ch'est viyant qu'il n'y a pas dé milleuthe biéthe en Jèrri.
Si, j'allions prendre une Mary-Ann pour nous rafraîchi?
Pouor seux, n'v'la qui n'est pon dé r'fus.
Pourtchi une Mary-Ann, car il n'y a rein dithèt.
Vèrr, viyant qu'il n'y a rein dé milleur en Jèrri qu'une Mary-Ann.
Et tches qu'ou fîtes après?
J'allîmes prendre chacun une Mary-Ann.
Tch'est ch'est, deux gout dé whiskey ou dé gin?
Nennin mercis, j'aime mus une Mary-Ann.
Selon la buanne et ancienne coutume Mess Jean?
Véthe, tréjous une Mary-Ann.
T'en vint-tu baithe une fais?
Véthe, et une Mary-Ann m'f'ra grand pliaîsi.

Almonas des Chroniques de Jersey, 1940

Jèrriais	Angliais
eune vèrrée	glassful
un vèrre à baithe	drinking glass
eune boutelle	bottle
eune boutillie	bottleful
dêbouchi eune boutelle	uncork a bottle
santé!	cheers!
trîntchi les vèrres	to clink glasses
baithe	to drink
un béthe	drink
eune bouaisson	drink
un brévage	drink
l'alcool	alcohol
lé cidre	cider
lé vîn	wine
lé bliane vîn	white wine
lé rouoge vîn	red wine
la biéthe	beer
l'esprit d'vîn	spirits
l'ieau-d'vie d'cidre	apple brandy, calvados
lé champangne	champagne
lé rhonme	rum
lé porteur	porter
lé vîn d'Porto	port
lé madère	madeira
l'absînthe	absinth
lé p'ré	perry
lé chaûdé chaûdé	
du nouvieau cidre	cider must
lé baûtchet	mead
lé vitoué	mead
lé génèvre	gin
lé dginne	gin
lé dginne sus des preunelles	sloe gin
la litcheu	liqueur
lé fout-bas	strong cider
lé vîn brûlé	mulled wine
lé whisky	whisky
lé martel	cognac
lé Bordgieaux	claret
lé clairète	claret
lé bracheux	brewer
la brach'chie	brewery
brachi	brew
un bouchon d'liège	cork
un bouochon	cork
l'êprouvette	wine taster
lé tire-bouchon	corkscrew

Jèrriais	Angliais
lé preinseu	cider press, press house
lé tou d'preinseu	cider crusher
du cidre d'souos l'amet	unfermented cider
du pur jus	unfermented cider
la distil'lie	distillery
distîler	to distil
la distillâtion	distillation
emboutilyi	to bottle
embout'ler	to bottle
l'emboutil'lie	bottling
un lèrmîn	a drop of drink
un filet	a drop of drink
un filot	a drop of drink
eune reinchette	a drop of drink
un sico	a drop of drink
eune dranme	a dram
soûl	drunk
gris	drunk
ivre	drunk
chonmé	drunk
envitoué	drunk
souîn	drunk
bringuesingue	drunk
gâté d'béthe	drunk
blindé	drunk
bragi	drunk
bédé-ouinne	drunk
alleunmé	tipsy
souard	tipsy
s'coincer	to get tipsy
s'coêffi	to get tipsy
sé soûler	to get drunk
bouaissonner	to get drunk
prendre eune tchuite	to get drunk
êt' en bouaisson	to be drunk
senti lé bouchon	to like a drink
toper	to tope
l'alcoolisme	alcoholism
alcoolique	alcoholic
un trop-pliein	a drunk man
eune biche	a drunk woman
un ivrouongne	a drunkard
un soûlard	a drunkard
un bouaissonneux	a drunkard
un riboteux	boozer

riboter	to booze	*l'ivrouongn'nie*	drunkenness
un b'veux	drinker	*baithe raide*	to drink heavily
un topeux	a heavy drinker	*gaûdgetter*	to drink heavily
un pînteux	a heavy drinker	*radaler*	to drink heavily
un chucheux	a heavy drinker	*piochi*	to drink heavily
la bouaissonn'nie	drunkenness	*l'ver l'coute*	to drink heavily
la béthie	drunkenness	*baithe à tare-larigot*	to drink heavily

Guinness

À eune rêunion d'la Section de la langue Jèrriaise d'la Société Jèrriaise, iun d'nos membres nos ramémouaithit qué quand i' tait mousse avant l'Otchupâtion, nou pouvait liéthe dans les beusses ch't' annonce: 'Guinness es bouan por te – ch'la donne la forche.'
Y'avait la même annonce à l'Aéroport étout – jusqu'ès années souaixante, i'sembl'ye.
Et nou-s'a veu à ches drein d's annonces des années chînquante:
Guinness à vendre îchin
Mon doux de la vie mon Guinness
Guinness a la forche

Né v'chîn chein tch'est app'lé en Angliais un "showcard" – eune carte d'annonce – fait pouor Jèrri:
(Chu portrait est copyrighté "Guinness Limited" et est fait sèrvi sus chutte page auve la pèrmission d'la compangnie Guinness Limited. ©Guinness Limited)

Et y'avait d's annonces pouor Guinness en Dgèrnésiais étout.

Le Masurier

Pouor la bordée d'l'grande tchéthue, faut baithe de LAMOTHE *** de sièz Le Masurier.

Pendant la plianterie, rein de dithèt pouor encouoragi que L'RHUM de siez Le Masurier.

Quand ch'est l'flu ou autre dithèt maladie, un p'tit de cognac LAMOTHE *** vos f'ra grand bein. Y faut tréjous en avèr sièz-sé. Vous pouvez l'acater à la boutique.

Pouor n'pon aver l'flu ou un fraid, deux d'gouts de RHUM de siez Le Masurier est l'millieur de tout.

Si vous allez à la pêque à basse iau un flask d'RHUM de siez Le Masurier vous empêchera d'être happé par une suée d'fraid.

Votre hardelle aimera bein un p'tit d'PORT CROFT'S de siez Le Masurier et chunna ly f'ra grand plaisi pour seur.

Pouor l'brancage, deux ou trais d'gouts de LAMOTHE *** vous ravigotera pouor faithe chu travas. Ch'est de siez Le Masurier et ch'est de tchi buan.

Es shows, pouor fathe pliaisi à vos amins ce s'ra un "JOHNNIE WALKER."

Quand vous avez une forte job, d'mandez au Vièrr "JOHNNIE WALKER," né en 1820 d'vous bailler un coup d'main.

Pendant la saison des patates deux d'gouts d'GIN de siez Le Masurier. N'v'là qui renforche.

Ch'est de sièz Le Masurier qu'nous a les milleurs litcheurs et d'mandez les à la boutique.

Es neuches, y faut tréjous de tchi bon et rein dithèt que l'SHERRY et l'PORT de siez Le Masurier, qui sont chein qu'il y a de milleur.

Touotes les litcheurs de sièz Le Masurier sont chein qu'il y a de milleur, et y faut les aver.

A la batterie faut d'la cognac LAMOTHE *** de siez Le Masurier.

LITCHEURS

Pouor les siens qui n'aiment que chein qu'est buan, d'mandez les litcheurs de siez Le Masurier.

Pouor un baptême, l'IEAU D'CANNELLE est d'coutume et vous pourrez en avèr siez Le Masurier.

Es élections faut plumper pouor "JOHNNIE WALKER," un vièr gars solide, né en 1820 et tréjous prumi.

Chaque fais qu'nous vos offrira à bêthe, d'mandez un "JOHNNIE WALKER," de sièz Le Masurier.

Es vendues rein de dithèt que "JOHNNIE WALKER" pouor faithe monter les prix.

Dans toute buanne bordée, ch'est "JOHNNIE WALKER," né en 1820, qui faut aver avec sé.

Pouor les séthées d'nièrr beurre ch'est l'amin "JOHNNIE WALKER" qui faut pouor vos ravigoter.

Es Carnavas faut "JOHNNIE WALKER," chu vièr, né en 1820 et tréjous en avant.

Un p'tit de LAMOTHE *** ou de PORT CROFT'S ravigotera les vièrrs et vous l'acaterez siez Le Masurier, qui ne vend que tchi bon.

Pouor fêter Noué, un raid buan port est l'sien CROFT'S de siez Le Masurier; ch'est l'milleur.

Almanac des Chroniques de Jersey, 1934

Whisky "Bianc Ch'va"

Morning News, 1939-1940

APPENDIX D

Chairman's address at the 36th Ordinary General Meeting of Ann Street Brewery Co Ltd held on 30 August 1940

This transcript of an 'Ordinary General Meeting of Ann Street Brewery held during the Occupation is fascinating in so far that it shows how a commercial company in occupied Jersey tried to carry on its normal affairs in unthinkable conditions.
It is also interesting to see the reference to 'making a fresh start', which might refer to the possibility of a future liberation ... but only very obliquely. There seems to be a slight confusion of dates in the text below, but what follows is an exact transcript of the address.

'Before proposing the adoption of the Accounts and the Report of the Directors, I would like to make a few remarks as to the events that led to the closing down of the business.

Up to the end of May, we carried large stocks of essentials required for brewing, and supplies were coming regularly, but from that period all cargoes were delayed or shut off altogether, due to ships being required for the evacuation of troops from France and Belgium.

For a time we were hopeful of getting malt from the Continent, but this did not materialise, although the authorities still have the matter in hand, and we also are trying to obtain to obtain supplies through other channels.

Our last delivery of beers was made on 9 August last, except for 400 dozen bottled beers which were reserved for the Army of Occupation.

Some of our extra hands were given notice, and the remainder are finishing tomorrow 31st August. A few men will be retained on part time to attend to the plant, premises etc and an allowance is being made to our employees, many of whom have been with the Company for many years.

As regards the Accounts, your Board considers these quite satisfactory. We must remember that we have had only ten weeks trading under normal conditions, and there is no doubt that had it not been for the Occupation of the Island, and the consequent cutting off of our supplies from the mainland, we should have carried on at a profit.

We hope that the time is not too far distant when we shall be able to make a fresh start, and you can rest assured that everything will be done to keep the Plant and Premises in good order, so that we can take advantage when the time comes.

Gentlemen – as you are all aware, this meeting is consequent upon the decision of the Extra-Ordinary General Meeting of October last to alter the financial year to 31 December, and, therefore, the accounts in your hands cover the Company's trading for six months only to 31 December 1941.

This six months working has resulted in a Net profit of £1,000 odd, and in view of the abnormal conditions under which we have been operating, we consider we have been fortunate in being able to show a balance on the right side.

The trade we have been able to do has been confined to the sale of a small amount of Foreign Beer and Cider to the Public, and the bottling of Foreign Beers for the Troops of Occupation. We have also had the sale of our quota of the Wines and Spirits purchased through the collective buyings made by the Jersey Wholesale Wine & Spirit Merchants' Association.

You will, no doubt, be aware that we expect to re-commence brewing in the near future, and in this respect it may not be out of place to say what the position is at the moment.

For some considerable time now, we have made several attempts to, and have explored the possibility of obtaining brewing materials from France, but found it impossible to obtain same, and moreover, we were informed that no fuel would be available for our use. The prospects, therefore, appeared to be extremely unfavourable.

In December last, however, we were asked by the German authorities to submit a list of the requirements necessary to re-open the brewing of beer locally, and this with a view of supplying the Troops of Occupation and the Civil Population of Jersey and Guernsey. This was done, and late in January we were informed that the materials were now available, but that our representative would be required to proceed to Paris and make arrangements for their purchase, also that fuel would be available.

Our managing director proceeded to France and was able to obtain the French government's permission to buy, and arranged for the brewing materials to be forwarded. We are now awaiting our first month's allocation of supplies, and we will commence brewing as soon as they arrive.

If the arrangements made become the 'en fait accompli' we will be again trading, although under far less favourable conditions than the past, but we will, at least, be assured of a profit on our working.

As to the Accounts before you, we have decided to propose a small dividend of 3%, seeing that we are only dealing with a six months result, and if the profits on the proposed new business justify it, the Board will consider the advisability of paying an interim dividend at the earliest possible moment.

I therefore propose that.......

"The Directors' report and the Statement of Accounts for the financial half-year ended 31 December 1941, duly audited, be taken as read and adopted, and that a dividend at the rate of three per cent, less Jersey Income Tax, be declared on the Ordinary Shares." '

BIBLIOGRAPHY

Ahier, Philip: *The Historical Hotels and Inns of Jersey; The Governorship of Sir Walter Raleigh in Jersey Sea Stories*

Amieson, A. G. (ed.): *A People of the Sea*

Anthony, Rowland (ed): *Grouville, The history of a country parish*

Balleine, G. R.: *A Biographical Dictionary of Jersey*

Black, Adam: *Guide to Jersey*, 1902

Bois, G. C.: *Jersey Folklore and Superstitions*

Channel Island Occupation Society: *Jersey's German bunkers*

Chevalier, Jean: *Journal*

Cross, Amanda: *Tastes of the Channel Islands*

Crowden, James: 'Jersey cider' in *Heritage* magazine, 2006

Davis, William: *The Harbour that failed*

De Gruchy, G. F. B.: *Mediaeval Land tenures in Jersey*

Falle, Rev. Philippe: *An Account of the Island of Jersey*

Faramus, Anthony: *A Journey into Darkness*

French, R. K.: *The History and Virtues of Cyder*

Frigot, Derrick: *Jersey's Rural Heritage*

Gastineau , Edward T.: *A Hobble though the Channel Islands in 1858*

Harris, Leo: *Boys Remember More*

Hillsdon, Sonia: *Jersey Witches, Ghosts and Traditions*

Holmes, Dennis: *Ready, Aye Ready, The St Helier's Fire Brigade 1900–1930*

Inglis, Henry D.: *The Channel Islands*, 1834

Langtry, Lillie: *The days I knew*

Lempriere, Raoul: *Customs, Ceremonies and Traditions of the Channel Islands*

Le Brocq, Edward: *Memoirs*

Le Feuvre, David: *Jersey: Not Quite British*

Le Sueur, Frances: *A Natural History of Jersey*

Jersey Island Federation of Women's Institutes: *Buon Appétit*

Knocker, G. S.: *Freemasonry in Jersey*

Lyte, Thomas: *A Sketch of the History and Present State of the Island of Jersey*, 1808

Nicolle, E. T.: *The town of St Helier, Its rise and Development*

Parish of St Brelade: *Saint Brelade, Jersey* (the parish's millennium book)

Parish of St Lawrence: *St Lawrence, Jersey* (the parish's millennium book)

Phillips, Mary: *Poor People*

Plees, W. : *An Account of the Island of Jersey*, 1817

Poingdestre, Jean: *Caesarea*, 1682

Roooke, Octavius: *The Channel Islands Pictorial, Legendary and Descriptive* (1858)

Sebire, Heather: *The Archaeology and Early History of the Channel Islands*

Simmons, Douglas A.: *Schweppes, the first 200 years*

Smith, Heather: *Celtic and Romano British Foods from the Isles* (www.academia.edu)

Stead, J.: *A Picture of Jersey*, 1809

Stevens, Joan: *Victorian Voices*; *Old Jersey Houses*, Vols I & II

Stevens-Cox, James and Gregory: *The Chanel Islands Annual Anthology 1972-1973*

A Stranger's Guide to Jersey, 1833

Tabb, Peter: *A Peculiar Occupation*

Trees for Life: *Trees on Jersey*

Turner, Barry: *An Outpost of Occupation*

William Gerard Walmesley: *A Pedestrian Tour through the Islands of Guernsey and Jersey 1821*, transcribed by Kenneth Renault (1992)

Wilson, Bee: *The Hive*

Woods, Jacqui: *Prehistoric Cooking*

Société Jersiaise Bulletins, especially 1970, 'Pommage' by J. G. Speer

The Jersey Critic Magazine

The Evening Post / Jersey Evening Post

Heritage Magazine

About the Author

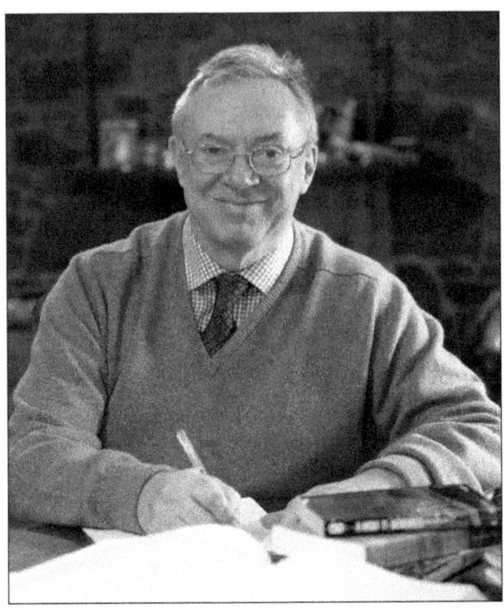

Alasdair Crosby is a writer and journalist who specialises in Channel Island subjects. He was for 14 years employed by the Jersey Evening Post newspaper, and is now the owner and editor of *RURAL - Jersey Country Life magazine*. He was brought up in Jersey and returned in 1991 to settle in the Island, where he lives with his wife and family.

He is the author of two previous books: *TITANIC - The Channel Islands Connection* and *A Community in Transition - The Catholic Church in Jersey in Modern Times.*